The
INDIVIDUAL
and the
NATURE
of
MASS
EVENTS

BOOKS BY JANE ROBERTS

The Rebellers (1963)

The Coming of Seth (How to Develop Your ESP Power) (1966)

The Seth Material (1970)

Seth Speaks: The Eternal Validity of the Soul, A Seth Book (1972)

The Education of Oversoul Seven (1973)

The Nature of Personal Reality, A Seth Book (1974)

Adventures in Consciousness: An Introduction to Aspect Psychology (1975)

Dialogues of The Soul and Mortal Self in Time (1975)

Psychic Politics: An Aspect Psychology Book (1976)

The World View of Paul Cézanne: A Psychic Interpretation (1977)

The Afterdeath Journal of an American Philosopher: The World View of William James (1978)

The "Unknown" Reality: Vol. 1, A Seth Book (1977)

The "Unknown" Reality: Vol. 2, A Seth Book (1979)

The Further Education of Oversoul Seven (1979)

Emir's Education in the Proper Use of Magical Powers (1979)

The Nature of the Psyche: Its Human Expression, A Seth Book (1979)

The Individual and the Nature of Mass Events, A Seth Book (1981)

The God of Jane: A Psychic Manifesto (1981)

If We Live Again: Or, Public Magic and Private Love (1982)

Oversoul Seven and the Museum of Time (1984)

Dreams, "Evolution," & Value Fulfillment: Vol. 1, A Seth Book (1986)

Dreams, "Evolution," & Value Fulfillment: Vol. 2, A Seth Book (1986)

Seth, Dreams, and Projection of Consciousness (1986)

The Magical Approach: Seth Speaks About the Art of Creative Living (1995)

The Way Toward Health, A Seth Book (1997)

A
Seth
BOOK

The
INDIVIDUAL
and the
NATURE
of
MASS
EVENTS

Jane Roberts

NOTES AND COVER ART BY ROBERT F. BUTTS

AMBER-ALLEN PUBLISHING
SAN RAFAEL, CALIFORNIA

Published by Amber-Allen Publishing
P.O. Box 6657
San Rafael, CA 94903

Cover Art: Robert F. Butts
Cover Design: Beth Hansen

Library of Congress Cataloging-in-Publication Data

Seth (Spirit)
    The individual and the nature of mass events / [channeled] by Jane Roberts ; notes by Robert F. Butts.
    p.   cm. — (A Seth book)
    Originally published: Englewood Cliffs, N.J. : Prentice-Hall, c1981.
    ISBN 978-1-878424-21-1 (alk. paper)
    1. Spirit writings.   I. Roberts, Jane 1929-1984.   II. Butts, Robert F.
III. Title.   IV. Series: Seth (Spirit).   Seth book.
BF1301.S376   1995
133.9'3 — dc20   95-25274
                                                CIP

ISBN 978-1-878424-21-1

23   22   21   20   19   18   17   16   15   14   13   12   11   10   9

To Rob

CONTENTS

"We have never told anybody to do anything, except to face up to the abilities of consciousness."

Seth
April 19, 1978

A note by R.F.B.: Seth was often pretty outspoken in Mass Events *when he discussed our medical beliefs and practices, and the unfortunate results they sometimes bring about. At the same time he tempered his ideas with passages like this one, from the 870th session for Chapter 10:*

"Generally speaking, for example, if you are seriously worried about a physical condition, go to a doctor, because your own beliefs may overfrighten you otherwise. Begin with innocuous but annoying physical conditions, however, and try to work those out for yourself. Try to discover why you are bothered. When you have a headache or a simple stomach upset, or if you have a chronic, annoying but not serious condition, such as trouble with your sinuses, or if you have hay fever — in those situations, remind yourself that your body does indeed have the capacity to heal itself."

A Psychic Manifesto

My life is its own definition.
So is yours.
Let us leave the priests
to their hells and heavens,
and confine
the scientists
to their dying universe,
with its
accidentally created stars.
Let us each dare
to open our dream's door,
and explore
the unofficial thresholds,
where we begin.

(A note by R.F.B.: This is the first verse of a long poem Jane wrote late in July 1979, as Seth was finishing his work on Mass Events. *Among other things, the poem is a passionate declaration of psychic independence, written in response to Seth's ideas in this book.)*

INTRODUCTION BY
JANE ROBERTS

A trance is a very private phenomenon. It represents a turning away of consciousness from ordinary reality toward an inner one. However private a trance may be, it must take place in a physical world of shared events. I am touched by those events and so are you; so even while I sit in trance, dictating books as Seth, I can't after all stray too far from our joint reality. The chair I sit in as I speak for Seth is a product of modern manufacture. The glass of wine on the coffee table before me, the cigarettes, and the mass-produced table itself, are all reminders that my most adventuresome journeys into other realities are rooted, for now at least, in the physical world of events that we all share together.

Robert F. Butts, my husband, sits on the couch across from me, taking verbatim notes of what I say as Seth, transcribing these "otherworldly" communications with a modern pen on good white bond paper. When I held ESP classes, Seth's sessions were always taped, and just this week he "came through" as I was being recorded for a radio program to be aired later. So technology, with all of its implications, is never really too far away.

While Seth was dictating *The Individual and the Nature of Mass Events,* for example, the Three Mile Island nuclear accident occurred; and had the affair turned into a disaster, our Chemung

County would have been used to house refugees. Many spectacular national events have happened, of course, since our first sessions took place late in 1963, but Seth seldom mentioned such issues, and then only in answer to our own questions. In this current book, however, he discusses in depth how our private realities merge into mass experience. For that reason he examines the public arena, and devotes a good deal of material to Three Mile Island and to the Jonestown mass suicides as well. Both situations occurred as Seth was dictating this book, and while they are contemporary, both cases are classic in their implications.

Rob's notes provide the necessary exterior orientation for this present volume, as they do for the previous Seth books, and hint at the framework of normal life in which Seth so gallantly "appears" twice weekly, tossing off my glasses and thereby signaling the beginning of my trance. Besides this, of course, my own moods, speculations, joys and sorrows have spun their earthly web through my mind on such days. I may have worked well or poorly at my own writing. The day may have been calm or distracted by unexpected guests, or marked by any of life's normal domestic ups and downs.

While Seth was dictating *Mass Events,* for example, another of our cats (Billy) died. Seth was discussing the Three Mile Island accident, but he left off book dictation for a while because we felt so badly, and gave us some excellent material on animal consciousness before and after death — because "tragedies" come in all shapes and sizes, and the most domestic events of our days offer Seth opportunities to comment on life itself.

So even if I was focused elsewhere and my consciousness turned inward, a spotlight was thrown upon our world from that other viewpoint, almost as if a character in one of our dreams suddenly came awake, walked out of the dream, and dared comment on our waking world. Perhaps this isn't a good analogy — Seth is far from a dream character, and in fact I hardly ever dream of him at all — but he *is* a personality whose platform of reality isn't the same as ours, a personality who writes books through me, but from his standpoint, not mine.

In this book he comments on our religions, sciences, cults, and on our medical beliefs as well, with an uncompromising wisdom —

as if — as if he represents some deep part of the human psyche that knows better, that has always known better — as if he speaks out not only with my voice but for many many other people — as if he represents the truths that we have allowed ourselves to forget.

What truths? That our dreams come alive at midday; that our feelings and beliefs turn into the reality we experience; that, in deeper terms, we are the events in which we participate, and that murder for the sake of an ideal is still murder. But more than this, Seth reminds us of something we knew as children: We are of good intent.

"You make your own reality." That statement is one of the cornerstones of Seth's material, stated almost from the beginning of our sessions and emphasized throughout his books. In *Mass Events,* though, Seth goes further, maintaining that our private impulses are meant to provide the impetus for the development of our own abilities in a way that will also contribute to the best interests of the species and the natural world as well. He's speaking of our normal impulses here, those that we've been taught are dangerous, chaotic, and contradictory. Seth maintains that we can't trust ourselves while distrusting our impulses at the same time. Much of this book is concerned with the purposes of our impulses, and the reasons for their poor reputations in the eyes of science and religion. What Seth is really saying here is that our impulses are meant to *help* us create our own realities on a personal basis in a way that will enhance both our private lives and our civilizations.

But if we are of good intent, how can we sometimes end up involved in the most reprehensible of actions? Seth faces such questions squarely, and deals with the motivations of both the fanatic and the idealist. And people *are* idealistic. Many readers of all ages write us, asking how they can develop their own potentials and also help bring about "a better world." They care deeply, and abhor the adverse conditions they see in society, whether or not they are intimately concerned with them. In this book Seth clearly shows how each of us can contribute to the mass reality, and concisely outlines the issues so that we don't fall prey to disillusionment or fanaticism.

Since we are all involved with world events, it is highly important that we also understand how we fit into those global actions, and see how our negative beliefs about ourselves and the species can result in situations far less than ideal, and quite different from our stated goals. For this reason, Seth explains how the theories of Freud and Darwin confine our imaginations and our abilities.

Rob and I grew up in the world of Freudian and Darwinian concepts too, of course. And we weren't given any magical immunity from the unfortunate results of such cramped vision. Those theories, along with religion's belief in the flawed self, have left their marks on all of our lives. Rob and I *have* been given a new, vaster philosophical structure through the Seth sessions, one that we share with our readers. And that structure is still emerging. It is far from finished. The answers are not all in. We are still learning how to ask the right questions.

When Seth began this manuscript, I was personally working with the idea of "heroic impulses" (those separate from our usual ones) that would operate as inner impetuses toward constructive action. In this book, though, Seth states that it is our *normal* everyday impulses that we must learn to trust. Even I was taken back! Our *usual* impulses? The ones I ignored while I was looking for the "heroic" ones? And finally I began to understand: Our normal impulses *are* heroic, despite our misunderstanding of them. In a way, this entire book is an introduction to our impulses, those we follow and those we deny.

I've had my own hassles with impulses, following only those I thought would lead me where I wanted to go, and drastically cutting down those I feared might distract me from my work. Like many other people, I thought that following my impulses was the least dependable way of achieving any goal — unless I was writing, when impulses of a "creative" kind were most acceptable. I didn't realize that all impulses were creative. As a result of such beliefs, I've had a most annoying arthritis-like condition for some years that was, among other things, the result of cutting down impulses toward physical motion.

In the past, when Seth told me to trust the spontaneous self, I said "Okay," and imagined some hypothetical inner self somehow apart from my conscious intents. But when Seth kept repeating "Trust your impulses" in this book, I finally got the message through my head — and I've already had considerable physical improvement as a result. This distant-seeming inner self wasn't so distant after all;

"it" communicated through *my* impulses. In a way, impulses *are* the language of the psyche.

But what about aggressive or contradictory or even murderous impulses? How can those be trusted? Seth answers those questions and many more, until as we read his explanations we wonder how we could have so misread our own nature as to distrust the very messages meant to lead us toward our own spiritual growth and that of the species as well.

And what is my own part in all of this? I see it as harking back to the poet's original role; to explore the reaches of his or her private psyche, pushing against usual psychological boundaries until they give, opening up a new mystical territory — the psyche of the people, of the species itself — perceiving a spectacular vision of inner reality that the poet then communicates to the people, translating that vision through words, rhythm, or songs.

The earliest poets were probably half shaman, half prophet, speaking for the forces of nature, for the "spirits" of the living and the dead, voicing their visions of man's unity with the universe. They spoke their messages, sang their songs, chanted their visions aloud. And maybe that's why Seth *speaks,* communicating first through words, rather than, say, through automatic writing. Seth's books are first of all spoken productions. Perhaps the Seth sessions themselves harken back to some ancient time when we received much of our pertinent information about ourselves in just such a fashion: one of us journeying for the others into the "mass unconsciousness" — a journey that somehow altered and expanded the personality — and then communicating our visions as best we could.

If so, though, such altered "between world" personalities can be remarkably stable; and if they form according to our ideas of individuality, they can certainly outdo us in their unique complexity. For if Seth is only a psychological model filled out by *my* unconscious trance material, then he certainly puts our usual concepts of personality to shame, and by implication shows that we ourselves have a long way to go if we are to use our full potential.

So I do think more is involved. I think that Seth *is* a model of ourselves as we know we can be; that he speaks for the part of ourselves that never for a minute believed all that nonsense about flawed selves.

As far as my relationship with Seth and his with me, because of our long-standing association I think we must have formed a unique psychological alliance; somehow I am part Seth, and in sessions at least, Seth must be part Jane, in a kind of psychological bonding on both sides. Seth must use my voice to speak and my life as reference, and certainly the contents of my mind are vastly expanded as a result of the sessions. My daily life is lived with the knowledge of that association, of course, and my normal routine now includes "turning into Seth" twice weekly, and has for years.

This Introduction represents my only conscious contribution to this entire book, for example. But certainly as Seth often states, even the unconscious portions of our personalities *are* actually conscious. It's all a matter of focus. Not that Seth is just another focus of mine, for it's quite legitimate to say that I'm a focus of *his* consciousness in that same context; but that Seth represents that larger portion of the psyche from which our own kind of consciousness emerges. The point of all of this *is* the exploration of human consciousness, its ranges and scopes. How much does it change as it approaches other levels of actuality?

But however we attempt to define Seth's reality, I'm convinced of one thing by now: He is delivering to our conscious minds our deepest unconscious knowledge about ourselves, the world, the universe, and the source of Being Itself. Not that Seth claims any kind of omnipotence, because he doesn't. His material, however, is clearly providing such translations of unconscious knowledge, and intuitive disclosures; disclosures, according to Seth, no more remarkable than those available in nature itself, but we have forgotten how to read nature's messages; disclosures no more mysterious than those available in our own states of inspiration, but we've forgotten how to decipher those communications too. Instead, many people are even frightened of inspiration itself.

I think that such phenomena were important in evolutionary terms, helping to shape man's consciousness. Not that such material wasn't often distorted, or just as often discounted: In any case, it would have to be interpreted again and again so that it applied to the species' experience in time's framework.

Talk about psychological complexities! I was just presented with an excellent example of the ideas I've been discussing. As I wrote the previous few paragraphs of this Introduction, the words themselves seemed to carry me on with a certain rhythm. I felt as if I were drawing on energy and knowledge beyond my usual capacities. Then, since it was late afternoon, I took a break for a brief nap. More ideas came to me that I scribbled down in the bedroom. The subjective pace quickened and kept accelerating — then I hit a psychological brick wall, and I could carry the concept no further. At that point I suddenly recognized Seth "around the edges" of my mind. The next moment, I fell asleep. When I awakened half an hour later, I prepared dinner. Rob and I ate and watched the television news. Then I went back to my study.

No sooner did I sit down than such a rich vein of material opened that I could hardly write fast enough to get it all down; and it began where my earlier ideas had ended off. I was being given many of the subject headings for — Seth's *next* book, even as I was writing the Introduction for this one! Behind each heading or subject, I sensed realms of information available to Seth, but not (in usual terms) to me. Yet there had been an earlier moment just before the onrush of material when I sensed an odd psychological threshold, a certain accelerated state, that in this case at least signaled the intersection of Seth's thoughts and mine. Then there was a brief point of psychological rest, an almost neutral psychological platform in which Seth's outline began to emerge.

Following this, in our next session, Seth confirmed that the material amounted to a partial outline for his projected new book, and that the title I'd "picked up" while he was still finishing *Mass Events* was correct. So though he hasn't begun it as of this writing, two days later, surely he will start dictating *Dreams, "Evolution," and Value Fulfillment* any day now. My glasses will go off. Seth will say again, "Now: Dictation," and Rob will make up a new title page for his notebook.

The Seth sessions and Seth's books are inevitably connected to my relationship with Rob, of course. He's far more than a recorder or transcriber of the material. Rob's remarkable mind with its questions and probing nature has always stimulated me to do my best, and has served as a kind of invisible but sturdy psychological screen, helping me view myself and the sessions as clearly as possible. If it hadn't been for his encouragement and active participation, I doubt that the Seth sessions would exist in their present form.

So while Seth's books go out into the public world, the sessions themselves rise from our private lives. Yet those lives are lived in coexistence with a mass arena of events that brush against us gently at times, or drastically affect our days on other occasions. In this book Seth describes the continuum of existence that holds us all together and blends our private experiences into world events. This is your world and ours. Hopefully, this book will help us all make it a better world.

Elmira, New York
September 22, 1979

PART ONE

THE EVENTS OF "NATURE." EPIDEMICS AND NATURAL DISASTERS

CHAPTER 1

THE NATURAL BODY AND ITS DEFENSES

SESSION 801, APRIL 18, 1977
9:31 P.M. MONDAY

(I*'ll preface the workaday notes for the first session of* Mass Events *with the following comments, just to briefly summarize the lifetime endeavor that my wife, Jane Roberts, and I are involved in with the Seth books. Seth is a highly creative "energy personality essence," as he calls himself, who speaks through Jane while she's in a trance or dissociated state. These notes, then, are written shortly after Seth finished dictating* Mass Events *in August 1979. I've discussed some of the same points while introducing earlier books in the series, of course, although on each occasion I did so in a different way for variety's sake. At the same time, Jane and I want each book to be complete in itself, so that the "new" reader can begin to understand what's happening from the very beginning. Details about some of the subjects I'll mention here can emerge as this book proceeds, or others are referred to. And these notes will also free Jane to deal with other matters in her Introduction for* Mass Events.

(By his own definition Seth is no longer a physical being, although he's told us he's lived a number of previous lives; thus, ideas of reincarnation enter into his material. Mass Events *is the sixth[1] book that Seth has produced — all of them with Jane's active cooperation, obviously, as well as my own, since I write down his material verbatim, then add my own notes.*

Often Jane has little memory of the information she delivers as, or for, Seth. She began speaking for him in December 1963, and shows no signs of slackening her output. At times her Seth voice can be very powerful indeed, with an accent I have yet to succeed in describing. When she's really into her trance state, her blue-gray eyes become much darker, much more luminous and penetrating. Seth calls Jane "Ruburt" and me "Joseph." According to him, these "entity names" mean only that in our present lives we identify more with the male aspects of our entities, or whole selves — which in themselves are neither male or female, but contain within them a number of other selves [of both sexes] to whom we're related, or a part of, reincarnationally and otherwise.

(We usually hold two "sessions," or meetings with Seth each week, totaling three or four hours, but we think that actually Seth could talk 24 hours a day for the rest of our lives, and still not cover all of the material he's capable of tuning in to for us. [The only trouble is that Jane and I wouldn't last long!] That astonishing creativity and energy in the sessions beckon us on constantly, then, regardless of what we think about Seth's "reality or nonreality," and even regardless of what he *tells us about himself.*

(Yet even producing the Seth books — along with a great amount of unpublished Seth material — doesn't call upon all of Jane's abilities, for she's also written 10 books "on her own." These include works of poetry, fiction, and psychic matters as experienced from her own conscious viewpoint. She has several more books in progress. It's safe to note, however, that now all of her work bears upon that unique, still-growing view of consciousness expressed by Seth and herself. And so does mine.

(That's saying a lot, really. We do intend to spend the rest of our lives studying the ramifications of that "unique, still-growing view of consciousness." We still have a host of questions about Seth's reality, his concepts, and Jane's role [and my own] in all of this — that is, questions about consciousness itself, basically: consciousness getting to know itself in endless variations, as I've written before, and whether or not it's couched in physical form.

(For now, let's postulate that Jane and I think we understand better than we used to that our consciousnesses have no limitations except those we've imposed upon them through our individual perceptions and understandings. Consciousness creates all, or all that we know reflects the particularized creations of consciousness, then, and potentially those sublime mental and physical achievements are without end. The idea of infinity is

implied here — a concept whose implications make us uneasy, for although Seth's material can be said to imply infinities of creation upon the part of each of us, still we realize the conscious mind's inability to truly grasp all of the qualities inherent within such a notion.

(At the same time, Jane and I are extremely grateful that we have the opportunity to study ideas about consciousness with Seth, and this opening up of our individual realities is something we couldn't have conceived of before 1963. Our appreciation of life has expanded greatly — and if the Seth material did nothing but help us grow in that respect, it would perform a very valuable service. We hope others feel they've gained something from the material too. [Actually, I think that what I've learned has saved me from bitterness and disillusionment in later life. Jane has also been helped a great deal.] So our aim with the Seth books is to let Seth have his say, to add some thoughts of our own, and to trust that the feelings and meanings in all of this will evoke beneficial responses in each reader. It's all we can do. I for one think that my own words are pretty inadequate tools of expression to convey the deeper, unspoken meanings within life that I sense but cannot really verbalize.

(I also think that Seth himself could have some pretty funny things to say here to Jane and me — some day I'll ask him — words with which he'd humorously caution us not to take the whole affair too seriously, to leave room in our daily lives for the simple, uninhibited joy of creative expression and living even while we study his unending outpouring of material. But maintaining such a balance isn't always easy. Seth has already offered Jane encouragement twice since he finished his part of the work for Mass Events *in August 1979. He came through with the following quotations when Jane began to express a renewed concern about her responsibility for his material, and for the reactions of others to it. Her feelings had arisen in large part because of the ever-increasing mail response the Seth books have generated. Interesting, then, the way the Seth portion of Jane's personality structure [whatever Seth's reality may be] reinforces those other portions that are meeting all of the challenges embodied in her current mental and physical existence — and we are continually seeking to learn more about how Seth is able to do this. In these excerpts Seth also touches upon certain other points that we think of often.*

(From a personal session held on August 29, 1979:

("There is a power of growth and value fulfillment within each individual that must be satisfied. It is the power that makes physical growth

possible, the power that is behind the fetus. You know ahead of time the nature of the period into which you will be born. You [Jane and Rob, or Ruburt and Joseph] were both born with certain abilities, and you knew ahead of time that you would have to enlarge the framework of conventional concepts if you were to have room to use those abilities. In a way, they gave you both a second life, for in the old framework there was no satisfying [underlined] or creative way to go.

("You have both used the material I have given you, and what you have learned on your own through the material, very well — some of it so smoothly that you are not even aware of your accomplishments. In some areas you still cling to old beliefs, but there is no end to what you can do, still, with growing comprehension. That is, you can still accomplish as much, if not more, than you already have.

("Think of yourselves, in important ways, as almost having been born in 1963 [when these sessions began]. The two of you — for you are both involved — have not only initiated a new framework from which you and others can view the nature of reality more clearly, but you also had to start from scratch, so to speak, to get the material, learn to trust it, and then to apply it to your own lives — even while 'the facts were not all in yet.' At no point did you have all of the material to draw upon, as for example, your readers do at any given point. So tell Ruburt not to judge himself too harshly, and in all of this have him try to remember his sense of play. . . . "

(From the regular, 877th session for September 3, 1979:

("All creativity is basically joyful. It is play in the highest sense of the term, and it is always alive with motion. The sessions and our work can help bring about a new mental species of men and women. Ideas change the chromosomes, but the sessions and Ruburt's books, and so forth, must first and foremost be joyful expressions of creativity, spontaneous expressions that fall into their own order . . . You paint because you love to paint, and forget what an artist is supposed to be or not to be. Have Ruburt forget what a writer or a psychic is supposed to be or not to be. Ruburt's spontaneity lets all of his creative abilities emerge. It is foolhardy to try and apply discipline, or secondary order to a spontaneous creativity that automatically gives you the finest order that nature could ever provide."

(Those two excerpts from Seth contain inspired thinking — especially portions about the power of value fulfillment, and the joy and spontaneity involved in creativity. As I typed his material I was reminded of the notes I wrote and played with the other day:

("There really isn't anything else like the sessions going on in the world today. Even now, while I'm thinking about how to put Mass Events *together for the reader, last night Seth came through with new material that he said will be part of* another *book. I should always remember that each time Jane and I sit for a session,* it's a unique event in the world.

· *("That isn't nearly as conceited a statement as it seems to be, of course, for each thing each person does is also unique in the world. Yet, at the same time I mean that the sessions are truly original and significant, with their contents offering new creative insights and hope to the human species in a way that most endeavors do not do. In that sense the Seth business is a remarkable achievement on Jane's part. I do believe that prolonged study of the Seth material would yield great results toward our understanding of ourselves. . . ."*

(And now for the notes I wrote in April 1977, opening the first session for Mass Events. *Although I've added to my notes for Seth's book since he finished dictating it, I've done so very briefly in order to keep them as contemporary as possible.)*

(One might say that Mass Events *had its origins two Seth books ago — way back in Volume I of* "Unknown" Reality, *which Seth finished dictating in June 1974. At 10:14 in the 697th session for that work, he made this statement: "I will have more to say concerning illnesses, epidemics, and mass disorders in this book."*

(It wasn't until I was checking the page [or printer's] proofs for Volume 1 last week that I realized Seth hadn't followed through on his promise. I'd also forgotten to remind him to do so. I asked Jane if Seth could devote the next session to that subject matter so that I could insert it in Volume 2 of "Unknown" Reality *as a note or an appendix, since I had plenty of work to do yet for that second volume. She agreed; we thought some very interesting material would result. We also thought it was a good time to pose questions for Seth — for just two weeks ago, in the 800th session, he'd finished dictating his own fifth book,* The Nature of the Psyche: Its Human Expression.[2]

(We gave up our regularly scheduled sessions last week, and spent a great deal of time correcting the proofs for Volume 1 of "Unknown".[3] *In fact, I didn't finish my part of the job until midnight Sunday; then early this morning I mailed the whole thing to Tam Mossman, Jane's editor at Prentice-Hall. By now both of us were bleary from all of those days and*

nights of concentrated labor, but still we wanted to hold the session. I sat opposite Jane in our quiet, softly-lit living room, working on these notes while I waited for her to take off her glasses and go easily into trance. I felt a familiar sense of anticipation as I thought of recording the excellent session to come. And that's when Seth surprised us.)

Now: Good evening.

("Good evening, Seth.")

You cannot begin to understand the nature of mass events of any kind unless you consider the even greater framework in which they have their existence.

A person's private experience happens in the context of his psychological and biological status, and basically cannot be separated from his religious and philosophical beliefs and sentiments, and his cultural environment and political framework —

(Our young tiger cat, Billy, had been sleeping on a nearby chair. Now he woke up, stretched, jumped down and walked over to Jane as she spoke for Seth. Billy crouched to jump up into her lap. I picked him up and headed for the cellar door. Jane remained in trance.)

Sweet creatures are difficult to find.

("Yes," I said to Seth over my shoulder. In a recent session Seth had remarked that Billy was "a sweet creature." And he is. I put him in the cellar, where he sleeps each night.)

All of the issues form together to make a trellis of behavior. Thorns or roses may grow therein. That is, the individual will grow outward toward the world, encountering and forming a practical experience, traveling outward from his center in almost vinelike fashion, forming from the fabric of physical reality a conglomeration of pleasant or aesthetic, and unpleasant or prickly events.

The vine of experience in this analogy is formed in quite a natural fashion from "psychic" elements that are as necessary to psychological experience as sun, air, and water are to plants. *(Loudly and humorously:)* I do not want to get too <u>entwined</u> (underlined) in this analogy, however; but as the individual's personal experience must be seen in the light of all of these issues, so mass events cannot be understood unless they are considered in a far greater context than usual.

The question of epidemics, for example, cannot be answered from a biological standpoint alone. It involves great sweeping psychological attitudes on the part of many, and meets the needs and desires of those involved — needs which, in your terms, arise in a framework of religious, psychological and cultural realities that cannot be isolated from biological results.

I have thus far stayed clear of many important and vital subjects, involving mass realities, because first of all the importance of the individual was to be stressed, and his power to form his private events. Only when the private nature of reality was emphasized sufficiently would I be ready to show how the magnification of individual reality combines and enlarges to form vast mass reactions — such as, say, the initiation of an obviously new historical and cultural period; the rise or overthrow of governments; the birth of a new religion that sweeps all others before it; mass conversions; mass murders in the form of wars; the sudden sweep of deadly epidemics; the scourge of earthquakes, floods, or other disasters; the inexplicable appearance of periods of great art or architecture or technology.

(Pause at 9:57, one of many.) I said there are no closed systems. This also means that in world terms, events spin like electrons, affecting all psychological and psychic systems as well as biological ones. It is true to say that each individual dies alone, for no one else can die that death. It is also true that part of the species dies with each death, and is reborn with each birth, and that each private death takes place within the greater context of the existence of the entire species. The death serves a purpose species-wise while it also serves the purposes of the individual, for no death comes unbidden.

An epidemic, for example, serves the purposes of each individual who is involved, while it also serves its own functions in the greater species framework.

When you consider epidemics to be the result of viruses, and emphasize their biological stances, then it seems that the solutions are very obvious: You learn the nature of each virus and develop an inoculation, giving [each member of] the populace a small dose of the disease so that a man's own body will combat it, and he will become immune.

The shortsightedness of such procedures is generally overlooked because of the definite short-term advantages. As a rule, for example, people inoculated against polio do not develop that disease. Using such procedures, tuberculosis has been largely conquered.

There are great insidious variables operating, however, and these are caused precisely by the small framework in which such mass epidemics are considered.

In the first place, the causes are not biological. Biology is simply the carrier of a "deadly intent." In the second place, there is a difference between a virus produced in the laboratory and that inhabiting the body — a difference recognized by the body but not by your laboratory instruments.

Give us a moment . . . In a way the body produces antibodies, and sets up natural immunization as a result of, say, inoculation. But the body's chemistry is also confused, for it "knows" it is reacting to a disease that is not "a true disease," but a biologically counterfeit intrusion.

To that extent — and I do not mean to overstate the case — the body's biological integrity is contaminated. It may at the same time produce antibodies also, for example, to other "similar" diseases, and so overextend its defenses that the individual later comes down with another disease.

(10:19.) Now, no person becomes ill unless that illness serves a psychic or psychological reason, so many people escape such complications. In the meantime, however, scientists and medical men find more and more viruses against which the population "must" be inoculated. Each one is considered singly. There is a rush to develop a new inoculation against the newest virus. Much of this is on a predictive basis: The scientists "predict" how many people might be "attacked" by, say, a virus that has caused a given number of deaths. Then as a preventative measure the populace is invited to the new inoculation.

(Emphatically:) Many people who would not get the disease in any case are then religiously inoculated with it. The body is exerted to use its immune system to the utmost, and sometimes, according to the inoculation, overextended [under such] conditions.[4] Those individuals who have psychologically decided upon death will die in any case, of that disease or another, or of the side effects of the inoculation.

Give us a moment . . . Inner reality and private experience give birth to all mass events. Man cannot disentangle himself from the natural context of his physical life. His culture, his religion, his psychologies, and his psychological nature together form the context within which both private and mass events occur. *(Loudly, then whispering so softly that I could barely hear:)* This book will, then, be devoted to the nature of the great sweeping emotional, religious, or biological events that often seem to engulf the individual, or to lift him or her willy-nilly in their power.

What is the relationship between the individual and the gigantic mass motions of nature, of government, or even of religion? What about mass conversions? Mass hysteria? Mass healings, mass murder, and the individual? Those are the questions we will devote ourselves to in this book.

It will be called: "The Individual and the Nature of Mass Events."

(Louder:) Take your break or end the session as you prefer.

(10:35. "We'll take the break, then."

(Immediately:) And you can say that your question about epidemics served as a convenient stimulus; for that question, coming from you, comes also from the readers of our books.

(Jane came out of her trance in a sort of amazed silence — which meant that she had some idea of what Seth had been talking about, as sometimes happens.

("Now just who in the heck is up to what?" I asked her. We laughed. "How can I use this material as an appendix or note in 'Unknown' *if it belongs in a new book? I thought you and your boy were up to something not long after the session started."*

("Oh, I don't believe it," she said. "This isn't anything like I consciously figured upon — and you can put that down for one of us to type, two or three years from now . . . I can't get over this. . . ."

(Jane had started doing some typing on the final manuscript for Seth's The Nature of the Psyche: Its Human Expression *a couple of days ago. She was also working on her own* The Afterdeath Journal of an American Philosopher: The World View of William James. *Yet I thought she needed the stimulus of Seth having something underway. There was more than a little irony in the situation, for I was the one who'd told her flat out, back in July 1975, that she was going to start* Psyche, *just so that she'd have a Seth book to play with. [I'd also wanted to see what she and Seth would come up with on demand.] But this time Seth fooled me and started* Mass Events *only a couple of weeks after finishing* Psyche. *I was all for it, though, I told Jane enthusiastically. It's always a pleasure to work on a Seth*

book, to explore with him his unique view of reality, and to try to put at least a few of his ideas to use in our everyday, "practical" world. I repeated my thought that it didn't matter how many Seth books she piled up ahead of contract, or publication: That was certainly a more creative and exciting position to be in than if one didn't have anything ahead. Jane agreed, while still worrying about what we were going to do with all of the material as it accumulated year after year. At this time there's no way we're going to see it all published.

("My mind works in sneaky little ways," she said. "I don't tell you everything. I was thinking of something like a question-and-answer format for a book, if we did a new one." Even that idea was a revelation to me, since she hadn't mentioned a book, period. Seth returned briefly as we talked:

(10:39.) We have begun Part 1, to be called: "The Events of 'Nature.' Epidemics and Natural Disasters."

(Then a moment later:) Chapter 1: "The Natural Body and Its Defenses."

("But I'm really surprised. I had no idea of this tonight," Jane said as soon as she was Jane again — thereupon emphasizing anew some of our endless questions about the Seth phenomenon: What portion of her personality, or entity, whether that portion might be called a Seth, or whatever, had been busy planning — organizing — this new endeavor? And how could such a creative process take place without her having at least some conscious intimations of it? What were the limits of human accomplishment?

(We had something to eat while we talked about the new book. I read Jane the title for it several times. She didn't seem to be very taken with it. "I don't know whether I'm going on with the session or not," she finally said. "I'm just waiting. So far I haven't gotten anything. . . ." Resume, eventually, at 11:25, with many pauses.)

Dying is a biological necessity, not only for the individual, but to insure the continued vitality of the species. Dying is a spiritual and psychological necessity, for after a while the exuberant, ever-renewed energies of the spirit can no longer be translated into flesh.

Inherently, each individual knows that he or she must die physically in order to survive spiritually and psychically (underlined). The self outgrows the flesh. Particularly since [the advent of Charles] Darwin's theories[5], the acceptance of the fact of death has come to imply a certain kind of weakness, for is it not said that only the strong survive?

To some degree, epidemics and recognized illnesses serve the sociological purpose of providing an acceptable reason for death — a face-saving device for those who have already decided to die. This does not mean that such individuals make a conscious decision to die, in your terms: But such decisions are often semiconscious *(intently)*. It might be that those individuals feel they have fulfilled their purposes — but such decisions may also be built upon a different kind of desire for survival than those understood in Darwinian terms.

It is not understood that before life an individual decides to live. A self is not simply the accidental personification of the body's biological mechanism. Each person born <u>desires</u> to be born. He dies when that desire no longer operates. No epidemic or illness or natural disaster — or stray bullet from a murderer's gun — will kill a person who does not want to die.

The desire for life has been most flaunted, yet human psychology has seldom dealt with the quite active desire for death. In its <u>natural</u> form this is not a morbid, frightened, neurotic, or cowardly attempt to escape life, but a definite, positive, "healthy" acceleration of the desire for survival, in which the individual strongly wants to leave physical life as once the child wanted to leave the parent's home.

(11:44.) I am not speaking here of the desire for suicide, which involves a definite killing of the body by self-deliberate means — often of a violent nature. Ideally this desire for death, however, would simply involve the slowing of the body's processes, the gradual disentanglement of psyche from flesh; or in other instances, according to individual characteristics, a sudden, <u>natural</u> stopping of the body's processes.

Left <u>alone</u>, the self and the body are so entwined that the separation would be smooth. The body would automatically follow the wishes of the inner self. In the case of suicide, for example, the self is to some extent acting out of context with the body, which still has its <u>own</u> will to live.

(Long pause, one of many.) I will have more to say about suicide, but I do not mean here to imply guilt on the part of a person who

takes his or her own life. In many such cases, a more natural death would have ensued in any event as the result of "diseases." Period. Often, for example, a person wanting to die originally intended to experience only a portion of earth life, say childhood. This purpose would be entwined with the parents' intent. Such a son or daughter might be born, for instance, through a woman who wanted to experience childbirth but who did not necessarily want to encounter the years of child-raising, for her own reasons.

(11:57. The telephone began to ring. The sudden noise was a shock, so deep was our mutual concentration. Yet Jane didn't come out of trance. As Seth, she stared at me; I stared back, making no effort to take the call. Fortunately, the ringing soon stopped.)

Such a mother would attract a consciousness who desired, perhaps, to reexperience childhood but not adulthood, or who might teach the mother lessons sorely needed. Such a child might naturally die at 10 or 12, or earlier. Yet the ministrations of science might keep the child alive far longer, until such a person [begins] encountering an adulthood thrust upon him or her, so to speak.

An automobile accident, suicide, or another kind of accident might result. The person might fall prey to an epidemic, but the smoothness of biological motion or psychological motion has been lost. I am not here condoning suicide, for too often in your society it is the unfortunate result of conflicting beliefs — and yet it is true to say that all deaths are suicide, and all births deliberate on the part of child and parent. To that extent, you cannot separate issues like a population explosion on the part of certain portions of the world, from epidemics, earthquakes, and other disasters.

(Long pause.) In wars, people automatically reproduce their kind to make up for those that are killed, and when the race overproduces there will be automatic controls set upon the population. Yet these will in all ways fit the intents and purposes of the individuals involved.

(Forcefully:) End of dictation, end of session, my heartiest regards . . .

(12:12 A.M. After giving a few lines of material for herself, Jane abruptly came out of a very deep trance without saying good night as Seth. "I haven't any memory of anything since break," she said. We were tired.

(I don't know yet how I'll go about producing my part of Mass Events, of course, but the reader, picking up the finished work, will be able to tell at

a glance all the decisions I made: whether the session notes are long or short, numerous or scarce, how often I referred to the other Seth books, and whether or not I added any appendix material.

("Well," I told Jane as we went to bed, "right now my idea is that we'll have only short notes and no appendixes. Doing things that way will speed up the publication date." I'm all too conscious of the great amount of physical time I'm spending on the two volumes of "Unknown" Reality; *I often feel responsible for holding up publication of Volume 2 especially, since Seth finished dictating it almost exactly two years ago. See the chronology of our activities in Note 2.)*

NOTES: SESSION 801

1. In the order of their publication the five previous Seth books are: *Seth Speaks: The Eternal Validity of the Soul; The Nature of Personal Reality: A Seth Book; Volumes 1 and 2 of the "Unknown" Reality: A Seth Book;* and *The Nature of the Psyche: Its Human Expression.* All of Jane's books, whether produced with or without Seth, are listed in the frontmatter of *Mass Events,* with publication dates.

2. I don't mean to confuse the reader by using the titles of Seth's "old" books, but rather to show how Jane's and my work encompasses a number of projects at once. That is, we have yet to manage to work on just one book of any kind at a time; that would be too simple! There's always a long slow rate of turnover in our labors, it seems: As one book or project is finished, another rises almost effortlessly to take its place, and everything rolls along together until the next large change comes about.

That progression in Jane's endeavors (and in my own to a lesser degree) may reflect her strong writing and psychic abilities, but it also reveals the way we constantly work with her work, and how we go about presenting it in the form of physical books so that we can show others what we've been up to.

Note that even though Seth finished dictating Volume 1 of *"Unknown" Reality* almost three years ago (in June 1974), and I completed my own notes and appendixes for it six months ago, we're just now coming to the end of the long, complicated process involved in following the manuscript through the editorial and production stages necessary to get the book out into the marketplace. Checking the page proofs is the last stage we go through before publication, and Volume 1 is due to be marketed this summer — probably in July.

In physical terms, three years is an important portion of one's life span. What were Jane and I each doing all that time? We were involved in a whole group of endeavors. I'll recap the major ones in order to place the beginning of Seth's latest book, *Mass Events,* in context. I do this for my own sake as well as the reader's, since I like to know exactly where I am in time, and what I mean and feel when writing even a short note for one of the Seth books.

This reconstruction of the past can be both fascinating and frustrating as I compare dates, session numbers, and our daily activities. Somehow, immersed in all of that minutiae of the past, I revive it so that it becomes part of the present once more — and that coexistence then reminds me of Seth's idea of simultaneous time; perhaps, outside of dreaming, it's the best approximation I can make of the paradoxical notion that all exists at once, and that all *changes* together, for each time I regard one of my past moments from the present, I change both that past and the present.

Another purpose is involved in presenting *Mass Events* in context, though: I plan to use current professional and personal events from our lives as a sort of background or framework for the book as Jane delivers it for Seth. But right now, here's a chronological list of our activities from June 17, 1974, when Seth finished his share of the work on Volume I of *"Unknown Reality"* to April 18, 1977 (today) when I mailed the corrected page proofs for that volume to Jane's publisher.

Beginning in June 1974, then, while writing notes and appendixes for Volume 1 of *"Unknown"*, and taking Seth's dictation for Volume 2, I spent eight months producing the art work for Jane's *Adventures in Consciousness* and for her book of poetry, *Dialogues of the Soul and Mortal Self in Time;* I finished all of those drawings in January 1975. In the meantime Jane completed *Adventures* in August 1974, and started *Psychic Politics* that October. In March 1975 we took time out to move from the apartment house in downtown Elmira to our "hill house" just outside the city. Jane finished dictating Volume 2 of *"Unknown"* for Seth in April 1975, and I started my notes and appendixes for it. In July 1975 Seth began *The Nature of the Psyche: Its Human Expression,* and in December of that year Jane initiated work on her own *The World View of Paul Cézanne: A Psychic Interpretation.* She finished *Politics* in February 1976, and *Cézanne* in September; *Politics* was published that September also. I completed my own writing for Volume 1 of *"Unknown"* in October. Our 16-year-old cat, Willy, died early in November, and two days later we obtained a kitten, Willy Two (or Billy, as we soon came to call him), from an area humane society. I finished typing the manuscript for Volume 1 late in November, spent December checking it, and mailed it to Prentice-Hall early in January 1977.

In January we obtained an unlisted telephone number, because we could no longer handle the 600-or-so calls a month that were coming in. Later in the month, Jane started writing *James.* In February 1977 we received from Prentice-Hall the copyedited manuscript for Volume 1 of *"Unknown" Reality.* (Copyediting is one of the earlier editorial stages a book goes through on its way to publication, and is meant to study all of the work that Jane and I and her editor, Tam Mossman, have already done on the manuscript: Before it's set into type, a reader who works independently of the publishing firm carefully checks the manuscript for grammar, contradictions, facts, consistency, and so forth, and makes suggestions for whatever changes he or she thinks are desirable. Jane and I are free, of course, to reject any alterations we don't agree with.) In March we checked the copyedited manuscript for *Cézanne*. Seth finished dictating *Psyche* early in April. A few days later we began correcting page proofs for Volume 1 of *"Unknown."*

In addition to these activities, Jane conducted her weekly ESP classes until we moved in March 1975, and kept up with her considerable correspondence. Her mail is accumulating at such a rate that I think it's becoming a valuable social document in its own right. An extremely interesting study could be done on the personal and social factors behind the great variety of responses her work has generated. We have on file most of the letters we've received over the years.

Through all of this, we've usually kept the sessions going, to get both book work and other, often private material, seen a number of scheduled visitors — and some who weren't scheduled — and participated in a few radio and newspaper interviews.

At this time, I'm still working on the notes and appendixes for Volume 2 of *"Unknown,"* even while Seth has begun *Mass Events.* Jane and I have already planned our approach to *Psyche* (which Seth has just finished), and it's to be published shortly after Volume 2 is. To top off our activities of the moment, we're having the front porch of the hill house rebuilt — with a new raised floor and screening all around, so that Jane can write there in the summertime. The workmen swarming around all day, and the noise involved, are both exciting and distracting. But I have a feeling that the front porch affair isn't the end of our construction odyssey: Jane has a certain speculative look when she notes that we have but one car — she doesn't drive — to occupy the large two-car garage attached to the rear of the house. What better idea than to convert half of the garage into a writing room, with sliding glass doors, and add a screened-in porch there also? After all, she commented recently, the porch would protect our back door, too, especially from all of that winter weather. . . .

3. Seth's delivery is remarkably clear and unambiguous, but once in a while he'll come through with an awkward sentence (as we all do), or one that combines the singular and the plural when one or the other should be used throughout, or he'll repeat a certain word too often. On such occasions Jane and I may recast the sentence slightly while maintaining the syntax, or add a clarifying word or phrase in brackets [like this].

If I catch anything amiss in Seth's delivery I'll ask him about it. He may omit a word, or I may misinterpret what he says while I'm concentrating on my notetaking. In these cases Jane always spots the error at once when she reads my typed session transcript. But except for such minor alterations, or in the case of personal information, which we may delete, Seth's material is presented as received, and we never arbitrarily eliminate any of it — occasionally to the pain of others, I'm afraid. We think it important that these sessions be given just as Jane delivers them, for after all the manner of that presentation, and its organization, are vital parts of the whole Seth phenomenon. So is the speed of delivery, for that matter. I want to remind the reader that the Seth books are *spoken* books rather than written ones, and that ordinarily Seth has no chance to revise his copy.

Jane's ability and training as a writer are obviously responsible for the form the sessions take. As she's said often: "I'm a writer who's psychic — not a psychic who's a writer."

4. I'm especially interested in Seth's material on inoculations, since on two separate occasions I underwent severe physical reactions after receiving them. Jane has also had some unfavorable experiences with inoculations.

As for myself, I took both preventative "treatments" before Jane began speaking for Seth in 1963. One led to a strong serum reaction that incapacitated me for two weeks; the other resulted in a partial paralysis lasting several days. I accepted the vaccines because I yielded (if somewhat reluctantly) to conventional parental and medical pressures, as well as my own beliefs of the time: I was "supposed" to take the inoculations; they would be "good" for me. Even now I must carry a warning card in my wallet. It bears a description of my reactions to at least some vaccines, as well as the most emphatic statement that if I'm found unconscious for any reason — after an accident, say — I must not be given an injection of any kind because I might have a fatal reaction to it. I haven't had a "shot" since living through those very unpleasant experiences, nor do I intend to. I no longer believe I'd succumb to one of the forbidden vaccines — but at the same time I don't want to find out what *might* happen, either!

Still, it would seem to be almost impossible to do without inoculation programs in our society — they're such a strong part of our national and private medical belief systems. I'm sure that Seth will elaborate upon the whole subject of mass inoculations as he proceeds with *Mass Events*.

He's commented before in his books on our medical practices and technology, of course. In Volume 1 of *"Unknown" Reality*, for instance, see Session 703, which was held on June 12, 1974. At 10:36, in part: "People will die when they are ready to, following inner dictates and dynamics. A person ready to die will, despite any medication. A person who wants to live will seize upon the tiniest hope, and respond. The dynamics of health have nothing to do with inoculations. They reside in the consciousness of each being."

5. Seth referred to evolution in both volumes of *"Unknown" Reality.* As it happens, I've just finished writing a rather long dissertation on the subject for Volume 2. It will be presented as Appendix 12.

SESSION 802, APRIL 25, 1977
9:47 P.M. MONDAY

(The regularly scheduled session for last Wednesday evening was not held. As I wrote in Note 2 for the first session of Mass Events, *which Seth-Jane gave a week ago, we're having the front porch of our hill house rebuilt. The workmen poured the cement for the new floor on Thursday. Today they installed the forms for the new porch steps, and poured again. The weather has been excellent.)*

Good evening.

("Good evening, Seth.")

Dictation: *(Pause, one of many.)* Now: To a certain extent (under-lined), epidemics are the result of a mass suicide phenomenon on the parts of those involved. Biological, sociological, or even economic factors may be involved, in that for a variety of reasons, and at different levels, whole groups of individuals want to die at any given time — but in such a way that their individual deaths amount to a mass statement.

On one level the deaths are a protest against the time in which they occur. Those involved have private reasons, however. The reasons, of course, vary from one individual to another, yet all involved "want their death to serve a purpose" beyond private concerns. Partially, then, such deaths are meant to make the survivors question the conditions (dash) — for unconsciously the species well knows there are reasons for such mass deaths that go beyond accepted beliefs.

In some historical periods the plight of the poor was so horrible, so unendurable, that outbreaks of the plague occurred, literally resulting in a complete destruction of large areas of the environment in which such social, political, and economic conditions existed. [Those] plagues took rich and poor alike, however, so the complacent well-to-do could see quite clearly, for example, that to some extent sanitary conditions, privacy, peace of mind, had to be granted to the poor alike, for the results of their dissatisfaction would have quite practical results. Those were deaths of protest.[1]

Individually, each "victim" was to one extent or another a "victim" of apathy, despair, or hopelessness, which automatically lowered bodily defenses.

Not only do such states of mind lower the defenses, however, but they activate and change the body's chemistries, alter its balances, and initiate disease conditions. Many viruses inherently capable of causing death, in normal conditions contribute to the overall health of the body, existing side by side as it were with other viruses, each contributing quite necessary activities that maintain bodily equilibrium.

If [certain viruses] are triggered, however, to higher activity or overproduction by mental states, they then become "deadly." Physically they may be passed on in whatever manner is peculiar to a specific strain. Literally, individual mental problems of sufficient severity emerge as social, mass diseases.

(Long pause.) The environment in which an outbreak occurs points at the political, sociological, and economic conditions that have evolved, causing such disorder. Often such outbreaks take place after ineffective political or social action — that is, after some unified mass social protest — has failed, or is considered hopeless. They often occur also in wartime on the part of a populace [that] is against a given war in which [its] country is involved.

Initially there is a psychic contagion: Despair moves faster than a mosquito, or any outward carrier of a given disease. The mental state brings about the activation of a virus that is, in those terms, passive.

(Pause at 10:16.) Despair may seem passive only because it feels that exterior action is hopeless — but its fires rage inwardly, and that kind of contagion can leap from bed to bed and from heart to heart. It touches those, however, who are in the same state only, and to some extent it brings about an acceleration in which something can indeed be done in terms of group action.

Now if you believe in one life only, then such conditions will seem most disastrous, and in your terms they clearly are not pretty. Yet, though each victim in an epidemic may die his or her own death, that death becomes part of a mass social protest. The lives of intimate survivors are shaken, and according to the extent of the epidemic the various elements of social life itself are disturbed, altered, rearranged. Sometimes such epidemics are eventually responsible for the overthrow of governments, the loss of wars.

There are also even deeper biological connections with the heart of nature. You are biological creatures. Your proud human consciousness rests on the vast "unconscious" integrity of your physical being. In that regard your consciousness is as natural as your toe. In terms of the species' integrity your mental states are, then, highly important. Despair or apathy is a biological "enemy." Social conditions, political states, economic policies, and even religious or philosophical frameworks that foster such mental states, bring about a biological retaliation. They act like fire applied to a plant.

The epidemics then serve many purposes — warning that certain conditions will not be tolerated. There is a biological outrage that will be continually expressed until the conditions are changed.

(Long pause at 10:31.) Give us a moment . . . Even in the days of the great plagues in England there were those smitten who did not die, and there were those untouched by the disease who dealt with the sick and dying. Those survivors, who were actively involved, saw themselves in a completely different light than those who succumbed, however: They were those, untouched by despair, who saw themselves as effective rather than ineffective. Often they roused themselves from lives of previously unheroic situations, and then performed with great bravery. The horror of the conditions overwhelmed them where earlier they were not involved.

The sight of the dying gave them visions of the meaning of life, and stirred new [ideas] of sociological, political, and spiritual natures, so that in your terms the dead did not die in vain. Epidemics by their public nature speak of public problems — problems that sociologically threaten to sweep the individual to psychic disaster as the physical materialization does biologically.

(Pause.) These are the reasons also for the range or the limits of various epidemics — why they sweep through one area and leave another clear. Why one in the family will die and another survive — for in this mass venture, the individual still forms his or her private reality.

(Pause at 10:42.) Give us a moment . . . In your society scientific medical beliefs operate, and a kind of preventative medicine,

mentioned earlier, in which procedures [of inoculation] are taken, bringing about in healthy individuals a minute disease condition that then gives immunity against a more massive visitation. In the case of any given disease this procedure might work quite well for those who believe in it. It is, however, the belief, and not the procedure, that works *(louder)*.[2]

I am not recommending that you abandon the procedure when it obviously works for so many — yet you should understand why it brings about the desired results.

Such medical technology is highly specific, however. You cannot be inoculated with the desire to live, or with the zest, delight, or contentment of the healthy animal. If you have decided to die, protected from one disease in such a manner, you will promptly come down with another, or have an accident. The immunization, while specifically effective, may only reinforce prior beliefs about the body's ineffectiveness. It may appear that left alone the body would surely develop whatever disease might be "fashionable" at the time, so that the specific victory might result in the ultimate defeat as far as your beliefs are concerned.

You have your own medical systems, however. I do not mean to undermine them, since they are undermining themselves. Some of my statements clearly cannot be proven, in your terms, and appear almost sacrilegious. Yet, throughout your history no man or woman has died who did not want to die, regardless of the state of medical technology. Specific diseases have certain symbolic meanings, varying with the times and the places.[3]

(10:56.) Give us a moment . . . Are your hands tired?

("No."

(Pause.) There has been great discussion in past years about the survival of the fittest, in Darwinian terms,[4] but little emphasis is placed upon the quality of life, or of survival itself; or in human terms, [there has been] little probing into the question of what makes life worthwhile. Quite simply, if life is not worthwhile *(louder)*, no species will have a reason to continue.

Civilizations are literally social species. They die when they see no reason to live, yet they seed other civilizations. Your private mental states *en masse* bring about the mass cultural stance of your civilization. To some extent, then, the survival of your civilization is quite literally dependent upon the condition of each individual; and that condition is initially a spiritual, psychic state that gives birth to the physical organism. That organism is intimately connected to the natural biological state of each other person, and to each other living thing, or entity, however minute.

New paragraph: Despite all "realistic" pragmatic tales to the contrary, the natural state of life itself is one of joy, acquiescence with itself — a state in which action is effective, and the power to act is a natural right. You would see this quite clearly with plants, animals, and all other life if you were not so blinded by beliefs to the contrary. You would feel it in the activity of your bodies, in which the vital individual affirmation of your cells brings about the mass, immensely complicated achievement of your physical being. That activity naturally promotes health and vitality.

I am not speaking of some romanticized, "passive," floppy, spiritual world, but of a clear reality without impediments, in which the opposite of despair and apathy reigns.

This book will be devoted, then, to those conditions that best promote spiritual, psychic, and physical zest, the biological and psychic components that make a species desire to continue its kind. Such aspects promote the cooperation of all kinds of life on all levels with one another. No species competes with another, but cooperates to form an environment in which all kinds can creatively exist.

(Forcefully:) End of dictation. We will have a rip-roaring book this time. You may end the session or take a break as you prefer.

("We'll take the break."

(11:17. Jane's delivery had been quite intent throughout, even though she'd taken many pauses; some of them had been long. Before the session she had wondered if she really wanted to have one, but as on other such occasions she came through with excellent material once she started.

(Resume in the same manner at 11:37.)

I will then briefly continue.

You live in a physical community, but you live first of all in a community of thoughts and feelings. These trigger your physical actions. They directly affect the behavior of your body. The experience of the animals is different, yet in their own ways animals have both individual intent and purpose. Their feelings are certainly as pertinent as yours. They dream, and in their way they reason.

They do not "worry." They do not anticipate disaster when no signs of it are apparent in their immediate environment. On their own they do not need preventative medicine. Pet animals are inoculated against diseases, however. In your society this almost becomes a necessity. In a "purely natural" setting you would not have as many living puppies or kittens. There are stages of physical existence, and in those terms nature knows what it is doing. When a species overproduces, the incidences of, say, epidemics grow. This applies to human populations as well as to the animals.

The quality of life is important above all. Newborn animals either die quickly and naturally, painlessly, before their consciousnesses are fully focused here, or are killed by their mothers — not because they are weak or unfit to survive, but because the [physical] conditions are not those that will produce the quality of life that makes survival "worthwhile."

The consciousness that became so briefly physical is not annihilated, however, but in your terms waits for better conditions.

There are also "trial runs" in human and animal species alike, in which peeks are taken, or glimpses, of physical life, and that is all. Epidemics sweeping through animal populations are also biological and psychic statements, then, in which each individual knows that only its own greatest fulfillment can satisfy the quality of life on an individual basis, and thus contribute to the mass survival of the species.

(Pause at 11:55.) Suffering is not necessarily good for the soul at all, and left alone natural creatures do not seek it. There is a natural compassion, a biological knowledge, so that the mother of an animal knows whether or not existing conditions will support the new offspring. Animals instinctively realize their relationship with the great forces of life. They will instinctively starve an offspring while its consciousness is still unfocused, rather than send it loose under adverse conditions.

In a natural state, many children would die stillborn for the same reasons, or would be naturally aborted. There is a give-and-take between all elements of nature, so that such individuals often choose mothers, for example, who perhaps wanted the experience of pregnancy but not of birth — where they choose the experience of the fetus but not necessarily [that] of the child. Often in such cases these are "fragment personalities," wanting to taste physical reality, but not being ready to deal with it. Each case is individual, however, so these are general statements.

Many children, who, it seems, should have died of disease, of "childhood epidemics," nevertheless survive because of their different intents. The world of thought and feeling may be invisible, and yet it activates all physical systems with which you are acquainted.

Animals as well as men can indeed make social statements, that appear in a biological context. Animals stricken by kitten and puppy diseases, for example, choose to die, pointing out the fact that the quality of their lives individually and *en masse* is vastly lacking. Their relationships with their own species is no longer in balance. They cannot use their full abilities or powers, nor are many of them given compensating elements in terms of a beneficial psychic relationship with man — but instead are shunted aside, unwanted and unloved. An unloved animal does not want to live.

Love involves self-respect, the trust in individual biological zest and integrity. To that extent, in their way animal epidemics have the same causes as human ones.

An animal can indeed commit suicide. So can a race or a species. The dignity of a spirited life demands that a certain quality of experience be maintained.

(Emphatically:) End of dictation, end of session. My heartiest regards. *(Whispering now:)* Trust the changes in Ruburt's [own condition]. A fond good evening.

("Thank you. The same to you, Seth. Good night.")

(12:17 A.M. See Jane's material on her "own condition" in her Introduction for this book. She's enjoyed a number of heartening improvements lately.)

NOTES: SESSION 802

1. In ordinary terms, various kinds of plague, including the bubonic and the infamous "Black Death," were (and still are) spread to man by fleas carrying a bacterium from infected rats. Other forms of the affliction are carried by other rodents. In Seth's terms, through the complicated interactions and communications involving all forms of life, man's deep dissatisfactions would have periodically helped trigger the resurgence of scourges like the plagues: In 3rd-century Rome, for instance, several thousand people were said to have died each day; estimates are that over a 20-year period in the 14th century, three-quarters of the population of Europe and Asia perished; there was the great plague of London in 1665, and so forth.

2. Occasionally, instead of calling for a particular word or phrase to be underlined for emphasis, Seth delivers it louder — sometimes much louder. I often underline such material so the reader will know just what's been stressed. On the printed page the results look pretty much like those words Seth himself wants underlined, but during the session they come through quite differently.

Jane has great energy and power at her disposal when speaking for Seth, and I can often feel those qualities as though they form a collective palpable entity in itself. During our private and book sessions Seth's voice effects are usually quite conversational in tone and emphasis, and he speaks slowly enough so that I can comfortably take notes. The Seth voice can be stunning in volume and rapidity of delivery, however, and can seemingly continue in those modes indefinitely: I've witnessed some truly remarkable demonstrations, lasting several hours. Such manifestations are practically never carried that far in our regular sessions, however. Nor is Jane ever exhausted by speaking for Seth — rather, she reports an infusion of energy, both subjectively and objectively. As she's often said, she "rides" the Seth voice, or the energy behind or within it.

Both of us have written about the Seth voice effects in other books, as we try to understand more about them.

3. See Note 4 for Session 801.

For all of the disadvantages of vaccination and inoculation programs, then, Seth obviously doesn't recommend that we abandon them at present, since most of us believe in their efficiency. It may be some time before private beliefs are strong enough to sustain us, without the use of those medical "crutches." Still, we can try to minimize such dependency (as Jane and I do now), and to avoid taking shots simply because they're "in vogue."

In Note 4 for Session 801, I quoted material Seth gave on inoculations in Session 703 for Volume 1 of *"Unknown" Reality.* Now let me cite some of his material from Session 704 in the same book. After 10:16: "You can point to diseases stamped out because of inoculations or other preventative measures. . . . It seems the worst kind of idiocy to suggest that the individual has any kind of <u>effective</u> protection against illness or disease . . .

"Again, many can thankfully praise a given doctor for discovering a disease condition 'in time,' so that effective countering measures were taken and the disease was eliminated. You cannot know for sure, of course, what would have happened otherwise . . . to those people who wanted to die. If they did not die of the disease, they may have 'fallen prey' to an accident, or died in a war, or in a natural disaster.

"They may have been 'cured' whether or not they had treatment, and gone on to lead productive lives. You do not know. A man or woman who is ready to die, if saved from one disease will promptly get another, or find a way of fulfilling that desire. Your problem there rests with the will to live, and with the mechanisms of the psyche."

Still, Jane and I do have our cats inoculated against feline distemper and respiratory viruses; pets acquired at humane societies (as ours often are) have already shared an infected environment. We suppose that if we had young children we'd see to their receiving the immunizations they "should" have, or are required to have by a school board, for example. It's very difficult in our society to rely upon beliefs alone where other people are involved, particularly in the face of medical and scientific propaganda. (Let me add, though, that there are available today numerous vaccines against childhood diseases, but that many parents ignore many of them. Some of those vaccines — for whooping cough, mumps, measles, German measles or rubella, for instance — are still quite controversial. They're often only partially effective, and can cause a variety of side effects: reactions ranging from the temporary to the permanent or fatal. Jane and I strongly recommend that parents thoroughly investigate and understand the pros and cons involved with *each* inoculation their children will receive.)

4. The English naturalist, Charles Darwin (1809–1882), maintained in his theory of organic evolution that all plants and animals develop from their own previous forms by inheriting minute variations through succeeding generations, with those forms best fitted to the environment being the ones most likely to survive.

Amazingly, another English naturalist, Alfred Wallace (1823–1913), independently developed a similar theory, and the two men had their work presented to science in the same paper in 1858. The next year Darwin published his *On the Origin of Species*.

I'm sure Seth would say that the whole affair was hardly a coincidence, since he's commented several times that new ideas often separately arise more than once in a given historical period.

SESSION 803, MAY 2, 1977
9:43 P.M. MONDAY

(Ever since she began dictating Mass Events *for Seth, Jane has felt like having book sessions but once a week — on Monday nights — and doing other things in between. So she's been working on her own* James, *writing poetry, painting, and helping me out with Seth's* Psyche *by doing some of the work I usually do when he's finished a book: typing sessions for the*

manuscript, checking my rough notes, rewriting some of them and making suggestions about others. But with all of this, she's been refreshing her physical and creative selves by simply enjoying the day-by-day magical ripening of another spring.)

Good evening.

("Good evening, Seth.")

Dictation: Your scientists are beginning to understand man's physical relationship with nature. The species is obviously a part of nature and not apart from it.

Environmental questions are being raised about man's effects upon the world in which he lives. There is, however, an inner environment that connects all consciousnesses that dwell upon your planet, in whatever form. This mental or psychic — or in any case nonphysical — environment is ever in a state of flux and motion. That activity provides you with all exterior phenomena.

Give us a moment . . . Your sense perception, physically speaking, is a result of behavior on the part of organs that seem to you to have no reality outside of their relationship with you. Those organs are themselves composed of atoms and molecules with their own consciousnesses. They have, then, their own states of sensation and cognition. They work for you, allowing you to perceive physical reality.

Your ears certainly seem to be permanent appendages, and so do your eyes. You say: "My eyes are blue," or "My ears are small." The physical matter of those sense organs changes constantly, however, with you none the wiser. While your body appears quite dependable, solid, [and] steady, you are not aware of the constant interchanges that occur between it and the physical environment. It does not bother you one whit that the physical substance of your body is made up of completely different atoms and molecules than it was composed of seven years ago, [say], or that your familiar hands are actually innocent of any smallest smidgen of matter that composed them [even in recent times past].

You perceive your body as solid. Again, the very senses that make such a deduction are the result of the behavior of atoms and molecules literally coming together to form the organs, filling a pattern of flesh. All other objects that you perceive are formed in their own way in the same fashion.

The physical world that you recognize is made up of invisible patterns. These patterns are "plastic," in that while they exist, their final form is a matter of probabilities directed by consciousness. Your senses perceive these patterns in their own ways. The patterns themselves can be "activated" in innumerable fashions. There is something out there *(humorously emphatic)* to observe.

(Long pause, one of many, at 10:04.) Your sense apparatus determines what form that something will take, however. The mass world rises up before your eyes, but your eyes are part of that mass world. You cannot see your thoughts, so you do not realize that they have shape and form, even as, say, clouds do. There are currents of thought as there are currents of air, and the mental patterns of men's feelings and thoughts rise up like flames from a fire, or steam from hot water, to fall like ashes or like rain.

All elements of the interior invisible environment work together, and they form the temporal weather patterns that are exteriorized mental states, presenting you locally and *en masse*, then, with a physical version of man's emotional states. Period.

(As he had during the 801st session, our cat, Billy, roused himself from a snooze and walked over to Jane. This time he jumped up into her lap, then positioned himself with his forelegs against her chest while examining her face. Jane, as Seth, petted him. I called Billy to me. He perched briefly on my own lap, then curled up on the cushion beside me.

(Amused:) You can say that I petted the pussy.

Now: The physical planet is obviously also ever-changing while it is operationally or realistically or pragmatically relatively stable. The physical matter of the planet is also composed of literally infinite hordes of consciousnesses — each experiencing its own reality while adding to the overall cooperative venture.

(Long pause.) Natural disasters represent an understandably prejudiced concept, in which the vast creative and rejuvenating elements important to planetary life, and therefore to mankind, are ignored. The stability of the planet rests upon such changes and alterations, even as the body's stability is dependent upon, say, the birth and death of the cells.

(10:20.) It is quite obvious that people must die — not only because otherwise you would overpopulate your world into extinction,

but because the nature of consciousness requires new experience, challenge, and accomplishment. This is everywhere apparent in nature itself. *(Pause.)* If there were no death, you would have to invent it *(smile)* — for the context of that selfhood would be as limited as the experience of a great sculptor given but one hunk of stone *(with quiet dramatic emphasis).*[1]

The sculptor's creation is pragmatically realistic, in that it exists as an object, and can be quite legitimately perceived, as can your world. The sculptor's statue, however, comes from the inner environment, the patterns of probabilities. These patterns are not themselves inactive. They are possessed by the desire to be-actualized (with a hyphen). Behind all realities there are mental states. These always seek form, though again there are other forms than those you recognize.

A chair is a chair for your purposes. As Ruburt speaks for me he sits in one. As you read this book you most probably lounge on a chair or couch or bench — all quite sturdy and real. The atoms and molecules within those chairs and couches are quite alert, though you do not grant them the quality of life. When children play ring-around-the-rosy, they form living circles in the air. In that game they enjoy the motion of their bodies, but they do not identify with those swirling circles. The atoms and molecules that make up a chair play a different kind of ring-around-the-rosy, and are involved in constant motion, forming a certain pattern that you perceive as a chair.

The differences in motion are so divergent that to you the chair, like your body, appears permanent. The atoms and molecules, like the children, enjoy their motion — solidly sketched in space from your perspective, however, with no "idea" that you consider that motion a chair, or so use it.

You perceive the atoms' activity in that fashion. [Nevertheless] the agreement takes place at mental levels, and is never completely "set," though it appears to be. No one perceives the same chair [all of the time], though perhaps a given chair will seem to be "the same one" seen from different angles.

The dance of the atoms and molecules is continuous in your area. In greater terms, any given chair is never the same chair. All of this must be taken into consideration when we discuss mass events.

Take your break.

(10:42. Jane's trance had been good, but she remembered Billy climbing into her lap, and how he'd put his face close to hers. "Seth thought it was great," she said. Resume at 11:14.)

The scientist probing the brain of an idiot or a genius will find only the physical matter of the brain itself.

Not one idea will be discovered residing in the brain cells. You can try to convey an idea, you can feel its effects, but you cannot see it as you can the chair. Only a fool would say that ideas were non-existent, however, or deny their importance.

You cannot find any given dream location, either, within the brain itself. The solid matter of your world is the result of the play of your senses upon an inner dimension of activity that exists as legitimately, and yet as tantalizingly hidden, as an idea or a dream location.

It is easy for you to see that seeds bring forth the fruit of the earth, each [of] their own kind. No seed is identical to any other, yet generally speaking there are species that serve to unite them. You do not mistake an orange for a grape. In the same way ideas or thoughts form general patterns, bringing forth in your world certain kinds of events. In this respect your thoughts and feelings "seed" physical reality, bringing forth materializations.

You operate quite nicely politically, living in villages, townships, countries, states, and so forth, each with certain customs and local ordinances. These in no way affect the land itself. They are designations for practical purposes, and they imply organization of intent or affiliation at one level. They are political patterns, invisible but highly effective. There are, however, far more vigorous invisible mental patterns, into which the thoughts and feelings of mankind are organized — or, naturally, organize themselves.

Each person's thoughts flow into that formation, forming part of the earth's psychic atmosphere. From that atmosphere flows the natural earthly patterns from which your seasons emerge with all of their variety and effects. You are never victims of natural disasters, though it may seem that you are, for you have your hand in forming them. You are creatively involved in the earth's cycles. No one can be born for you, or die for you, and yet no birth or death is really an isolated event, but one in which the entire planet participates. In personal terms, again, each species is concerned not only with survival but with the quality of its life and experience.

In those terms, natural disasters <u>ultimately</u> end up righting a condition that earlier blighted the desired quality of life, so that adjustments were made.

Am I going too fast?

("No," I said, although Seth-Jane's pace was pretty good as far as my writing speed was concerned.)

The "victims" choose to participate in those conditions at spiritual, psychological, and biological levels. Many of those who are counted among the fatalities might otherwise die of extended illnesses, for example. At cellular levels such knowledge is available, and in one way or another imparted, often in dreams, to the individual. Conscious comprehension need not follow, for many people know such things, and pretend not to know them at the same time.

(11:44.) Others have finished with their challenges; they want to die and are looking for an excuse — a face-saving device. However, those who choose such deaths want to die in terms of drama, in the middle of their activities, and are in a strange way filled with the exultant inner knowledge of life's strength even at the point of death. At the last they identify with the power of nature that <u>seemingly</u> destroyed them.

That identification often brings about in death — but not always — an added acceleration of consciousness, and involves such individuals in a kind of "group death experience," where all of the victims more or less embark into another level of reality "at the same time."

Those people were aware just beneath consciousness of the possibilities of such an event long before the disaster occurred, and could until the last moment choose to avoid the encounter. Animals know of weather conditions ahead of time, as old tales say. This perception is a biological part of your heritage also. The body is prepared, though consciously it seems you are ignorant.

There are innumerable relationships that exist between the interior environment of the body and the weather patterns. The ancient feelings of identification with storms are quite valid, and in that respect the "realism" of feelings is far superior to the realism of logic. When a person feels a part of a storm, those feelings speak a literal truth. Logic deals with exterior conditions, with cause-and-effect relationships. Intuitions deal with immediate experience of the most intimate nature, with subjective motions and activities that in your

terms move far quicker than the speed of light, and with simultaneous events that your cause-and-effect level is far too slow to perceive.[2]

(Long pause.) In that regard also, the activities of the inner environment are too fast for you to follow intellectually. Your intuitions,
however, can give you clues to such behavior. A country is responsible
for its own droughts, earthquakes, floods, hurricanes — and for its
own harvests and rich display of products, its industry and cultural
achievements, and each of these elements is related to each other one.

If the quality of life that is considered spiritually and biologically
necessary fails, then adjustments occur. A political problem might be
altered by a natural disaster if political means fail. On the other
hand, the rousing creative energies of the people will emerge.

Excellence will show itself through the arts, cultural creativity,
technological or sociological accomplishments. The species tries to
fulfill its great capacities. Each physical body in its own way is like the
world. It has its own defenses and abilities, and each portion of it
strives for a quality of existence that will bring to the smallest parts of
it the spiritual and biological fulfillment of its own nature.

(Heartily:) End of dictation. End of session unless you have
questions.

("I guess not, Seth.")

My fondest regards, then, and a hearty good evening.

("Thank you. The same to you, Seth."

(12:08 A.M. Jane was out of an excellent trance before I finished
writing. . . .)

NOTES: SESSION 803

1. Seth's material on dying and the nature of consciousness immediately
reminded me of what he'd said at 11:20 in the 801st session: "Dying is a biological necessity . . . Inherently, each individual knows that he or she must die
physically in order to survive spiritually and psychically . . . The self outgrows
the flesh." I'd been thinking about those passages, and when Seth returned
to the subject tonight I decided to have some fun with our accepted social
and scientific establishments by writing this note.

Seth's ideas about the true nature — the necessity — of dying directly contradict more and more of what we read these days. Now a number of scientists
tell us that long before the end of this century we'll have the ability to prolong
our physical lives forever — or at least indefinitely, to be more "practical"

about it. We're told again and again that technically we're on the verge of producing artificial versions of many bodily parts, as well as microcomputers that
will be implanted within the body to regulate its performance; these advances,
plus our "conquering" of disease, pain, and suffering, plus genetic engineer-
ing, will soon make it possible for human beings to live indefinitely. Those in
the know maintain that if you are fortunate enough to be a younger person,
you may never have to die.

What grandiose claims these are, however — at least at this time — for
Jane and I also read that in the last three-quarters of a century science has
managed to bring about an increase of only four years in the life expectancy
of the adult white male: from 69 to 73 years. Granted that the medical establishment has learned a lot since 1900, still it'll have to move awfully fast now
to make all of those predictions come true before the year 2000, say.

But nowhere do we see anything about any spiritual dilemmas that may
be involved with all of this, or about the enormous social problems — challenges, to be sure — that could soon begin to manifest themselves if anything
even approaching "eternal life" comes within the reach of numbers of
people. Think of the legalities alone involved. (People might even have to
change their marriage vows!) Science-fiction ideas abound. What about population control? What about those who want to live on, but can't afford to?
How will decisions be made about who receives the favored treatment and
who doesn't? Will families qualify, or just individuals? Geniuses or dolts? If the
services necessary to extend life are free — paid for by the government, that
is — will government decide that certain families simply cannot be allowed to
have children, that they'll be left to die out? In view of our present world challenges, it might even be said that there are already too many people in the
world. And what about animals and other forms of life? Perhaps in their own
collective wisdom the animals will look upon us as though we've altogether
given up our powers of intuitive understanding.

Right now I'd bet that man will most certainly try with all of his might
every technique he can devise in order to prolong physical life as long as possible — so great is his conscious fear of death as the consummate extinction
for all time to come. Through all of his recorded history, man has created
that fear, that *belief*, with the greatest tenacity imaginable.

There's much irony involved in the whole idea of living indefinitely. If
such a possibility is ever achieved, I think that on conscious levels the members of the species will come to fear the chance of *accidental death* more than
anything else, and that this powerful concern may seriously circumscribe
behavior. For who, knowing that for all practical purposes he or she is
"immortal," will want to risk that most precious gift of all — life — by doing
anything that could rudely take it away? Even contact sports, let alone activities like air, sea, or space travel, or any dangerous occupation, could be

abhorred. Disease of any kind, as well as aging itself, would have to be controlled absolutely.

As for Jane and me, we really don't think it necessary that we live forever physically, or even to be 200 years old — an attitude that may be no more than a sign of our own conditioning. We may even be a little sad and jealous that we chose to be born a few decades too soon. "I wouldn't mind seeing the age of 100, though, if I were in good shape," Jane said as we discussed this note. Those of approaching generations, we thought, may have no hesitation at all about opting to live as long as possible. At least for a while, consciousness would accommodate them very well. The final irony of all may develop, however: Jane added that the suicide rate would rise considerably after the many implications associated with extended lifetimes began to penetrate human consciousness. People, she said, at last openly recognizing the great necessity and desirability of biological death, would in many instances simply "turn themselves off."

2. Seth and Jane have both referred to faster-than-light effects in earlier books. Seth did so while discussing his CU's, or units of consciousness, for instance. Albert Einstein, in his special theory of relativity, demonstrated that nothing else in the universe can quite reach — let alone surpass — the speed of light. Some physicists have theorized about certain faster-than-light "particles," however, that by some unknown process are *created* traveling at such enormous velocities; thus in that way they try to get around the limits set by Einstein. There have also been recent astronomical observations of several far-distant objects that appear to be "superluminous," or traveling considerably faster than the speed of light. These effects have yet to be satisfactorily explained.

Of course, when one leaves the realm of "particles," no matter how small they may be, or how they behave or how tenuous their "physical" construction, then all restraints could well be off. As in the case of his CU's, Seth's "subjective motions and activities," his "simultaneous events," would easily be the rule in the basic nonphysical universe.

SESSION 804, MAY 9, 1977
9:44 P.M. MONDAY

(Jane's birthday was yesterday, and a couple of events that made pretty nice presents revolved around that date. Two days ago, she worked on our new front porch for the first time; she sat in the slanting sunlight and wrote down the information she psychically picked up from the "world view" of William James, the American psychologist and philosopher who lived from 1842–1910. She now has considerable material for her book on James. [In

the note she's making for her Introduction to Seth's The Nature of the Psyche, *Jane describes a world view as "... a living psychological picture of an individual life, with its knowledge and experience, which remains responsive and viable long after the physical life itself is over."]*

(Then today she received the contract for Psyche *from her publisher, Prentice-Hall. Now she prefers to formally sign for a book only after she — and/or Seth — has finished most of the work on that project.*

(Seth abruptly came through without greetings:)

Now — dictation. The body is a spiritual, psychic, and social statement, biologically spoken. It is obviously private, yet it cannot be concealed, in that "it is where you are," in usual terms.

The individual body is what it is because it exists in the context of others like it. By this I mean that a given present body presupposes a biological past of like creatures. It presupposes contemporaries. If, for example, one adult human being were perceived by an alien from another world, certain facts would be apparent. Even though such an alien came upon a lone member of your species in otherwise uninhabited land, the alien could make certain assumptions from the individual's appearance and behavior.

(Long pause.) If the "earthling" spoke, the alien would of course instantly know that you were communicating creatures, and in the vocal sounds recognize patterns that contained purpose and intent. To one extent or another, all creatures use language (underlined), implying a far vaster sociobiological relationship than is usually supposed. From [the earthling's] appearance the alien would be able to deduce — if it did not already know — the proportions of the various elements upon your planet; this being surmised from your method of locomotion, appendages, and the nature of your physical vision.

While each individual springs privately into the world at birth, then, each birth also represents quite literally an effort — a triumphant one — on the part of each member of each species, for the delicate balance of life requires for each birth quite precise conditions that no one species can guarantee alone, even to its own kind. The grain must grow. The animals must produce. The plants must do their part. Photosynthesis,[1] in those terms, reigns.

The seasons must retain some stability. The rains must fall, but not too much. The storms must rage, but not too devastatingly. Behind all of this lies a biological and psychic cooperative venture.

All of this <u>could</u> be perceived by our hypothetical alien from one lone human individual; and we will return to our alien later on.

(Long pause at 10:05.) Cells possess "social" characteristics. They have a tendency to unite with others. They naturally communicate. They naturally <u>want</u> to move. Period. In making such statements I am not personifying the cell, for the desire for communication and motion does not belong to man, or even animals, alone. Man's desire to journey into other worlds is in its way as natural as the plant's urge to turn its leaves toward the sun.

Man's physical world, with all of its civilizations and cultural aspects, and even with its technologies and sciences, basically represents the species' innate drive to communicate, to move outward, to create, and to objectify sensed inner realities. The most private life imaginable is a very social affair. The most secluded recluse must still depend upon the biological sociability of not only his own body cells, but of the natural world with all of its creatures. The body, then, no matter how private, is also a public, social, biological statement. A spoken sentence has a certain structure in any language. It presupposes a mouth and a tongue, the kind of physical organization necessary; a mind; a certain kind of world in which sounds have meaning; and a very precise, quite practical knowledge of the nature of sounds, the combination of their patterns, the use of repetition, and a knowledge of the nervous system. Few of my readers possess such conscious knowledge, yet the majority speak quite well.

In one way or another, therefore, it certainly seems that your body possesses a kind of quite pragmatic information, and acts upon it. You can express almost any idea that you want in vocal terms, even if you have hardly any conception at all of the way in which your own speech is executed.

The body is geared then to act. It is pragmatically practical, and above all it wants to explore and to communicate. Communication implies a social nature. The body has within it inherently everything necessary for its own defense. The body itself will tease the child to speak, to crawl and walk, to seek its fellows. Through biological communication the child's cells are made aware of its physical environment, the temperature, air pressure, weather conditions, food supplies — and the body reacts to these conditions, making some adjustments with great rapidity.

At cellular levels the world exists with a kind of social inter-
change, in which the birth and death of cells are known to all others,
and in which the death of a frog and a star gain equal weight. But at
your level of activity your thoughts, feelings, and intents, however
private, form part of the inner environment of communication. This
inner environment is as pertinent and vital to the species' well-being
as is the physical one. It represents the psychic, mass bank of potential, even as the planet provides a physical bank of potential. When
there is an earthquake in another area of the world, the land mass in
your own country is in one way or another affected. When there are
psychic earthquakes in other areas of the world, then you are also
affected, and usually to the same degree.

In the same way, if one portion of your own body is injured, then
other portions feel the effects of the wound. An earthquake can be a
disaster in the area where it occurs, even though its existence cor-
rects imbalances, and therefore promotes the life of the planet.
Emergency actions are quite rigorous in the immediate area of an
earthquake, and aid is sent in from other countries. When an area of
the body "erupts," there are also emergency measures taken locally,
and aid sent from other portions of the body to afflicted parts.

The physical eruption, while it may appear to be a disaster in the
area of the disease, is also, however, a part of the body's defense
system, taken to insure the whole balance of the body. Biologically,
illness therefore represents the overall body defense system at work.

(10:42.) I am trying to put this simply — but without some illnesses, the body could not endure. Give us a moment . . . First of all,
the body must be in a state of constant change, making decisions far
too fast for you to follow, adjusting hormonal levels, maintaining balances between all of its systems; not only in relationship to itself —
the body — but to an environment that is also in constant change.
At biological levels the body often produces its own "preventative
medicine," or "inoculations," by seeking out, for example, new or
foreign substances in its environment [that are] due to nature,
science or technology; it assimilates such properties in small doses,
coming down with an "illness" which, left alone, would soon vanish
as the body utilized what it could [of it], or socialized "a seeming
invader."

The person might feel indisposed, but in such ways the body assimilates and uses properties that would otherwise be called alien ones. It immunizes itself through such methods. The body, however, exists with the mind to contend with — and the mind produces an inner environment of concepts. The cells that compose the body do not try to make sense of the cultural world. They rely upon your interpretation, therefore, for the existence of threats of a non-biological nature. So they depend upon your assessment.

(Long pause.) If that assessment correlates with biological ones, you have a good working relationship with the body. It can react swiftly and clearly. When you sense threat or danger for which the body can find no biological correlation, even as through cellular communication it scans the environment physically, then it must rely upon your assessment and react to danger conditions. The body will, therefore, react to imagined dangers to some degree, as well as to those that are biologically pertinent. Its defense system often becomes overexerted as a result.

The body is, therefore, quite well equipped to deal with its physical stance in the physical world, and its defense systems are unerring in that respect. Your conscious mind, however, directs your temporal perception and interprets that perception, organizing it into mental patterns. The body, again, must depend upon those interpretations. The biological basis of all life is a loving, divine and cooperative one, and presupposes a safe physical stance from which any member of any species feels actively free to seek out its needs and to communicate with others of its kind.

(Pause at 11:01.) Give us a moment . . . It is fashionable to believe that the animals do not possess imagination, but this is a quite erroneous belief. They anticipate mating, for example, before its time. They all learn through experience, and despite all of your concepts, learning is impossible without imagination at any level.

In your terms, the imagination of the animals is limited. Theirs is not merely confined to the elements of previous experience, however. They can imagine events that have never happened to them. Man's abilities in this respect are far more complicated, for in his imagination he deals with probabilities. In any given period of time, with one physical body, he can anticipate or perform an infinitely vaster number of events — each one remaining probable until he activates it.

The body, responding to his thoughts, feelings, and beliefs, has much more data to deal with, therefore, and must have a clear area in which concise action is possible.

Take your break.

("Thank you."

(11:09 to 11:35.)

The body's defense system is automatic, and yet to a certain degree it is a secondary rather than primary system, coming into mobilization as such only when the body is threatened.

The body's main purpose is not only to survive but to maintain a quality of existence at certain levels, and that quality itself promotes health and fulfillment. A definite, biologically pertinent fear alerts the body, and allows it to react completely and naturally. You might be reading a newspaper headline, for example, as you cross a busy street. Long before you are consciously aware of the circumstances, your body might leap out of the path of an approaching car. The body is doing what it is supposed to do. Though consciously you were not afraid, there was a biologically pertinent fear that was acted upon.

If, however, you dwell mentally in a generalized environment of fear, the body is given no clear line of action, allowed no appropriate response. Look at it this way: An animal, not necessarily just a wild one in some native forest, but an ordinary dog or cat, reacts in a certain fashion. It is alert to everything in its environment. A cat does not anticipate danger from a penned dog four blocks away, however, nor bother wondering what would happen if that dog were to escape and find the cat's cozy yard.

Many people, however, do not pay attention to everything in their environments, but through their beliefs concentrate only upon "the ferocious dog four blocks away." That is, they do not respond to what is physically present or perceivable in either space or time, but instead [dwell] upon the threats that may or may not exist, ignoring at the same time other pertinent data that are immediately at hand.

The mind then signals threat — but a threat that is nowhere physically present, so that the body cannot clearly respond. It therefore reacts to a pseudothreatening situation, and is caught between gears, so to speak, with resulting biological confusion. The body's responses must be specific.

The overall sense of health, vitality, and resiliency is a generalized condition of contentment — brought about, however, by multitudinous specific responses. Left alone, the body can defend itself against any disease, but it cannot defend itself appropriately against an exaggerated general fear of disease on the individual's part. It must mirror your own feelings and assessments. Usually, now, your entire medical systems literally <u>generate</u> as much disease as is cured — for you are everywhere hounded by the symptoms of various diseases, and filled with the fear of disease, overwhelmed by what seems to be the body's propensity toward illness — and nowhere is the body's vitality or natural defense system stressed.

Private disease, then, happens also in a social context. This context is the result of personal and mass beliefs that are intertwined at all cultural levels, and so to that extent serve private and public purposes.

(Pause at 11:56.) The illnesses generally attributed to all different ages are involved. Those of the elderly, again, fit in with your social and cultural beliefs, the structure of your family life. Old animals have their own dignity, and so should old men and women. Senility is a mental and physical epidemic — a needless one. You "catch" it because when you are young you believe that old people cannot perform. There are no inoculations against beliefs, so when young people with such beliefs grow old they become "victims."[2]

The kinds of diseases change through historical periods. Some become fashionable, others go out of style. All epidemics, however, are mass statements both biologically and psychically. They point to mass beliefs that have brought about certain physical conditions that are abhorrent at all levels. They often go hand-in-hand with war, and represent biological protests.

(Long pause.) Whenever the conditions of life are such that its quality is threatened, there will be such a mass statement. The quality of life must be at a certain level so that the individuals of a species — of any and all species — can develop. In your species the spiritual, mental and psychic abilities add a dimension that is biologically pertinent.

There simply must be, for example, a freedom to express ideas, an individual tendency, a worldwide social and political context in which each individual can develop his or her abilities and contribute to the species as a whole. Such a climate depends, however, upon many ideas not universally accepted — and yet the species is so formed that the biological importance of ideas cannot be stressed too strongly.

More and more, the quality of your lives is formed through the subjective realities of your feelings and mental constructions. Again, beliefs that foster despair are biologically destructive. They cause the physical system to shut down. If mass action against appalling social or political conditions is not effective, then other means are taken, and these are often in the guise of epidemics or natural disasters. The blight is wiped out in one way or another.

Such conditions, however, are the results of beliefs, which are mental, and so the most vital work must always be done in that area.

(Emphatically:) End of session.

("Okay.")

My heartiest regards, and a most fond good evening.

("Thank you, Seth. Good night."

(12:15 A.M. Seth ended the session as abruptly as he'd started it. Jane was doing so well delivering the material for him at a steady, intent pace that I'd expected her to continue for some little while. She said the session stopped because I asked Seth to repeat the word "vital" — just above — which I hadn't understood the first time.

(Jane explained that when I did this she was "already three or four sentences ahead" in the material, and the question forced her to look back at what she'd just said. Then, knowing it was late even though she was in trance, she suddenly decided to close out the session. At the same time, she'd felt quite capable of continuing for another hour.)

NOTES: SESSION 804

1. Photosynthesis is the imperfectly understood process by which the green chlorophyll in plants uses the energy of sunlight to manufacture carbohydrates from water and carbon dioxide. This "stored sunlight" can then be used as food.

2. Seth is certainly right when he says that "senility is a mental and physical epidemic," considering the many millions of people who have suffered —

and perished — from it in the past. I watched my father go through the ravages of senility; he died in November 1971, at the age of 81. See Jane's very evocative passages about him, as well as my drawing of him in old age, in Part Three of her book of poetry, *Dialogues.*

The beliefs people acquire when young can be changed, of course, and according to Seth (and the ideas Jane and I have also) this process of change would be the best "inoculation" there is against senility. As I watched my father grow older, with an accompanying progressive loss of memory and function, I used to wonder why he didn't consciously revise his response to life — and why I never saw any indication that he *wanted* to. I clearly sensed that it was possible for him to improve his beliefs about life, and that the benefits from such a course of action would be great. Nor did I merely *wish* he would change just so that I could avoid the pain I felt watching him deteriorate. My father's chosen withdrawal from the world was all too plain for everyone to see. In our imperfect understanding, Jane and I and other family members saw this process go on: We did not feel there was much any of us could do.

Now, there's very recent discussion in medical circles that many cases of senility are caused by a "slow virus infection," rather than just heredity or the traditional aging and oxygen starvation of the brain. The hope, and the unproven speculation, are that eventually such an infection might be treatable medically. But either way (whether senility arises through aging or infection), beliefs would come first, helping the whole body maintain its healthy performance well into old age, or encouraging it to deteriorate unnecessarily.

As I wrote this note Jane pointed out that some of my material in Note 1 for the 803rd session is applicable here. For, obviously, senility will have to be conquered by some combination of physical and/or mental techniques if men and women are to live a lot longer, let alone "forever."

SESSION 805, MAY 16, 1977
9:28 P.M. MONDAY

(Jane's ideas — and mine, too — have matured considerably since I wrote a month ago that she was thinking of converting half of our garage into a writing room, with its attendant back porch. In fact, we've agreed to go ahead with that project this summer. It will certainly be a long and noisy endeavor. Now that he's finished the front porch, our contractor is free to begin work at the back of the house as soon as possible.)

Good evening.

("Good evening, Seth.")

Dictation: An animal has a sense of its own biological integrity. So does a child. In all forms of life each individual is born into a world already provided for it, with circumstances favorable to its growth and development; a world in which its own existence rests upon the equally valid existence of all other individuals and species, so that each contributes to nature's whole.

In that environment there is a cooperative sociability of a biological nature, that is understood by the animals in their way, and taken for granted by the young of your own species. The means are given so that the needs of the individual can be met. The granting of those needs furthers the development of the individual, its species, and by inference all others in the fabric of nature.

Survival, of course, is important, but it is not the prime purpose of a species, in that it is a necessary means by which that species can attain its main goals. Of course [a species] must survive to do so, but it will, however, purposefully avoid survival if the conditions are not practically favorable to maintain the quality of life or existence that is considered basic.

A species that senses a lack of this quality can in one way or another destroy its offspring — not because they could not survive otherwise, but because the quality of that survival would bring about vast suffering, for example, so distorting the nature of life as to almost make a mockery of it. Each species seeks for the development of its abilities and capacities in a framework in which safety is a medium for action. Danger in that context exists under certain conditions clearly known to the animals, clearly defined: The prey is known, for example, as is the hunter. But even the natural prey of another animal does not fear the "hunter" when the hunter animal is full of belly, nor will the hunter then attack.

There are also emotional interactions among the animals that completely escape you, and biological mechanisms, so that animals felled as natural prey by other animals "understand" their part in nature. They do not anticipate death before it happens, however. The fatal act propels the consciousness out from the flesh, so that in those terms it is merciful.

During their lifetimes animals in their natural state enjoy their vigor and accept their worth. They regulate their own births — and their own deaths. The quality of their lives is such that their abilities are challenged. They enjoy contrasts: that between rest and motion, heat and cold, being in direct contact with natural phenomena that everywhere quickens their experience. They will migrate if necessary to seek conditions more auspicious. They are aware of approaching natural disasters, and when possible will leave such areas. They will protect their own, and according to circumstances and conditions they will tend their own wounded. Even in contests between young and old males for control of a group, under natural conditions the loser is seldom killed. Dangers are pinpointed clearly so that bodily reactions are concise.

The animal knows he has the right to exist, and a place in the fabric of nature. This sense of biological integrity supports him.

Man, on the other hand, has more to contend with. He must deal with beliefs and feelings often so ambiguous that no clear line of action seems possible. The body often does not know how to react. If you believe that the body is sinful, for example, you cannot expect to be happy, and health will most likely elude you, for your dark beliefs will blemish the psychological and biological integrity with which you were born.

The species is in a state of transition, one of many. This one began, generally speaking, when the species tried to step apart from nature in order to develop the unique kind of consciousness that is presently your own. That consciousness is not a finished product, however, but one meant to change, [to] evolve and develop." Certain artificial divisions were made along the way that must now be dispensed with.

(10:03.) You must return, wiser creatures, to the nature that spawned you — not only as loving caretakers but as partners with the other species of the earth. You must discover once again the spirituality of your biological heritage. The majority of accepted beliefs — religious, scientific, and cultural — have tended to stress a sense of powerlessness, impotence, and impending doom — a picture in which man and his world is an accidental production with little meaning, isolated yet seemingly ruled by a capricious God. Life is seen as "a valley of tears" — almost as a low-grade infection from which the soul can be cured only by death.

Religious, scientific, medical, and cultural communications stress the existence of danger, minimize the purpose of the species or of any individual member of it, or see mankind as the one erratic, half-insane member of an otherwise orderly realm of nature. Any or all of the above beliefs are held by various systems of thought. All of these, however, strain the individual's biological sense of integrity, reinforce ideas of danger, and shrink the area of psychological safety that is necessary to maintain the quality possible in life. The body's defense systems become confused to varying degrees.

I do not intend to give a treatise upon the biological structures of the body and their interworkings, but only to add such information in that line that is not currently known, and is otherwise important to the ideas I have in mind. I am far more concerned [with] more basic issues. The body's defenses will take care of themselves if they are allowed to, and if the psychological air is cleared of the true "carriers" of disease.

CHAPTER 2

"Mass Meditations." "Health" Plans for Disease.
Epidemics of Beliefs, and Effective Mental
"Inoculations" Against Despair

(Pause at 10:15.) Chapter 2: "'Mass Meditations.' *(A one-minute pause.)* 'Health' Plans for Disease. Epidemics of Beliefs, and Effective Mental 'Inoculations' Against Despair."

(Long pause at 10:20.) While in this book I will point out some of the unfortunate areas of private and mass experience, I will also provide some suggestions for effective solutions. "You get what you concentrate upon."[1] Your mental images bring about their own fulfillment. These are ancient dictums, but you must understand the ways in which your mass communication systems amplify both the "positive and the negative" issues.

I may for a while stress the ways in which individually, and as a civilization, you have undermined your own feelings of safety; yet I will also give you methods to reinforce those necessary feelings of biological integrity and spiritual comprehension that can vastly increase your spiritual and physical existence.

Your beliefs have generated feelings of unworth. Having artificially separated yourselves from nature, you do not trust it, but often experience it as an adversary. Your religions granted man a soul, while denying any to other species. Your bodies then were relegated to nature and your souls to God, who stood immaculately apart from His creations.

Your scientific beliefs tell you that your entire world happened accidentally. Your religions tell you that man is sinful: The body is not to be trusted; the senses can lead you astray. In this maze of beliefs you have largely lost a sense of your own worth and purpose. A generalized fear and suspicion is generated, and life too often becomes stripped of any heroic qualities. The body cannot react to generalized threats. It is, therefore, put under constant strain in such circumstances, and seeks to specify the danger. It is geared to act in your protection. It builds up strong stresses, therefore, so that on many occasions a specific disease or threat situation is "manufactured" to rid the body of a tension grown too strong to bear.

Many of my readers are familiar with private meditation, when concentration is focused in one particular area. There are many methods and schools of thought here, but a highly suggestive state of mind results, in which spiritual, mental, and physical goals are sought. It is impossible to meditate without a goal, for that intent is itself a purpose. Unfortunately, many of your public health programs, and commercial statements through the various media, provide you with mass meditations of a most deplorable kind. I refer to those in which the specific symptoms of various diseases are given, in which the individual is further told to examine the body with those symptoms in mind. I also refer to those statements that just as unfortunately specify diseases for which the individual may experience no symptoms of an observable kind, but is cautioned that these disastrous physical events may be happening despite his or her feelings of good health. Here the generalized fears fostered by religious, scientific, and cultural beliefs are often given as blueprints of diseases in which a person can find a specific focus — the individual can say: "Of course, I feel listless, or panicky, or unsafe since I have such-and-such a disease."

The breast cancer suggestions associated with self-examinations have caused more cancers than any treatments have cured (*most emphatically*). They involve intense meditation of the body, and adverse imagery that itself affects the bodily cells.[2] Public health announcements about high blood pressure themselves raise the blood pressure of millions of television viewers (*even more emphatically*).

Your current ideas of preventative medicine, therefore, generate the very kind of fear that causes disease. They all undermine the

individual's sense of bodily security and increase stress, while offering the body a specific, detailed disease plan. But most of all, they
operate to increase the individual sense of alienation from the body,
and to promote a sense of powerlessness and duality.

Take your break.

(10:45 to 11:09.)

Your "medical commercials" are equally disease-promoting.
Many, meaning to offer you relief through a product, instead actually promote the condition through suggestion, thereby generating
a need for the product itself.

Headache remedies are a case in point here. Nowhere do any
medically-oriented commercial or public service announcements
mention the body's natural defenses, its integrity, vitality, or
strength. Nowhere in your television or radio matter is any emphasis
put upon the healthy. Medical statistics deal with the diseased. Studies upon the healthy are not carried out.

More and more foods, drugs, and natural environmental conditions are being added to the list of disease-causing elements. Different
reports place dairy products, red meats, coffee, tea, eggs, and fats on
the list. Period. Generations before you managed to subsist on many
such foods, and they were in fact promoted as additive to health.
Indeed, man almost seems to be allergic to his own natural environment, a prey to the weather itself.

It is true that your food contains chemicals it did not in years
past. Yet within reason man is biologically capable of assimilating
such materials, and using them to his advantage.

When man feels powerless, however, and in a state of generalized
fear, he can even turn the most natural earthly ingredients against
himself. Your television, and your arts and sciences as well, add up to
mass meditations. In your culture, at least, the educated in the literary
arts provide you with novels featuring antiheroes, and often portray
an individual existence [as being] without meaning, in which no
action is sufficient to mitigate the private puzzlement or anguish.

Many — not all — plotless novels or movies are the result of this
belief in man's powerlessness. In that context no action is heroic,
and man is everywhere the victim of an alien universe. On the other
hand your common, unlettered, violent television dramas do indeed
provide a service, for they imaginatively specify a generalized fear in

a given situation, which is then resolved through drama. Individual action counts. The plots may be stereotyped or the acting horrendous, but in the most conventional terms the "good" man wins.

(11:30.) Such programs do indeed pick up the generalized fears of the nation, but they also represent folk dramas — disdained by the intelligentsia — in which the common man can portray heroic capabilities, act concisely toward a desired end, and triumph.

Those programs often portray your cultural world in exaggerated terms, and most resolution is indeed through violence. Yet your more educated beliefs lead you to an even more pessimistic picture, in which even the violent action of men and women who are driven to the extreme serves no purpose. The individual must feel that his actions count. He is driven to violent action only as a last resort — and illness often is that last resort.

(Long pause.) Your television dramas, the cops-and-robbers shows, the spy productions, are simplistic, yet they relieve tension in a way that your public health announcements cannot do. The viewer can say: "Of course I feel panicky, unsafe, and frightened, because I live in such a violent world." The generalized fear can find a reason [for its existence]. But the programs at least provide a resolution dramatically set, while the public health announcements continue to generate unease. Those mass meditations therefore reinforce negative conditions.

In the overall, then, violent shows provide a service, in that they usually promote the sense of a man's or a woman's individual power over a given set of circumstances. At best the public service announcements introduce the doctor as mediator: You are supposed to take your body to a doctor as you take your car to a garage, to have its parts serviced. Your body is seen as a vehicle out of control, that needs constant scrutiny.

The doctor is like a biological mechanic, who knows your body far better than you. Now these medical beliefs are intertwined with your economic and cultural structures, so you cannot lay the blame upon medical men or their profession alone. Your economic well-being is also a part of your personal reality. Many dedicated doctors use medical technology with spiritual understanding, and they are themselves the victims of the beliefs they hold.

If you do not buy headache potions, your uncle or your neighbor may be out of business and not able to support his family, and therefore lack the means to buy your wares. You cannot disconnect one area of life from another. *En masse*, your private beliefs form your cultural reality. Your society is not a thing in itself apart from you, but the result of the individual beliefs of each person in it. There is no stratum of society that you do not in one way or another affect. Your religions stress sin. Your medical profession stresses disease. Your orderly sciences stress the chaotic and accidental theories of creation. Your psychologies stress men as victims of their backgrounds. Your most advanced thinkers emphasize man's rape of the planet, or focus upon the future disaster that will overtake the world, or see men once again as victims of the stars.

Many of your resurrected occult schools speak of a recommended death of desire, the annihilation of the ego, for the transmutation of physical elements to finer levels. In all such cases the clear spiritual and biological integrity of the individual suffers, and the precious immediacy of your moments is largely lost.

Earth life is seen as murky, a dim translation of greater existence, rather than portrayed as the unique, creative, living experience that it should be. The body becomes disoriented, sabotaged. The clear lines of communication between spirit and body become cluttered. Individually and *en masse,* diseases and conditions result that are meant to lead you into other realizations.

(Abruptly:) End of session.

("Very good material.")

My fondest regards.

("Good night, Seth," I said at 11:59 P.M. I'd expected him to continue for a while longer.)

NOTES: SESSION 805

1. When Seth came through with "You get what you concentrate upon," I remembered that he'd first spoken that sentence some years ago — and that soon afterward I'd made a little paper sign bearing those words and taped it to a wall in one of the two apartments we occupied in Elmira, New York. Had I dated the excerpt? I knew that a few years later the sign had accompanied us on our move to the hill house just outside the city, where we live now. After tonight's session I found it — again upon a wall — with the date: February 26, 1972. From our records I learned that I'd taken Seth's quotation from a personal session Jane held while we were on vacation in Marathon, a resort community in the Florida Keys.

The session had been an impromptu one, and developed on our last night in Marathon because we'd been worrying about our goals in life, and how significant a part the Seth material might play in our affairs. We'd felt strong attractions toward what seemed to be a simpler, more open and pleasant life in the Keys, where the weather was excellent all year, and living in a trailer was an accepted way of life. Yet we didn't think we could afford it. *The Seth Material* had been published in mid-1970, but sales were slow, and *Seth Speaks* wasn't out yet; we'd just finished correcting the page proofs for that work. I'd given up my commercial art job before we went on vacation, and didn't know what I'd end up doing, besides helping Jane as much as I could.

As I suppose is almost always the case with tourists in romantic, faraway places, we had many ties back home. Although Jane's father, and my own, had died the previous year (in 1971), our mothers were still living: Jane's in a nursing home in upstate New York, and mine at the Butts family home in Sayre, Pennsylvania, which is only 18 miles from Elmira and just south of the New York State border. (While Jane and I were away my mother stayed with one of my brothers, who lives some 60 miles below Sayre.)

All of our possessions were in Elmira. To convert to trailer living meant that we'd have to dispose of most of what we owned, including paintings and manuscripts, furniture, files, books, and many written records — something we probably couldn't have brought ourselves to do. And how could we go to Florida and leave all of our friends, and how inconvenient would it be to deal with a publisher (Prentice-Hall) headquartered way up north in New Jersey? Jane was much more willing to attempt the move than I was, but I think we knew all along that beneath our questions and feelings the idea of moving was more like a shared dream, or a probable reality we chose not to explore during our current physical lives. Jane's mother was to die within three months of our return home, mine over a year later (in November 1973).

Seth gave an excellent session for us on that last warm night in Marathon. He did his best to reassure us. The following excerpt leads up to the quotation that inspired this note:

"You have a relationship not only unique, the two of you, but one that also serves as a springboard for creativity. You have talents and abilities that carry with them satisfactions that you both often blithely take for granted: They are so a part of your existences that you are not even aware of them.

"Do not confuse your [joint] position with anyone else's. It is unique. Because it is, the possibilities are endless. If you magnify your limitations you create your own prisons. If you enjoy those freedoms that are yours now, you automatically increase them. You are in a clear position at this moment. You cannot expect a blissful time innocent of problems. That is not the nature of life or of existence.

"Your set of problems are of the most creative kind. They are challenges from which great potentials can emerge. Your full energy for work and your creative drives are released, and will be, as you creatively use and understand your problems. But do not concentrate upon them, nor let them close your eyes to the joys and freedoms that you have. You get what you concentrate upon. There is no other main rule *(my emphasis)*."

2. As Jane wrote for this note: "We think that the dangers of negative suggestion are as real as the physical ones that are connected with the overuse of X-rays, say. Certainly some women have uncovered cancers through self-examinations, and in so doing perhaps saved their lives. There's no way of knowing, though, what part negative suggestion might have played in their diseased conditions to begin with.

"With some women, not conducting regular self-examinations would rouse as many fears as doing them — and since those women's beliefs follow official medical ones so strictly, they're much better off with the examinations. In this and all instances regarding health, each woman should weigh all the evidence, examine her beliefs, and make her own decisions."

I remind the reader that after break ended at 11:35 in the last session (the 804th in Chapter 1), Seth had this to say: "Left alone, the body can defend itself against any disease, but it cannot defend itself appropriately against an exaggerated general fear of disease on the individual's part. It must mirror your own feelings and assessments. Usually, now, your entire medical systems literally generate as much disease as is cured — for you are everywhere hounded by the symptoms of various diseases, and filled with the fear of disease, overwhelmed by what seems to be the body's propensity toward illness — and nowhere is the body's vitality or natural defense system stressed."

Seth didn't mention it in the session tonight, but Jane and I find it extremely interesting that just last week much national publicity was given to the ongoing two-year-old controversy among cancer specialists over whether women — especially those under 50 years of age — should be given routine mammograms (X-ray examinations) in efforts to detect breast cancer in its early stages.

Involved in the arguments are the leading cancer investigative organizations in the country. For example: Scientific advisers to the government's National Cancer Institute, which is conducting elaborate studies of many thousands of women of varying ages, have called for a halt to the routine screening of younger women. These scientists are on record as stating that such X-raying may *cause* more breast cancer than it cures. Many millions of dollars, and much time and effort, have been and are being given to such research programs. It will be difficult to alter those studies because of entrenched belief systems. Even the economic factors become important: Beside the great sums involved in the "official" programs, for instance, many private radiologists have also found mammography screening to be quite profitable.

Now, there's much confusion on the part of women over whether to have mammograms. The process isn't infallible, unfortunately; also, misinterpretations of its results have caused a number of cancer-free women to undergo mastectomies — often radical ones — when they didn't have to. Moreover, each of these individuals has to live with the belief that they've had cancer, and must constantly be on the alert for any signs of its recurrence — signs they do not find. At the same time, they are subjected to even *more* X-ray examinations on a regular basis. They can also have insurance and employment problems (as can many other cancer patients).

A controversy related to that over mammograms, but one that hasn't been nearly as well publicized, concerns "prophylactic subcutaneous mastectomy" — the process by which some women elect to have their breasts removed *before* they actually develop cancer in one or both of them. These women have been told that statistically they're "high risk" prospects for cancer. Involved here are recent diagnostic procedures: the study of the "patient's" family history, the study of the "density" and structure of her breast tissues as determined by mammogram patterns, and the detection of *possibly* premalignant cellular changes. In this preventative operation, the surgeon leaves the nipple and the skin of the breasts, and restores their bulk with implants of plastic or silicone.

At this time many more doctors disagree than agree with the need for prophylactic mastectomies. Those against the procedure cite the errors possible in diagnosis, including the misinterpretation of mammographic patterns. Once again, negative suggestion rules in the present and is projected into the future, for the individual is told that she is at the mercy of her own bodily processes, which might go awry at any moment.

Even when resorted to, prophylactic mastectomies are not foolproof, for a few women have still developed cancer in the area of the nipple. What Jane and I are very curious about, however, is how many "statistically vulnerable" women submitted to operations they didn't need — for surely a significant number of them wouldn't have developed cancer in the first place. The percentage is unknowable, of course. If it could be shown that most of the "high risk" women would get cancer, there wouldn't be arguments about whether such mastectomies are of general value. As things are, though, because of the controversy women once again end up confused as to who is right and what to do. Large scale studies, including one by the National Cancer Institute, are planned to explore the whole question of prophylactic mastectomies.

I'll conclude this note by making three quick points. The first is that other agencies and individuals in the medical and psychological fields are conducting studies of the ties that exist between emotional states and cancer. The second is that Jane and I are perfectly aware of all the good things that medical science has contributed to our worldwide civilization; given our species' present collective beliefs about the vulnerability of the individual to outside forces, medicine as it's now practiced is a vital component of that civilization. The third point is that with *his* views, Seth is simply trying to open our eyes to a much wider understanding of human capacities.

Apropos of that final item, Jane and I refer the reader to the *entire* last session. For in it Seth not only discussed the body's natural defenses and how it "immunizes itself," but also examined our negative cultural beliefs about the body and disease. We think his material is so good that it deserves more than one reading.

SESSION 806, JULY 30, 1977
9:31 P.M. SATURDAY

(This is the first session for Mass Events *since the last one, obviously — but with an 11-week gap between the two. How come? What were Jane and I doing all of that "time" — that nearly one-quarter of a year of our physical lives?*

(First, after holding session 805 we took a six-week break from sessions of any kind. We didn't plan to do this; it just developed, and we eventually realized that it did so through Jane's simple need for a change in routine. We had plenty of other things to do: I was still occupied daily with writing notes and appendixes for Volume 2 of "Unknown" Reality; *on June 4 Jane received the page proofs for* Cézanne, *and began correcting them for the printer; on the 14th of the month "our" contractor began converting half of our garage into a writing room for Jane, and adding a large back porch [see the end of Note 2 for Session 801]. All of that building activity was much noisier and more disruptive than the work had been for the front porch, and forced some changes in our schedules, including more night work, as we manipulated around those distractions.*

(On July 9 we received from Prentice-Hall our first press copies of Volume 1 of "Unknown." *This made us feel good indeed, for it signaled the first publication of a Seth book in three years [since* Personal Reality *came out in 1974]. In mid-July our friend Sue Watkins[1] began typing the rest of*

the final manuscript for Psyche; *Jane had managed to help me out by find-*
ing the time to prepare the first five chapters for the publisher, but since we
were both so busy we asked Sue for assistance. [Sue is a writer also, and
knows about things like manuscripts.] Then by the time this 806th session
came about, Jane estimated that she was practically through with the first
handwritten draft of James. *She's also started her Introduction for it.*

(Going back to the end of our stay-at-home vacation, on June 25 Seth-
Jane began delivering a series of 10 sessions that we held on Monday and
Saturday evenings for a change, instead of following our usual Monday-
Wednesday routine. We finally decided to classify these sessions as private,
or at least as not being work for Mass Events. *Some of that material is*
intensely personal, and some only generally so. But a lot of it isn't intimate
at all — meaning that it could help others if it were published. This real-
ization brought up questions we've encountered before: Which sessions apply
to a particular project, and which ones don't? What if they're related in
oblique ways, yet Seth doesn't call them book dictation? I may not realize I
should ask him about this at the time, or only later begin to speculate about
using certain material. We know that Seth will specify a given number of
sessions for this book, for instance, yet we keep the freedom to consider adding
other material.

(This 806th session is such an example. Strictly speaking, it isn't dicta-
tion for Mass Events, *but Jane and I are presenting portions of it here*
because Seth discussed events and memory with a different emphasis, and
touched upon aspects of reincarnation[2] — all subjects that spring out of
that ineffable, really undefinable quality he calls simultaneous time. I ask
the reader to always keep in mind that no matter what subject he's dis-
cussing, or from what viewpoint, Seth's kind of "time" underlies all that
our present physical senses translate into linear, concrete experience and
history. For clarification, I also keep this in mind: Seth isn't physical, as he
defines himself, and that "energy personality essence" seemingly isn't all
that focused on the passage of time — as we are — yet way back in the 14th
session for January 8, 1964, he told us that time "is therefore still a reality
of some kind to me." In these notes for Mass Events, *I plan to refer to time*
— all kinds of it — from "time to time.")

Good evening.

("Good evening, Seth.")

Part 1 of the session.

Because events do not exist in the concrete, done-and-finished versions about which you have been taught, then memory must also be a different story.

You must remember the creativity and the open-ended nature of events, for even in one life a given memory is seldom a "true version" of a past event. The original happening is experienced from a different perspective on the part of each person involved, of course, so that the event's implications and basic meanings may differ according to the focus of each participant. That given event, in your terms happening for the first time, say, begins to "work upon" the participants. Each one brings to it his or her own background, temperament, and literally a thousand different colorations — so that the event, while shared by others, is still primarily original to each person.

The moment it occurs, it begins to change as it is filtered through all of those other ingredients, and it is minutely altered furthermore by each succeeding event. The memory of an event, then, is shaped as much by the present as it is by the past. Association triggers memories, of course, and organizes memory events. It also helps color and form such events.

You are used to a time structure, so that you remember something that happened at a particular time in the past. Usually you can place events in that fashion. There are neurological pockets, so to speak, so that biologically the body can place events as it perceives activity. Those neurological pulses are geared to the biological world you know.

In those terms, past or future-life memories usually remain like ghost images by contrast. Overall, this is necessary so that immediate body response can be focused in the time period you recognize. Other life memories are carried along, so to speak, beneath those other pulses — never, in certain terms, coming to rest so that they can be examined, but forming, say, the undercurrents upon which the memories of your current life ride.

When such other-life memories do come to the surface, they are of course colored by it, and their rhythm is not synchronized. They are not tied into your nervous system as precisely as your regular memories. Your present gains its feeling of depth because of your past as you understand it. In certain terms, however, the future represents, say, another kind of depth that belongs to events. A root goes out in all directions. Events do also. But the roots of events go through your past, present, and future.

Often by purposefully trying to slow down your thought processes, or playfully trying to speed them up, you can become aware of memories from other lives — past or future. To some extent you allow other neurological impulses to make themselves known. There may often be a feeling of vagueness, because you have no ready-made scheme of time or place with which to structure such memories. Such exercises also involve you with the facts of the events of your own life, for you automatically are following probabilities from the point of your own focus.

It would be most difficult to operate within your sphere of reality without the pretension of concrete, finished events. You form your past lives now in this life as surely as you form your future ones now also.

Simultaneously, each of your past and future selves dwell in their own way now, and for them the last sentence also applies. It is theoretically possible to understand much of this through an examination-in-depth of the events of your own life. Throwing away many taken-for-granted concepts, you can pick a memory. But try not to structure it — a most difficult task — for such structuring is by now almost automatic.

(10:01.) The memory, left alone, not structured, will shimmer, shake, take other forms, and transform itself before your [mental] eyes, so that its shape will seem like a psychological kaleidoscope through whose focus the other events of your life will also shimmer and change. Such a memory exercise can also serve to bring in other-life memories. Edges, corners, and reflections will appear, however, perhaps superimposed upon memories that you recognize as belonging to this life.

Your memories serve to organize your experience and, again, follow recognized neurological sequences. Other-life memories from the future and past often bounce off of these with a motion too quick for you to follow.

In a quiet moment, off guard, you might remember an event from this life, but there may be a strange feeling to it, as if something about it, some sensation, does not fit into the time slot in which the event belongs. In such cases that [present-life] memory is often tinged by another, so that a future or past life memory sheds its cast upon the recalled event. There is a floating quality about one portion of the memory.

This happens more often than is recognized, because usually you simply discount the feeling of strangeness, and drop the part of the memory that does not fit. Such instances involve definite bleed-throughs, however. By being alert and catching such feelings, you can learn to use the floating part of the otherwise-recognizable memory as a focus. Through association that focus can then trigger further past or future recall. Clues also appear in the dreaming state, with greater frequency, because then you are already accustomed to that kind of floating sensation in which events can seem to happen in their own relatively independent context.

Dreams in which past and present are both involved are an example; also dreams in which the future and the past merge, and dreams in which time seems to be a changing ingredient.

Now take your break.

(10:14 to 10:44.)

Now: In certain terms the past, present, and future [of your present life] are all compressed in any given moment of your experience.

Any such moment is therefore a gateway into all of your existence. The events that you recognize as happening now are simply specific and objective, but the most minute element in any given moment's experience is also symbolic of other events and other times. Each moment is then like a mosaic, only in your current life history you follow but one color or pattern, and ignore the others. As I have mentioned [in other books], you can indeed change the present to some extent by purposefully altering a memory event. That kind of synthesis can be used in many instances with many people.

Such an exercise is not some theoretical, esoteric, impractical method, but a very precise, volatile, and dynamic way of helping the present self by calming the fears of a past self. That past self is not hypothetical, either, but still exists, capable of being reached and of changing its reactions. You do not need a time machine to alter the past or the future.

Such a technique is highly valuable. Not only are memories not "dead," they are themselves ever-changing. Many alter themselves almost completely without your notice. In his *(unpublished)* apprentice novels, Ruburt *(Jane)* did two or three versions of an episode with a priest he had known in his youth. Each version at the time he wrote it represented his honest memory of the event. While the bare facts were more or less the same, the entire meaning and interpretation of each version differed so drastically that those differences far outweighed the similarities.

Because the episode was used on two or three different occasions, Ruburt could see how this memory changed. In most cases, however, people are not aware that memory changes in such a fashion, or that the events they think they recall are so different.

The point is that past events grow. They are not finished. With that in mind, you can see that future lives are very difficult to explain from within your framework. A completed life in your terms is no more completed or done than any event. There is simply a cutoff point in your focus from your framework, but it is as artificial as, basically, perspective is applied to painting.

It is not that the inner self is not aware of all of this, but that it has already chosen a framework, or a given frame of existence, that emphasizes certain kinds of experience over others.

(11:05. Now Seth went into the more personal Part 2 of the session, explaining how in her own case Jane could give her past self in this life her current knowledge, so that through the resulting "psychological synthesis" she would be better equipped to handle certain challenges.

(End at 11:44 P.M.)

NOTES: SESSION 806

1. Sue Watkins has been mentioned, and at times quoted, in a number of Jane's books: *The Seth Material, Seth Speaks, Adventures in Consciousness, Psychic Politics,* and both volumes of *"Unknown" Reality.* Jane started her ESP class in September 1967. We met Sue in September 1968; she began attending class a month later, and did so more or less regularly until the end of class in February 1975. At this time Sue is working on a novel of her own and co-editing a weekly newspaper in a small town some 50 miles north of Elmira, New York (where Jane and I live).

2. Jane spent considerable time before my birthday (I turned 58 on June 20) preparing a sketch book of poems and colored drawings as a present for me. She touched upon many subjects in her highly original poetry and art. On reincarnation she wrote:

To Rob

Were you born once in winter,
in Europe's ice and snow,
when villages were dark at night
and wolves roamed the towering hills?
Or dark-skinned, did your swaddling cry
pierce Egypt's early dawn?
How many birthdays come and gone,
how many homelands, each your own?
How many loves have whispered through
the patterns of your mind?
How many sons and daughters have grown
from your womb or loins?
What voices merge with mine
to wish you happy birthday,
and what loves within your past
lay out a feast of wine and cakes?

And in a more "modern" vein:

To Rob

We parked here today
and the green world swirled
jungle-quick, downtown
across the river, and like
a city bushman I was in tune,
swinging through thought's treetops
while the traffic stopped and started,
precise as a ceremony of animals,
almost formal, engines thundering
then purring, wheels pausing,
headlights hypnotized in sun.
You walked into the bank,
making an exchange as ancient
as any tribal dance.

SESSION 814, OCTOBER 8, 1977
9:43 P.M. SATURDAY

(With one exception, which I'll get to later, we've spent another long period — 9 weeks — without holding book sessions. Seth-Jane was certainly busy on all of those Monday and Saturday nights, though, and came through with another separate series of sessions after I inserted the 806th session into Mass Events *— 17 of them this time, as compared to the 10 sessions delivered before the 806th was held. Once again, these were private or nonbook sessions, and once again they covered a wide range of subjects other than personal ones.*

(Including the 806th session, those two blocks of material mean that in the last 20 weeks [or 4 1/2 months], Seth has held but one session for Mass Events, *and 28 on other subjects. "Maybe he's already finished the book, and forgot to tell us," I joked with Jane. "Maybe it's going to be his shortest one yet."*

("That constant book stuff can get confining, though," she said, then reminded me that Seth — with her obvious consent — had plunged into Mass Events *only a couple of weeks after finishing* Psyche. *"It gets so he concentrates on book subjects so much that a lot of other things are left out . . . At least breaks in dictation give us chances to go off in other directions — the sessions are more flexible that way."*

(This flexibility also generates some challenges, however, for the great amount of material we've accumulated during the Mass Events *hiatus gave us the urge to see what we could do about getting at least some of it published, so that others could benefit. The problem — the challenge — would be to find the physical time to do the necessary editing and notes to put such a manuscript in shape for publication; this would be a job that could easily take a year. Jane and I considered combining that hypothetical book with* Mass Events, *but figured out that the resulting volume would almost surely be too long; longer even than Volume 2 of* "Unknown" Reality, *which in our opinion is bulky enough.*

(The two sets of material are also different in certain subtle ways, although one can always justifiably say that each subject Seth discusses is in some fashion a part of his overall philosophy. It would have to be that way, of course. In other words, it's somewhat ironic that during the break in dictating Mass Events *Seth-Jane actually produced the equivalent of* another *book, but one that we can't do much about, at least at this time.*[1]

(Since the 806th session was held 10 weeks ago [on July 30], then, I've worked steadily on Volume 2 of "Unknown." Late in August Jane interrupted her work on James to move all of her writing paraphernalia into her new room at the back of the house. Sue Watkins delivered the finished manuscript for several chapters of Psyche, and picked up more to type. Jane, who was to work on James all through September, prepared a presentation for that book so that in the meantime her editor, Tam Mossman, could show it to his associates at Prentice-Hall. On September 12, Jane had a very vivid dream that she believes was rooted in a past life of hers in Turkey: Her dream involved a little boy, Prince Emir, who lived in a brand-new world in which death hadn't been invented yet. Over the telephone three days later, Tam suggested that Jane do a children's book, or one for "readers of all ages," based on her dream about Emir[2]; the next day he called again, this time to give her the delightful news that he'd accepted James for publication.

(Then, in a private session held on the evening of September 17, 1977, Seth came through with a very exciting concept called "Framework 1 and Framework 2." Jane and I were so struck by the practical, far-reaching implications of this proposition that we began a concerted effort to put it to use in daily life. Briefly and very simply, Seth maintains that Framework 2, or inner reality, contains the creative source from which we form all events, and that by the proper focusing of attention we can draw from that vast subjective medium everything we need for a constructive, positive life in Framework 1, or physical reality. We've already made known to Seth our desires that he go into his Frameworks 1 and 2 material much more extensively in Mass Events, *since those concepts are so closely involved with the individual and collective experiences surrounding the lives of everyone.[3]*

(Now for the "one exception" I referred to at the beginning of this note. It's the 812th session for October 1, and at least some of it is book dictation. It was triggered by a visit we had recently from a reader who obviously had strong tendencies toward paranoia. Seth gave a session on paranoia in response to that encounter [but not for the individual concerned, although Jane later wrote to him], then instructed us to lay the session aside for inclusion in a later chapter of Mass Events.

(Finally: Just before tonight's session Jane said she thought Seth might do some work on Mass Events. *She had a question about herself, and I asked for a few lines from Seth on whether she just might have been born left-handed.*

I want to use the material in connection with a passage I'm putting together
for Volume 2 of "Unknown" Reality. *[See the excerpts from Session 211, in*
Appendix 18 of that work.] However, Seth didn't answer my question.)

Now, good evening —

("Good evening, Seth.")

— and as Ruburt supposed, dictation, as from our last formal
book session *(the 805th).*

In order from the beginning — the passages on paranoia *(in the*
812th session) will come later. While Ruburt was working at one of his
books a few days ago, he heard a public service announcement. The
official told all listeners that the flu season had officially begun. He
sternly suggested that the elderly and those with certain diseases
make appointments at once for flu shots.

The official mentioned, by the way, that there was indeed no
direct evidence connecting past flu shots with the occurrence of a
rather bizarre disease that some of those inoculated with the flu
vaccine happened to come down with.[4] All in all, it was quite an
interesting announcement, with implications that straddle biology,
religion, and economics. "The flu season" is in a way an example of
a psychologically-manufactured pattern that can at times bring
about a manufactured epidemic.

Behind such announcements there is the authority of the medical profession, and the very authority of your systems of communication as well. You cannot question the voice over the radio. It is
disembodied and presumes to know.

Once again, the elderly were singled out. It seems obvious that
they are more susceptible to diseases. That susceptibility is a medical
fact of life. It is a fact, however, without a basic foundation in the
truth of man's biological reality. It is a fact brought about through
suggestion. The doctors see the bodily results, which are quite definite, and then those results are taken as evidence.

In a few isolated areas of the world even today, the old are not
disease-ridden, nor do their vital signs weaken. They remain quite
healthy until the time of death.

Their belief systems, therefore, you must admit, are quite practical. Nor are they surrounded by medical professions. Later in the
book we will return to the subject. Here, you have, however, what

almost amounts to a social program for illness — the flu season. A mass meditation, it has an economic structure in back of it: The scientific and medical foundations are involved. Not only this, however, but the economic concerns, from the largest pharmacies to the tiniest drugstores, the supermarkets and the corner groceries — all of these elements are involved.

Pills, potions, and shots supposed to combat [colds and the] flu are given prominent displays, serving to remind those who might have missed them otherwise of the announcements [about] the coming time of difficulty. Commercials on television bring a new barrage, so that *(amused)* you can go from the hay fever season to the flu season without missing any personal medications.

A cough in June may be laughed off and quickly forgotten. A cough in the flu season, however, is far more suspect — and under such conditions one might think, particularly in the midst of a poor week: "Who wants to go out tomorrow anyhow?"

You are literally expected to come down with the flu. It can serve as an excuse for not facing many kinds of problems. Many people are almost consciously aware of what they are doing. All they have to do is pay attention to the suggestions offered so freely by the society. The temperature does rise. Concern causes the throat to become dry. Dormant viruses — which up to now have done no harm — are activated.

(10:10.) Coat, glove, and boot manufacturers also push their wares. Yet in those categories there is more sanity, for their ads often stress wholesome activities, portraying the happy skier, the tramper through the woods in winter. Sometimes, however, they suggest that their wares will protect you against the flu and colds, and against the vulnerability of your nature.

The inoculations themselves do little good overall, and they can be potentially dangerous, particularly when they are given to prevent an epidemic which has not in fact occurred. They may have specific value, but overall they are detrimental, confusing bodily mechanisms and setting off other biological reactions that might not show up, say, for some time.[5]

The flu season intersects with the Christmas season, of course, when Christians are told to be merry and [wish] their fellows a happy return to the natural wonders of childhood, in thought at least. [They are also told] to pay homage to God. Christianity has become, however, a tangled sorry tale, its cohesiveness largely vanished. Such a religion becomes isolated from daily life. Many individuals cannot unify the various areas of their belief and feeling, and at Christmas they partially recognize the vast gulf that exists between their scientific beliefs and their religious beliefs. They find themselves unable to cope with such a mental and spiritual dilemma. A psychic depression often results, one that is deepened by the Christmas music and the commercial displays, by the religious reminders that the species is made in God's image, and by the other reminders that the body so given is seemingly incapable of caring for itself and is a natural prey to disease and disaster.

So the Christmas season carries a man's hopes in your society, and the flu season mirrors his fears and shows the gulf between the two.

The physician is also a private person, so I speak of him only in his professional capacity, for he usually does the best he can in the belief system that he shares with his fellows. Those beliefs do not exist alone, but are of course intertwined with religious and scientific ones, as separate as they might appear. Christianity has conventionally treated illness as the punishment of God, or as a trial sent by God, to be borne stoically. It has considered man a sinful creature, flawed by original sin, <u>forced</u> to work by the sweat of his brow.

Science has seen man as an accidental product of an uncaring universe, a creature literally without a center of meaning, where consciousness was the result of a physical mechanism that only <u>happened</u> to come into existence, and that had no reality outside of that structure. Science has at least been consistent in that respect. Christianity, however, officially asks children of sorrow to be joyful and sinners to find a childlike purity; it asks them to love a God who one day will destroy the world, and who will condemn them to hell if they do not adore him.

Many people, caught between such conflicting beliefs, fall prey to physical ills during the Christmas season particularly. The churches and the hospitals are often the largest buildings in any town, and the only ones open on Sunday without recourse to city ordinances. You cannot divorce your private value systems from your health, and the hospitals often profit from the guilt that religions have instilled in their people.

I am speaking now of religions so intertwined with social life and community ventures that all sense of basic religious integrity becomes lost. Man is by nature a religious creature.

Take your break.

(10:40 to 11:10.)

Dictation: One of man's strongest attributes is religious feeling. It is the part of psychology most often overlooked. There is a natural religious knowledge with which you are born. Ruburt's book *The Afterdeath Journal of an American Philosopher: The World View of William James* explains that feeling very well. It is a biological spirituality translated into verbal terms. It says: "Life is a gift (and not a curse). I am a unique, worthy creature in the natural world, which everywhere surrounds me, gives me sustenance, and reminds me of the greater source from which I myself and the world both emerge. My body is delightfully suited to its environment, and comes to me, again, from that unknown source which shows itself through all of the events of the physical world."

That feeling gives the organism the optimism, the joy, and the ever-abundant energy to grow. It encourages curiosity and creativity, and places the individual in a spiritual world and a natural one at once.

Organized religions are always attempts to redefine that kind of feeling in cultural terms. They seldom succeed because they become too narrow in their concepts, too dogmatic, and the cultural structures finally overweigh the finer substance within them.

The more tolerant a religion is, the closer it comes to expressing those inner truths. The individual, however, has a private biological and spiritual integrity that is a part of man's heritage, and is indeed any creature's right. Man cannot mistrust his own nature and at the same time trust the nature of God, for God is his word for the source of his being — and if his being is tainted, then so must be his God.

Your private beliefs merge with those of others, and form your cultural reality. The distorted ideas of the medical profession or the scientists, or of any other group, are not thrust upon you, therefore. They are the result of your mass beliefs — isolated in the form of separate disciplines. Medical men, for example, are often extremely unhealthy because they are so saddled with those specific health beliefs that their attention is concentrated in that area more than others not so involved. The idea of prevention is always based upon fear — for you do not want to prevent something that is joyful. Often, therefore, preventative medicine causes what it hopes to avoid. Not only does the idea [of prevention] continually promote the entire system of fear, but specific steps taken to prevent a disease in a body not already stricken, again, often set up reactions that bring about side effects that would occur if the disease had in fact been suffered.

(11:32.) A specific disease will of course have its effects on other portions of the body as well, [effects] which have not been studied, or even known. Such inoculations, therefore, cannot take that into consideration. There are also cases where alterations occur after inoculation, so that for a while people actually become carriers of diseases, and can infect others.

There are individuals who very rarely get ill whether or not they are inoculated, and who are not sensitive in the health area. I am not implying, therefore, that all people react negatively to inoculations. In the most basic of terms, however, inoculations do no good, either, though I am aware that medical history would seem to contradict me.

At certain times, and most particularly at the birth of medical science in modern times, the belief in inoculation, if not by the populace then by the doctors, did possess the great strength of new suggestion and hope — but I am afraid that scientific medicine has caused as many new diseases as it has cured. When it saves lives, it does so because of the intuitive healing understanding of the physician, or because the patient is so impressed by the great efforts taken in his behalf, and therefore is convinced secondhandedly of his own worth.

Give us a moment . . . Physicians, of course, are also constantly at the beck and call of many people who will take no responsibility at all for their own well-being, who will plead for operations they do not need. The physician is also visited by people who do not want to get well, and use the doctor and his methods as justification for further illness, saying: "The doctor is no good," or "The medicine will not work," therefore blaming the doctor for a way of life they have no intention of changing.

The physician is also caught between his religious beliefs and his scientific beliefs. Sometimes these conflict, and sometimes they only serve to deepen his feelings that the body, left alone, will get any disease possible.

Take your break.

(11:45 to 12:01.)

Again, you cannot separate your systems of values and your most intimate philosophical judgments from the other areas of your private or mass experience.

In this country, your tax dollars go for many medical experiments and preventative-medicine drives — because you do not trust the good intent of your own bodies. In the same way, your government funds [also] go into military defenses to prevent war, because if you do not trust your own body's good intent toward you, you can hardly trust any good intent on the part of your fellow men.

In fact, then, preventative medicine and outlandish expenditures for preventative defense are quite similar. In each case there is the anticipation of disaster — in one case from the familiar body, which can be attacked by deadly diseases at any time, and is seemingly at least without defenses; and in the other case from the danger without: exaggerated, ever-threatening, and ever to be contended with.

(Intently:) Disease must be combatted, fought against, assaulted, wiped out. In many ways the body becomes almost like an alien battleground, for many people trust it so little that it becomes highly suspect. Man then seems pitted against nature. Some people think of themselves as patients, as others, for example, might think of themselves as students. Such people are those who are apt to take preventative measures against whatever disease is in fashion or in season, and hence take the brunt of medicine's unfortunate aspects, when there is no cause.

(12:13.) Give us a moment. . . .

(Now Seth delivered a few paragraphs for Jane and me, then ended the session at 12:22 A.M.)

NOTES: SESSION 814

1. Here are a few comments I've always wanted to make about writing and painting, both of which I usually do each day.

As I sorted through the mass of material Seth-Jane has produced these last weeks, I found myself once again charmed and mystified by the challenges contained in the art of writing. The painted image can be taken in at a glance, at any stage of its development, but the cognition of the written word takes much more time, no matter how fast one reads or absorbs new material. With a single look the artist has an immediate grasp of the entire work before him; he (or she) can tell what he's done and has to do, what he may have to change or "fix up," even if he fails at it. Not so the writer, who while reading must pass up the artist's simultaneous perception for his own linear cognition as he makes a multitude of decisions involving sentence structure, what to use or eliminate, and so forth.

Sometimes the artist in me visually comes to the aid of the writer by laying out pages of material and notes side by side upon a table or two. Then I can see what I'm trying to do as a whole, and half intuitively, half intellectually make decisions about how to organize passages I may be having problems with. This process is always very challenging and thrilling to me. It always seems to work, although progress may still be slow at times. This method also helps greatly in counteracting that initial impatience the artist part of me strongly feels when my writer self comes upon a complex situation.

I'm well aware of current scientific theories about the supposed separate functions of the two hemispheres of the brain: The left half is said to control logical activities like writing, while the right half is responsible for the intuitive artistic abilities. Perhaps — but after all, writing can be intuitively based, and art can be logically produced. At least the whole brain (its hemispheres are connected deep within by the corpus callosum) must contain that necessary basic creative ability that may then be apportioned out — but only to an extent, I think — between the hemispheres. Barring physical injury/surgery, there must be more communication between its halves (via the corpus callosum) than the brain is given credit for. There's so much we don't know yet about the brain (let alone the mind!). What about telepathy between the hemispheres? I think the divisions charted for the brain so far may be too strict, that *beliefs* about such separations may get in the way of our perception of the brain's beautifully *whole* operation.

"But Seth apparently just delivers his material verbally, and that's it," Jane wrote after reading my first draft of this note. "Even in a long book, he doesn't go through any of those cognitive processes Rob mentions. I do when I'm writing, editing, or rewriting my own work. If I do any of that work as Seth, it's so unconscious and fast that I'm not aware of it. And Seth's 'writing' needs hardly any changes."

I also wrote in Note 3 for Session 801: ". . . that ordinarily Seth has no chance to revise his copy."

2. I'll remind the reader that Jane has already received inspiration and material for two books from her amazingly creative dream state: her novel, *The Education of Oversoul Seven,* and *James.* While dreaming she tuned into whole chapters of *Seven,* for instance.

3. I should also note that Seth has made one short, rather mysterious reference to the existence of Frameworks 3 and 4. Two days after he'd first talked about his concept of Frameworks 1 and 2, he came through with the following statement in another private session. Jane and I have yet to ask him to elaborate upon it: "There is, incidentally, a Framework 3 and a Framework 4, in the terms of our discussion — but all such labels are, again, only for the sake of explanation. The realities are merged."

4. Seth referred to the paralyzing Guillain-Barre syndrome, which struck a tiny proportion of those receiving shots in the 1976 swine flu program in this country. For many reasons, the federal government suddenly ended the very expensive and controversial program last December. Then in May of this year a number of scientists, working both in and outside of government, agreed that the flu shots *triggered* the Guillain-Barre syndrome, but that the reasons for such reactions in certain individuals are unknown. Jane and I didn't take the shots.

5. Earlier material on inoculations can be found in Chapter 1. See Session 801 with Note 4, and Session 802 with Note 3.

SESSION 815, DECEMBER 17, 1977
9:22 P.M. SATURDAY

(*All right. Another long period — 10 weeks this time — has passed following Seth's last session for* Mass Events. *Since this is the third such break between book sessions, it seems that Jane and I would be used to the idea by now. Actually, I'm more bothered than she is by such long intervals. I like to follow an endeavor through from start to finish in a reasonably direct manner. When the sessions don't work out that way I can feel somewhat uneasy, while realizing at the same time that a number of compensating factors may be at work. In this case two distinct notions, one factual and one philosophical, helped keep me at ease.*

(*First, during that 10-week break Seth-Jane held a series of 18 sessions — excellent ones — that once again did not constitute dictation for* Mass Events. *Second, if one keeps in mind Seth's ideas about simultaneous time, that basically all happens at once [even considering Seth's own acknowledgment that time ". . . is therefore still a reality of some kind to me"], then it hardly matters how long a break transpires between particular sessions; there is no real separation; dictation on any subject or project can be resumed whenever all involved — Jane, Seth, and myself — choose, and it will be as though the break never existed. For in trance, Jane will once again be in accord with Seth in that nearly "timeless" environment in which he has a large portion of his being.*[1]

(So we've decided to simply go along with however Mass Events *works out in terms of length, whether that length involves time or the number of sessions. We do not plan to ask Seth when the book will be done. We have asked him to discuss his Framework 1 and 2 concepts for it, though, and he's promised to do so; he's had a good deal to say about those structures in the nonbook material Jane has delivered since the 814th session was held.*

(As of now: I'm practically through with the appendixes for Volume 2 of "Unknown" Reality — *which means I still have a number of notes to write for the book's sessions per se, as well as much work to do for the Introductory Notes and the Epilogue. Soon after Tam Mossman suggested in early October that she do a book on her dream about Emir,*[2] *Jane began work on that project with her usual enthusiasm. The dream became Chapter 1 of the book, and inspired the rest of it; she's having great fun writing the story, and is sending it to Tam chapter by chapter as it comes out of her typewriter — a procedure she's never followed before. She doesn't know how long* Emir *will be. Late in October she signed her contracts for the publication of* James, *and delivered the finished manuscript at the end of November. Besides doing all of her own writing and newspaper work, Sue Watkins is close to finishing her part of the typing on the final manuscript for Seth's* Psyche; *I still have to spend more time on some of the notes for it. Sue has also agreed that next year she'll start helping me type my notes and appendix material for Volume 2 of* "Unknown."

(While we've been busy with our endeavors, the shortening, brilliantly colored and often warm days of October passed into November and turned progressively colder through the month; we've already had more than a little snow since Thanksgiving; and now in a few days [about December 22] winter will officially arrive. I've raked leaves, stacked wood in the garage, installed storm windows, and made sure our hill house is otherwise all set for cold weather.

(We're still holding the sessions on Monday and Saturday evenings, which is the routine we initiated after the 805th session was held just seven months ago [on May 16]. As we sat for tonight's session Jane told me — somewhat to my surprise — that she felt Seth might give some material for Mass Events. *She wasn't positive, however. Today she'd reread his sessions for the book. Then:)*

Good evening.

("Good evening, Seth.")

Dictation. I do not want to shock you, but dictation — continuation of our last chapter *(2: "Mass Meditations," etc.)*.

(With some humor:) Ruburt and Joseph have recently purchased a color television set, so now their television world is no longer in black and white. I have used television as an analogy at various times, and I would like to do so again, to show the ways in which physical events are formed, and to try to describe the many methods used by individuals in choosing those particular events that will be personally encountered.

Not only does television actually serve as a mass means of communal meditation, but it also presents you with highly detailed, manufactured dreams, in which each viewer shares to some extent. We will use some distinctions here, and so I am going to introduce the terms "Framework 1" and "Framework 2," to make my discussion clear.

We will call the world as you physically experience it, Framework 1. In Framework 1, you watch television programs, for example. You have your choice of many channels. You have favorite programs. You follow certain scenes or actors. You watch all of these dramas, hardly understanding how it is that they appear on your screen to begin with. You are certain, however, that if you do buy a television set it will perform in an adequate fashion, whether or not you are familiar with electronics. Period.

You switch from channel to channel with predictable results. The programming for Channel 9, for example, does not suddenly intrude on Channel 6. Even the actors themselves, taking part in such sagas, have but the remotest idea of events that are involved in order that their own images will appear on your television screen. Their jobs are to act, taking it for granted that the technicians are following through.

Now somewhere there is a program director, who must take care of the entire programming. Shows must be done on time, actors assigned their roles. Our hypothetical director will know which actors are free, which actors prefer character roles, which ones are heroes or heroines, and which smiling Don Juan always gets the girl — and in general who plays the good guys and the bad guys.

There is no need in my outlining in detail the multitudinous events that must occur so that you can watch your favorite program. You flip the switch and there it is, while all of that background work is unknown to you. You take it for granted. Your job is simply to choose the programs of your choice on any evening. Many others are watching the same programs, of course, yet each person will react quite individually.

(9:40.) Now for a moment let us imagine that physical events occur in the same fashion — that you choose those which flash upon the screen of your experience. You are quite familiar with the events of your own life, for you are of course your own main hero or heroine, villain or victim, or whatever. As you do not know what happens in the television studio before you observe a program, however, so you do not know what happens in the creative framework of reality before you experience physical events. We will call that vast "unconscious" mental and universal studio Framework 2.

In this book I will try to tell you what goes on behind the scenes — to show you the ways in which you choose your daily physical programs, and to describe how those personal choices mix and merge to form a mass reality. For now, we will go back to television again. You can turn off a program that offends you. You can choose to buy or not buy a product whose virtues are being praised. Television presents you with a mirror of your society. It reflects and rereflects through millions of homes the giant dreams and fears, the hopes and terrors of events in the most private individual.

Television interacts with your lives, but it does not cause your lives. It does not cause the events that it depicts. With your great belief in technology, it often seems to many people that television causes violence, for example, or that it causes a love of overmaterialism, or that it causes "loose morals." Television reflects. In a manner of speaking it does not even distort, though it may reflect distortions. The writers and actors of television dramas are attuned to the "mass mind." They are not leaders or followers. They are creative reflectors, acutely aware of the overall, generalized emotional and psychic patterns of the age.

They also make choices as to which plays they will take part in. [Each has his or her] own favorite kind of role, even if the role be that of a maverick. To the actors, of course, their roles become strong parts of their personal experiences, while those who observe the plays take part largely as observers.

You are aware through your newspapers and magazines of the dramas, news broadcasts, or other programs that are presently being offered. In the same way you are aware, generally speaking, of the "programs" being physically presented in your own nation and throughout the world. You decide which of these adventures you want to take part in — and those you will experience in normal life, or in Framework 1.

The inner mechanisms that happen prior to your experience will take place in the vast mental studio of Framework 2. There, all the details will be arranged, the seemingly chance encounters, for example, the unexplained coincidences that might have to occur before a given physical event takes place.

Take your break.

(10:02 to 10:19.)

On a conscious level, and with your conscious reserves alone, you could not keep your body alive an hour. You would not know how to do it, for your life flows through you automatically and spontaneously. You take the details for granted — the breathing, the inner mechanisms of nourishment and elimination, the circulation, and the maintenance of your psychological continuity. All of that is taken care of for you in what I have termed as Framework 2.

In that regard, certainly, everything works to your advantage. Indeed, often the more concerned you become with your body the less smoothly it functions. In the spontaneity of your body's operation there is obviously a fine sense of order. When you turn on a television set the picture seems to come out of nowhere onto the screen — yet that picture is the result of order precisely focused.

Actors visit casting agencies so that they know what plays need their services. In your dreams you visit "casting agencies." You are aware of the various plays being considered for physical production. In the dream state, then, often you familiarize yourself with dramas that are of a probable nature. If enough interest is shown, if enough actors apply, if enough resources are accumulated, the play will go on. When you are in other than your normally conscious state, you visit that creative inner agency in which all physical productions must have their beginning. You meet with others, who for their own reasons are interested in the same kind of drama. Following our analogy, the technicians, the actors, the writers all assemble — only in this case the result will be a live event rather than a televised one. There are disaster films being planned, educational programs, religious dramas. All of these will be encountered in full-blown physical reality.

Such events occur as a result of individual beliefs, desires, and intents. There is no such thing as a chance encounter. No death occurs by chance, nor any birth. In the creative atmosphere of Framework 2, intents are known. In a manner of speaking, no act is private. Your communication systems bring to your living room notices of events that occur throughout the world. Yet that larger inner system of communications is far more powerful in scope, and each mental act is imprinted in the multidimensional screen of Framework 2. That screen is available to all, and in other levels of consciousness, particularly in the sleep and dreaming stages, the events of that inner reality are as ever-present and easily accessible as physical events are when you are awake.

(10:40.) It is as if Framework 2 contains an infinite information service, that instantly puts you in contact with whatever knowledge you require, that sets up circuits between you and others, that computes probabilities with blinding speed. Not with the impersonality of a computer, however, but with a loving intent that has your best purposes in mind — yours and also those of each other individual.

You cannot gain what you want at someone else's detriment, then. You cannot use Framework 2 to force an event upon another person. Certain prerequisites must be met, you see, before a desired end can become physically experienced.

(10:45.) Give us a moment . . .

I will try to begin work on our book in a more predictable fashion, while still maintaining our own discussions, and answering any questions you may have. I do want to use our Framework 2 material, however, in a more general fashion for the book.[3] You may use any of our [other] material you want, but the book itself will not rely upon that information.

(The balance of the session, then, is deleted. Seth said good night at 11:12 P.M.)

NOTES: SESSION 815

1. The basic simultaneity of time is the most fascinating of all of Seth's ideas, I think. That "spacious present" holds all events side by side, ready to be interpreted in cause-and-effect fashion by the organizational abilities of our more limited physical senses. I wrote about reconstructing the past, simultaneous time, and dreams early in Note 2 for Session 801. Also see the material on Seth and his simultaneous time in the opening notes for the 806th session.

2. See the opening notes for the 814th session. Jane is calling her new book *Emir's Education in the Proper Use of Magical Powers.*

3. Although this is the first session for *Mass Events* in which Seth had discussed Framework 1 and Framework 2, at the moment Jane and I are a good deal more familiar with his ideas concerning those fields of action than the reader is; see the opening notes for the last (814th) session. Since introducing them in the deleted, or nonbook session for September 17, Seth has at least mentioned the two frameworks in 17 of the 23 deleted sessions he's given us since then.

He'd dealt with Frameworks 1 and 2 in only seven sessions, however, when I wrote a paragraph of suggestions about them on October 26. This spontaneous creation not only summarized what I'd learned from his new material so far, but gave me something I could read daily. I've pinned copies to walls in both my painting and writing rooms.

My piece is naturally tailored to my own beliefs and needs, of course, and some of its implications may become clearer to readers as Seth continues with his framework material in *Mass Events.* But I'm presenting my effort as close as possible to its time of conception so that each interested person can keep it in mind, and eventually write his or her own version of it for personal use. Jane has done this; we find that a daily casual reading of our respective "credos" concerning Frameworks 1 and 2 is valuable indeed. I wrote on October 26:

> "I have the simple, profound faith that anything I desire in this life can come to me from Framework 2. There are no impediments in Framework 2. Framework 2 can creatively produce everything I desire to have in Framework 1 — my excellent health, painting, and writing, my excellent relationship with Jane, Jane's own spontaneous and glowing physical health and creativity, the greater and greater sales of all her books. I know that all of these positive goals are worked out in Framework 2, regardless

of their seeming complexity, and that they can then show themselves in Framework 1. I have the simple, profound faith that everything I desire in life can come to me from the miraculous workings of Framework 2. I do not need to be concerned with details of any kind, knowing that Framework 2 possesses the infinite creative capacity to handle and produce everything I can possibly ask of it. My simple, profound faith in the creative goodness of Framework 2 is all that is necessary."

PART TWO

FRAMEWORK 1
AND
FRAMEWORK 2

CHAPTER 3

MYTHS AND PHYSICAL EVENTS.
THE INTERIOR MEDIUM
IN WHICH SOCIETY EXISTS

SESSION 817, JANUARY 30, 1978
9:35 P.M. MONDAY

(*S* *eth's statement at the end of dictation for the 815th session, "I will try to begin work on our book in a more predictable fashion," reflected his good intent, but things didn't turn out that way. Jane and I let the holiday season intervene to some extent, and Session 816, which came through the day after Christmas, didn't concern book work at all. Then, starting in early January, we held eight sessions having to do with questions we'd put off dealing with for a long time; some were personal and some were not. We stayed with our Monday–Saturday evening session routine, though, and kept busy with all of our other projects.[1]*

(We also experienced a very cold wintry month indeed, including a series of massive snowstorms within the week just ended — "the worst in over a decade," as I wrote in a note for last Saturday night's private session.)

Good evening.

("Good evening, Seth.")

Dictation: A new chapter *(3)*, to be titled: "Myths and Physical Events." *(Long pause.)* Then: "The Interior Medium in Which Society Exists."

Give us a moment . . . Before we discuss man's and woman's private roles in the nature of mass events — no matter what they are — we must first look into the medium in which events appear concrete and real. The great sweep of the events of nature can be understood only by looking into a portion of their reality that is not apparent to you. We want to examine, therefore, the inner power of natural occurrences.

A scientist examining nature studies its exterior, observing the outsideness of nature. Even investigative work involving atoms and molecules, or [theoretical[2]] faster-than-light particles, concerns the particle nature of reality. The scientist does not usually look for nature's heart. He certainly does not pursue the study of its soul.

All being is manifestation of energy — an emotional manifestation of energy. Man can interpret the weather in terms of air pressure and wind currents. He can look to fault lines in an effort to understand earthquakes. All of this works at a certain level, to a certain degree. Man's psyche, however, is emotionally not only a part of his physical environment, but intimately connected with all of nature's manifestations. Using the terms begun in the last chapter, I will say then that man's emotional identification with nature is a strongly-felt reality in Framework 2. And there we must look for the answers regarding man's relationship with nature. There in Framework 2 the nature of the psyche appears quite clearly, so that its sweeps and rhythms can be understood. The manifestations of physical energy follow emotional rhythms that cannot be ascertained with gadgets or instruments, however fine.

Why is one man killed and not another? Why does an earthquake disrupt an entire area? What is the relationship between the individual and such mass events of nature?

Before we can begin to consider such questions, we must take another look at your own world, and ascertain its source, for surely its source and nature's are the same. We will also along this line, and throughout this book, have to make some distinctions between events and your interpretations of them.

It certainly seems that your world is concrete, factual, definite, and that its daily life rests upon known events and facts. You make a clear distinction between fact and fantasy. You take it for granted as a rule that your current knowledge as a people rests upon scientific

data, at least, that is unassailable. Certainly technological development appears to have been built most securely upon a body of
concrete ideas.

The world's ideas, fantasies, or myths may seem far divorced from
current experience — yet all that you know or experience has its
origin in that creative dimension of existence that I am terming Framework 2. In a manner of speaking your factual world rises on a bed of
fantasy, myth, and imagination, from which all of your detailed paraphernalia emerge. What then is myth, and what do I mean by the term?

Myth is not a distortion of fact, but the womb through which fact
must come. Myth involves an intrinsic understanding of the nature
of reality, couched in imaginative terms, carrying a power as strong
as nature itself. Myth-making is a natural psychic characteristic, a psychic element that combines with other such elements to form a
mythical representation of inner reality. That representation is then
used as a model upon which your civilizations are organized, and also
as a perceptual tool through whose lens you interpret the private
events of your life in their historical context.

(10:06.) When you *accept* myths you call them facts, of course, for
they become so a part of your lives, of societies and your professions,
that their basis seems self-apparent. Myths are vast psychic dramas,
more truthful than facts. They provide an ever-enduring theater of
reality. It must be clearly understood, then, that when I speak of
myths I mean to imply the nature of psychic events whose enduring
reality exists in Framework 2, and forms the patterns that are then
interpreted in your world.

If someone is caught in a natural disaster, the following questions might be asked: "Am I being punished by God, and for what
reason? Is the disaster the result of God's vengeance?" A scientist
might ask instead: "With better technology and information, could
we somehow have predicted the disaster, and saved many lives?" He
might try to dissociate himself from emotion, and to see the disaster
simply as the result of a nonpersonal nature that did not know or
care what lay in its path.

In all cases, however, such situations instantly bring to mind
questions of man's own reality and source, his connections with God,
his planet, and the universe. He interprets those questions according to his own beliefs. Let us then look at some of them.

Take your break.

(10:18 to 10:27.)

Now: Myths are natural phenomena, rising from the psyche of man as surely as giant mountain ranges emerge from the physical planet. Their deeper reality exists, however, in Framework 2 as source material for the world that you know.

In those terms, the great religions of your civilizations rise from myths that change their character through the centuries, even as mountain ranges rise and fall. You can see mountain ranges. It would be ridiculous to ignore their reality. You see your myths somewhat less directly, yet they are apparent within all of your activities, and they form the inner structures of all of your civilizations with their multitudinous parts.

In those terms, then, Christianity and your other religions are myths, rising in response to an inner knowledge that is too vast to be clothed by facts alone. In those terms also, your science is also quite mythical in nature. This may be more difficult for some of you to perceive, since it appears to work so well. Others will be willing enough to see science in its mythical characteristics, but will be most reluctant to see religion as you know it in the same light. To some extent or another, however, all of these ideas program your interpretation of events.

In this part *(2)* of the book, we are more or less dealing with the events of nature as you understand it. It will seem obvious to some, again, that a natural disaster is caused by God's vengeance, or is at least a divine reminder to repent, while others will take it for granted that such a catastrophe is completely neutral in character, impersonal and [quite] divorced from man's own emotional reality. The Christian scientist is caught in between. Because you divorce yourselves from nature, you are not able to understand its manifestations. Often your myths get in the way. When myths become standardized, and too literal, when you begin to tie them too tightly to the world of facts, then you misread them entirely. When myths become most factual they are already becoming less real. Their power becomes constrained.

(10:43.) Give us a moment . . . Most people interpret the realities of their lives, their triumphs and failures, their health or illness, their fortune or misfortune, then, in the light of a mythical reality that is

not understood as such. What is behind these myths, and what is their source of power?

Facts are a very handy but weak brew of reality. They immediately consign certain kinds of experiences as real and others as not. The psyche, however, will not be so limited. It exists in a medium of reality, a realm of being in which all possibilities exist. It creates myths the way the ocean creates spray. Myths are originally psychic fabrications of such power and strength that whole civilizations can rise from their source. They involve symbols and known emotional validities that are then connected to the physical world, so that that world is never the same again.

They cast their light over historical events because they are responsible for those events. They mix and merge the inner, unseen but felt, eternal psychic experience of man with the temporal events of his physical days, and form a combination that structures thoughts and beliefs from civilization to civilization. In Framework 2 the interior power of nature is ever-changing. The dreams, hopes, aspirations and fears of man interact in a constant motion that then forms the events of your world. That interaction includes not only man, of course, but the emotional reality of all earthly consciousnesses as well, from a microbe to a scholar, from a frog to a star. You interpret the phenomena of your world according to the mythic characteristics that you have accepted. You organize physical reality, then, through ideas. You use only those perceptions that serve to give those ideas validity. The physical body itself is quite capable of putting the world together in different fashions than the one that is familiar to you.

You divorce yourselves from nature and nature's intents far more than the animals do. Nature in its stormy manifestations seems like an adversary. You must either look for reasons outside of yourselves to explain what seems to be nature's ill intent at such times, or its utter lack of concern.

Science often says that nature cares little for the individual, only for the species, so then you must often see yourselves as victims in a larger struggle for survival, in which your own intents do not carry even the puniest sway.

End of dictation. End of session, unless you have questions.

(*"No, I guess not."*)

There are good things coming. That is all I have to say.

(*"Okay."*)

My heartiest regards, and a fond good evening.

(*"Thank you, Seth. Good night."*)

(*11:02 P.M. Jane's delivery in trance had been excellent — concentrated and steady.*)

NOTES: SESSION 817

1. Those "other projects" included work by Jane and me on *Emir* and Volume 2 of *"Unknown" Reality*, respectively. (Jane has been told that everyone at Prentice-Hall, her publishing house, "just loves" *Emir*.) A couple of weeks ago Sue Watkins delivered the last two chapters of the manuscript for *Psyche* that she's been typing for us; we still have to check that book and finish the notes for it. Then yesterday Jane received from her publisher the copyedited manuscript for *James*, so during the next week or so we'll be very carefully going over that work, too.

2. See Note 2 for the 803rd session.

SESSION 818, FEBRUARY 6, 1978
10:19 P.M. MONDAY

(*No session was held last Wednesday night because Jane and I were so busy checking the copyedited manuscript for* James. *I had the book wrapped for mailing today, but I didn't leave the house. A massive snowstorm had developed by noon. It was raging stronger than ever as we sat for the session at 9:15; drifts were piled several feet high against the northern side of the house, and against our new screened-in back porch facing the west. Now the forecasts were for the storm to continue through the night.*

(*We waited for the session to begin for an hour and four minutes — something neither of us could recall having done in the past. Both of us were silent for long periods. At 10:05 Jane remarked: "I feel like there's a whole lot of material out there getting organized, but it just hasn't gotten here yet. Weird . . . I don't think I've ever felt quite this way before. Otherwise I'd just say the hell with it and do something else. But if I don't have a session tonight, then in the next one I'll want to know why it didn't happen this time. It's as though I could wake up at 2 A.M. and say, 'Oh my god, here it is. . . .'"*)

(And those strange feelings of Jane's are precisely why we're presenting this session in Mass Events, *even though it isn't book dictation. Seth came through with some very interesting material on the relationship involving the three of us, as well as the communication between his reality and ours. The session contains just the kind of insights we're always looking for as we seek to understand the whole ambience of the Seth experience, and when we receive such information we want others to know about it too. We hardly expected Seth to discuss Framework 3, though, since we're still assimilating his material on Frameworks 1 and 2.*

("It would be really frustrating, waiting, except that everything seems so timeless," Jane said as we continued to sit. "Do you feel that way?" I did. The warm living room with its soft lights, and the storm outside, seemed to have persisted forever. Our house on the hill is so well-insulated that we heard the weather's assaults as though from a great distance, except for an occasional sharp clatter from one of the metal window awnings as its slats vibrated in a blast of icy wind. Then finally:)

Good evening.

("Good evening, Seth.")

Now: In explanation, I do not know exactly how to word this, but in a manner of speaking I take tours — through psychological realities, however, or through psychic lands rather than physical ones. Such journeys "take no time" in your terms. Yet for our sessions I must synchronize many activities, so that on some occasions I am with you, and I am also involved elsewhere.

You have a storm. Weathermen speak of local conditions and merging air currents — but my journeys are in a realm where consciousnesses merge. I do not know if I have specifically mentioned it, but you should understand my constant state of growth, expansion, and development. Recall Ruburt's episodes with the [psychic] library.[1] Those are examples of far lesser versions of my activities, and yet in those terms, and using an analogy, I travel to many great universities of the mind.

Much of this is difficult to explain, again, for information and knowledge is constantly transformed — almost completely reborn, so to speak, through characteristics that are inherently a part of thought itself. Knowledge is changed automatically through the auspices of each consciousness who perceives it. It is magnified and yet refined. It is a constant language, yet one that transforms itself. When I "attend these sessions," or "speak," then I exchange with others a more complicated system of reality than any computer could handle. You do not understand or perceive the ways in which your reality contributes to the foundation of the mass-world reality that you experience. Unconsciously, each individual participates in forming that world. In my case, however, I am aware of the same kind of activities, only in regard to many realities rather than one.[2]

As I try to increase your capacity for understanding, and to expand the scopes of your abilities, so in other kinds of worlds I do the same thing. While our meetings take place in your time, and in the physical space of your house, say, the primary encounter must be a subjective inner one, an intersection of consciousnesses that is then physically experienced.

The encounters themselves occur in a Framework 3 environment. That framework of course, again in terms of an analogy, exists another step away from your own Framework 2.[3] I do not want to get into a higher-or-lower hierarchy here, but the frameworks represent spheres of action. Our encounters initially take place, then, beyond the sphere that deals exclusively with either your physical world or the inner mental and psychic realm from which your present experience springs.

On a very few occasions over the past years, before a session Ruburt has felt a distance between us, or that our material was not quite ready. I have already explained that sometimes I leave you a "tape." Usually that takes care of any such instances. This evening, however, Ruburt somewhat sensed not only a distance but also the larger complications of my activities.

(10:45.) Give us a moment . . . Now to some extent, you see, you are both involved, but in ways almost impossible for me to explain. Do not take this literally by any means. Portions of your consciousness are alive in mine, so you are to some extent carried along where I go, as motes of dust might be swept along with a brisk autumn wind from one area to another. *(Humorously:)* I am not comparing you with motes of dust by any means; to some extent, however, you do share in my journeys. You are carried above the land of your usual perception so that portions of you glimpse subjective states. These

arouse your curiosity even when consciously you are not aware of perceiving them. That curiosity acts as impetus.

Your intents and concerns, your interests, your needs and desires, your characteristics and abilities, directly influence our material, for they lead you to it to begin with.

You want to make the material workable in your world — a natural and quite understandable desire: The proof is in the pudding, and so forth. Yet of course you are also participators in an immense drama in which the main actions occur outside of your world, in those realms from which your world originated — and you are, foremost, natives of those other realms, as each individual is; as each being is.

Those realms are far from lonely, dark, and chaotic. They are also quite different from any concept of nirvana or nothingness. They are composed of ever-spiralling states of existence in which different kinds of consciousnesses meet and communicate. They are not impersonal realms, but are involved in the most highly intimate interactions. Those interactions exist about you all the while, and I would like you in your thoughts to aspire toward them, to try to stretch your perceptions enough so that you become at least somewhat aware of their existence.

These frameworks, while I speak of them separately, exist one within the other, and each one impinges upon the other. To some extent you are immersed in all realities. In a strange fashion, and in this particular case, your conflict with your notes[4] had to do with a sense of orderliness aroused by the need to assemble facts. But [this was] then carried over so that you wanted to keep your Roman *(reincarnational)* world and this [present] one separate and not merge them through association — as you did — so that it was difficult to know this when you did your sketches. Subjectively you wanted to put the worlds together, to explore the similarities and so forth, but practically you wanted to divide them for your notes.

If you can, try to sense this greater context in which you have your being. Your rewards will be astonishing. The emotional realization is what is important, of course, not simply an intellectual acceptance of the idea. Ruburt wanted material on this book, and that is well and good. The book is important. The book has its meaning in your world, but I do not want you to forget the vaster context in which these sessions originate. This kind of information can at least trigger responses on your part, increasing still further the scope of knowledge that you can receive from me.

In your world knowledge must be translated into specifics, yet we also deal with emotional realities that cannot be so easily deciphered. In this session, in the words I speak — but more importantly in the atmosphere of the session — there are hints of those undecipherable yet powerful realities that will then, in your time, gradually be described in verbal terms that make sense to you.

(11:13.) There is more, but it will have to wait simply because it is not presently translatable. According to the impact of this session, your own comprehensions and perceptions will bring other clues, either in the waking or the dream state. Keep your minds open for them, but without any preconceived ideas of how they might appear. Ruburt's own development triggers certain psychic activity that then triggers further growth. He has been participating in his library, for example, whether or not he is always aware of it.

End of session.

("Thank you, Seth. Good night."

(11:15 P.M. "Boy, I really felt different while that was going on," Jane said as soon as she was out of trance. "I had a sense of power that I usually don't get. I'm glad I waited. I guess I feel like I've been someplace else, or something like that. I have a feeling there's something new in the session, but I'll have to figure it out. . . . ")

NOTES: SESSION 818

1. In *Psychic Politics* Jane thoroughly described her discovery and use of her nonphysical library.

2. Jane and I plan to eventually ask Seth to explain to us, in ways that will let us at least approach an understanding of them, some of those other realities in which he exists and "speaks."

3. This is the second time that Seth has very briefly referred to Framework 3. See Note 3 for the 814th session.

4. When Volume 2 of *"Unknown" Reality* is published a year or so from now (early in 1979), the reader can refer to certain notes I wrote for sessions 715–16. In them I described a series of episodes during which I saw myself as a captain in a Roman military force, early in the first century A.D.

SESSION 820, FEBRUARY 13, 1978
9:40 P.M. MONDAY

(This morning I mailed to Prentice-Hall the eighth and last chapter of Jane's book, Emir's Education in the Proper Use of Magical Powers.

(Session 819, which was held last Saturday evening, had nothing to do with Mass Events. *In our opinion tonight's session* did, *however, and for a number of reasons that will become obvious as it's read. Yet Seth didn't call it dictation.*

(At lunch today I suggested to Jane that she put together a short book on the Frameworks 1 and 2 material Seth has given us since he introduced that concept in a private session last September 17, 1977. We've had 31 private or nonbook sessions since then, and a number of them contain information on Frameworks 1 and 2 — much of it relevant to that presented in Mass Events. *I thought Jane might consider such a book project along with her other work. In a way the suggestion was my idea of trying to do something about Seth producing books within books, as I discussed in my opening notes for the 814th session; but Seth is so prolific that it seems we'll never get all of his material published at this time.*

(Jane showed more interest in my idea than I'd thought she would, and spent the afternoon going over those private sessions. As the hours passed she reacted to Seth's data by becoming very loose and relaxed. She "felt funny," she said. Still, she wanted to try for the session. We began waiting at 9:30. Then, without greetings:)

Now: How nice that you remembered Framework 2 again.

To some extent the material on Frameworks 1 and 2 is of course an example of the entire idea, for you receive a good deal of information in sessions not given to book dictation — simply because, while our books are extremely free, still they must be colored by your ideas of what books are.

Even your concepts of creativity are necessarily influenced by Framework 1 thinking, of course, so our sessions do indeed follow a larger pattern than that, giving you certain perspectives from different angles in book dictation, and in other material. To some extent the larger creative pattern of the material, which does exist and is sensed, is nevertheless not directly perceived, for you are bound to perceive it piecemeal.

I have said that acts of creativity best approach the workings of Framework 2, for [those] acts always involve leaps of faith and inspiration, and the breaking of barriers.

Each of our books adds to the others. That includes Ruburt's as well — and that also includes of course books not yet written, in your terms, so that the future books also influence what you think of as the past ones. Again, while appearing in your time, the contents of the books come from outside of your time.

When you are writing a regular book you draw upon associations, memories, and events that are known to you and others, that perhaps you had forgotten but that suddenly spring to mind in answer to your intent and following your associations. When an artist is painting a landscape, he might unconsciously compare hundreds of landscapes viewed in the past in multitudinous, seemingly forgotten hues that splashed upon the grass or trees, or as he seeks for a new creative combination. Art is his focus so that he draws from Framework 2 all of those pertinent data that are necessary for his painting. Not just technique is concerned, but the entire visual experience of his life.

Framework 2 involves a far vaster creative activity, in which your life is the art involved — and all [of the] ingredients for its success are there, available. When you are creating a product or a work of art, the results will have much to do with your ideas of what the product is, or what the work of art is — so your ideas about your life, or life itself, will also have much to do with your experience of it as a living art.

If you believe in the laws of cause and effect, as accepted, or in the laws of polarity, as accepted *(and explained in a letter we received today),* then you will be bound by those laws, for they will represent your artistic technique. You will believe that you must use them in order to, say, paint the living portrait of your life. You will therefore structure your experience, drawing to yourself from Framework 2 only that which fits. You will not have the "technique" to attract other experience, and as long as you stick with one technique your life-pictures will more or less have a certain monotony.

Again, the writer or the artist also brings more into his work than the simple ability to write or paint. In one way or another all of his experience is involved. When you pay attention to Framework 1 primarily, it is as if you have learned to write simple sentences with one word neatly before the other. You have not really learned true expression. In your life you are writing sentences like "See Tommy run." Your mind is not really dealing with concepts but with the simple perception of objects, so that little imagination is involved. You can express the location of objects in space, and you can communicate to others in a similar fashion, confirming the physical, obvious properties that others also perceive.

In those terms, using our analogy, the recognition of Framework 2 would bring you from that point to the production of great art, where words served to express not only the seen but the unseen — not simply facts but feelings and emotions — and where the words themselves escaped their consecutive patterns, sending the emotions into realms that quite defied both space and time.

(10:13.) Now and then people have such moments, and yet each private reality has its existence in an eternal creativity from which, again, your world springs.

It is not as if that vaster reality were utterly closed to your perception, for it is not. To some extent it is everywhere apparent in each person's private experience, and it is obviously stated in the very existence of your world itself. The religions, in one way or another, have always perceived it, although the attempt to interpret that reality in terms of the recognized facts of the world is bound to distort it.

Give us a moment . . . Your world, then, is the result of a multidimensional creative venture, a work of art in terms almost impossible for you to presently understand, in which each person and creature, and each particle, plays a living part. Again, in Framework 2 each event is known, from the falling of a leaf to the falling of a star, from the smallest insect's experience on a summer day to the horrendous murder of an individual on a city street. Those events each have their meaning in a larger pattern of activity. That pattern is not divorced from your reality, not thrust upon you, not apart from your experience. It often only seems to be because you so compartmentalize your own experience that you automatically separate yourself from such knowledge.

Creativity does not deal with compartments. It throws aside barriers. Even most people who are involved in creative work often apply their additional insights and knowledge only to their art, however — not to their lives. Period. They fall back to cause and effect.

Your Framework 1 life is, again, based on the idea that you have only so much energy, that you will wear out, and that a certain expenditure of energy will produce a given amount of work — in other words, that applied effort of a certain kind will produce the best results. In the same way, it is believed that the energy of the universe will die out. All of this presupposes "the fact" that no new energy is inserted into the world. The source of the world would therefore seem no longer to exist, having worn itself out in the effort to produce physical phenomena. In the light of such thinking, Framework 2 would be an impossibility.

Instead, the energy of life is inserted constantly into your world, in a way that has nothing to do with your so-called physical laws. I said *(14 years ago)* that the universe expands as an idea does, and that is exactly what I mean.

The greater life of each creature exists in that framework that "originally" gave it birth, and in a greater manner of speaking each creature, regardless of its age, is indeed being constantly reborn. I am couching all of this in terms of your world's known reality, which means that I am dealing with the local properties of Framework 2 as they have impact in your experience.

(Pause at 10:39.) Rest your fingers.

We will most probably have to end the session, for there are points where the translation becomes most difficult. You [both] are privately at a time where you are ready to go ahead again, where the information given is catching up to you in time, so that there can be renewed bursts of comprehension, dream experiences, and other such events.

End of session.

("Thank you, Seth."

(10:43 P.M. "That was really strange," Jane said, when she'd finished her excellent delivery for Seth. I was surprised to see that she looked more than a little queasy. "That's the first time that ever happened: I started to feel really sick, as though the material really got to me while he was giving it. Toward the end there was a strain, involving things I couldn't translate. As though I was on the edge of getting some great stuff I've never heard of before. I still feel that way. . . .

("Maybe my feelings weren't caused by any thing, but some kind of acceleration toward a state I couldn't reach, instead of any great disclosure for the world," Jane said a little later. "But I really felt sick there."

(Her comments fit in well with Seth's closing statement about the difficulty of translation; otherwise, we couldn't find a reason for her reactions in the session material itself. I suggested that the necessary insights would come to her later. It did seem that her odd state had its origins in her feelings of the afternoon and early evening.)

SESSION 821, FEBRUARY 20, 1978
9:30 P.M. MONDAY

(In Note 1 for the 817th session, which was held on January 30, I wrote that Sue Watkins had recently delivered the last of the typed manuscript for Seth's The Nature of the Psyche. *Actually, she had converted my original typed sessions making up* Psyche *into standard manuscript form for the publisher; I still have to do many of the notes for the book after I finish my work on Volume 2 of* "Unknown" Reality *several months from now.*

(On the other hand, with the copyedited manuscript for James *and the concluding chapters of* Emir *mailed to Prentice-Hall earlier this month, Jane found herself with some unexpected free time. [We don't expect to receive the page proofs for* James, *for correcting, until late next month.] Jane began to enjoy her break by writing poetry and doing some painting — but she surprised me when she also spontaneously began to rough out some of the notes for* Psyche. *She still planned to leave up to me the detailed, even painstaking work that she doesn't care for: the endless checking and rechecking of dates and events in order to get each note just right. Yet I was more than happy with whatever help she could give, I told her, since it would let us get* Psyche *published that much sooner after Volume 2.*

(I don't know how long I'll continue to benefit from Jane's assistance, though, since poetry, painting, and notes can all be quickly laid aside if she starts a new project, or resumes work on one that she's kept in abeyance for some time. One such delayed endeavor is an autobiography that she began several years ago. Another is the sequel to her novel, The Education of Oversoul Seven; *that first Seven book was published in April 1973 — and lately she's been thinking of resuming work on* Seven Two, *as we usually call it.[1] One thing is certain:* Jane will see to it that something *creative happens to change the status quo, for she's much too restless and energetic to leave things as they are.*

(In line with doing things differently, no session was held last Saturday night because over the weekend we decided to give up the Monday–Saturday session routine we've followed for the last eight months, and return to our original practice of holding sessions on Monday and Wednesday evenings. The change was made to give Jane more time on weekends to handle the mail. I don't think my own daily work patterns will be affected much; I help her with the correspondence, but don't spend nearly the time at it that she does.)

Now: Dictation: You are, of course, a part of nature, and a part of nature's source.

Growing from an infant to a full adult was probably one of the most difficult, and yet the most easy of feats that you will ever accomplish in a life. As a child you identified with your own nature. You intuitively realized that your being was immersed in <u>and a part</u> of the process of growth.

No amount of intellectual information, no accumulation of facts however vast, could give you the inner knowledge necessary to accomplish the physical events involved in that growth process. You learn to read, but the seeing itself is an accomplishment of far greater magnitude — one that seemingly happens all by itself. It happens because each of you is, again, indeed a part of nature and of nature's source.

In various ways your religions have always implied your relationship with nature's source, even though they often divorced nature herself from any place of prime importance. For religions have often hinged themselves upon one or another quite valid perception, but then distorted it, excluding anything else that did not seem to fit. "You are children of the universe." This is an often-heard sentence — and yet the main point of the Christ <u>story</u>[2] was not Christ's death but his <u>birth</u>, and the often-stated proposition that each person was indeed "a child of the father."

There are many later-appended references in the Bible, such as the fig tree story, in which nature is played down. Christ's "father" was, however, the God who was indeed aware of every sparrow that fell, who knew of every creature's existence, whatever its species or kind. The story of the shepherds and flocks comes much closer to Christ's intent, where each creature looked out for the others.

The officials of the Roman Catholic Church altered many records — cleansing them, in their terms, of anything that might suggest pagan practices, or nature worship as they thought of it. In terms of your civilization, nature and spirit became divided so that you encounter the events of your lives largely in that context. To some degree or another, then, you must feel divorced from your bodies and from the events of nature. The great sweeps of emotional identification with nature itself do not sustain you, therefore. You study those processes as if you somehow stood apart from them.

(Long pause, one of many, at 9:51.) Give us a moment . . . To some extent your society's beliefs allow you enough freedom so that most of you trust your bodies while they are growing toward adulthood. Then, however, many of you no longer rely upon the processes of life within you. Certain scientific treatises often make you believe that the attainment of your adulthood has little purpose, except to insure the further existence of the species through parenthood — when nature is then quite willing to dispense with your services. You are quite simply told that you have no other purpose.[3] The species itself must then appear to have no reason except a mindless determination to exist. The religions do insist that man has a purpose, yet in their own confusion they often speak as if that purpose must be achieved by denying the physical body in which man has his life's existence, or by "rising above" "gross, blunted," earthly characteristics. Period. In both cases man's nature, and nature in general, take short shrift.

Such tales are myths. They do indeed have power and strength. In those terms they represent the darker side of myths, however — yet through their casts you presently view your world. You will interpret the private events of your lives, and the spectacular range of history, in the light of those assumptions about reality. They not only color your experience, but you create those events that more or less conform to those assumptions.

(Long pause.) Those who "lose" their lives in natural disasters become victims of nature. You see in such stories examples of meaningless deaths, and further proof of nature's indifference to man. You may, on the other hand, see the vengeful hand of an angry God in such instances, where the deity once again uses nature to bring man to his knees. Man's nature is to live and to die. Death is not an affront to life, but means its continuation — not only inside the framework of nature as you understand it, but in terms of nature's source. It is, of course, natural then to die.

The natural contours of your psyche are quite aware of the inner sweep and flow of your life, and its relationship with every other creature alive. Intuitively, each person is born with the knowledge that he or she is not only worthwhile, but fits into the context of the universe in the most precise and beautiful of fashions. The most elegant timing is involved in each individual's birth and death. The exquisite play of your own inner nature inherently allows you to identify with all of the aspects of nature in general — and that identification leads you into the deeper knowledge of your own part in nature's source.

(10:19.) The myths upon which you base your lives so program your existence that often you verbally deny what you inwardly know. When people are hurt in a natural disaster, for example, they will often profess to have no idea at all for such involvement. They will ignore or deny the inner feelings that alone would give the event any meaning in their lives. The reasons for such involvement would be endless, or course — all valid, yet in each and every case, man and nature in those terms would meet in an encounter that had meaning, from the largest global effects to the smallest, most private aspects of the individuals involved. You have made certain divisions because of your myths, of course, that make this kind of explanation extremely important and difficult. You think of rain or earthquakes as natural events, for example, while you do not consider thoughts or emotions as natural events in the same terms. Therefore it is difficult for you to see how there can be any valid interactions between, say, emotional states and physical ones.

You might say: "Of course, I realize that the weather affects my mood," yet it will occur to very few of you that your moods have any effect upon the weather. You have so concentrated upon the categorization, delineation, and exploration of the objective world that it surely seems to be "the only real one." It seems to exert force or pressure against you, or to impinge upon you, or at least almost to happen by itself, so that you sometimes feel powerless against it. Your myths have given great energy to the outsideness of things.

In exasperation some of you see nature as good and enduring, filled with an innocence and joy, while on the other hand you envision man as a bastard species, a blight upon the face of the earth, a creature bound to do everything wrong regardless of any strong good intent. Therefore you do not trust man's nature either.

This myth finds great value in the larger processes of nature in general, and yet sees man alone as the villain of an otherwise edifying tale. A true identification with nature, however, would show glimpses of man's place in the context of his physical planet, and would bring to the forefront accomplishments that he has achieved almost without his knowing.

Take your break.

(10:40. Jane's pace in trance had been quite slow, with many long pauses. I thought the material excellent, however, with plenty of "bite" to it. Resume in the same manner at 10:51.)

Dictation: I will return to those accomplishments somewhat later. For now I would like to mention some other issues, involving the individual's connection either with natural disasters or with epidemics of one kind or another, that by definition concern large groups of people.

You form your own reality. If you are tired of having me stress that point, I can only say that I hope the repetition will serve to make you understand that the statement applies to the most minute and the most important of the events that you experience.

Some people believe that they must be punished, and so they seek [out] unfortunate circumstances. They [go] to one event after another in which they meet retribution. They may seek out areas of the country in which natural disasters are frequent, or their behavior may be such that they attract from other people reactions of an explosive kind. Often, however, individuals use disasters quite for their own purposes, as an exteriorized force that brings their lives into clear focus. Some may be flirting with the idea of death, and choose a dramatic encounter with nature in the final act. Others change their minds at the last moment.

Those involved in such disasters — the survivors — often use such "larger-than-life" circumstances in order to participate in affairs that seem to have greater import than those possessed by previous humdrum existences. They seek the excitement, whatever its consequences. They become a part of history to whatever extent. For once their private lives are identified with a greater source — and from it many derive new strength and vitality. Social barriers are dropped, economic positions forgotten. The range of private emotions is given greater, fuller, sweep.

To some extent or another man's desires and emotions merge with the physical aspects of nature as you understand it, so that such storms or disasters are as much the result of psychological activity as they are of weather conditions.

Objectively — whatever the appearances — storms, earthquakes, floods, *et cetera,* are quite necessary to the well-being of the earth. Both man's and nature's purposes are served, then, though generally speaking man's myths make him blind to those interactions. People's thoughts and emotions always give clear clues whenever illness is involved, yet most people ignore such information. They censor their own thoughts. Many therefore "fall prey" to epidemics of one kind or another because they want to, though they might deny this quite vigorously.

I am speaking particularly of epidemics that are less than deadly, though danger is involved. In your times, hospitals, you must realize, are important parts of the community. They provide a social as well as a medical service. Many people are simply lonely, or overworked. Some are rebelling against commonly held ideas of competition. Flu epidemics become social excuses for much needed rest, therefore, and serve as face-saving devices so that the individuals can hide from themselves their inner difficulties. In a way, such epidemics provide their own kind of fellowship — giving common meeting grounds for those of disparate circumstances. The [epidemics] serve as accepted states of illness, in which people are given an excuse for the rest or quiet self-examination they desperately need but do not feel entitled to otherwise.

(Long pause at 11:21.) I do not mean to assign any hint of accusation against those so involved, but mainly to state some of the reasons for such behavior. If you do not trust your nature, then any illness or indisposition will be interpreted as an onslaught against health. Your body faithfully reflects your inner psychological reality. The nature of your emotions means that in the course of a lifetime you will experience the full range of feelings. Your subjective state has variety. Sometimes sad or depressing thoughts provide a refreshing change of pace, leading you to periods of quiet reflection, and to a quieting of the body so that it rests.

Fears, sometimes even seemingly irrational ones, can serve to rouse the body if you have been too lethargic, or have been in a rut psychologically or physically. If you trusted your nature you would be able to trust such feelings, and following their own rhythms and routes they would change into others. Ideally even illnesses are a part of the body's health, representing needed adjustments, and also following the needs of the subjective person at any given time. *(Long pause.)* They are a part of the interplay between the body and mind, or spirit.

The majority of my readers have come down with one or another . disease usually considered very dangerous, and without ever knowing it, because the body healed itself normally and naturally. The disease was not labeled. It was not given recognition as a condition. Worries or fears were not aroused, yet the disease came and vanished.

In such instances natural healing processes occurred, for which the body is seldom given credit. Such healings do not just involve changes in the body, for example, for a physical healing can take place because of events that seem utterly disconnected.

Some portion of each individual is in direct contact with the very source of its own existence. Each individual is innately aware that help is available in every situation, and that information does not need to come through the physical senses alone. Many illnesses are cured, then, through quite natural methods that not only involve physical healings, but bring into play other events — events that have great bearing on the psychological elements that may be involved behind the scenes. For those interactions we will have to look to Framework 2.

End of session.

("Very good.")

Thank you. A fond good evening.

("The same to you. Good night."

(11:47 P.M. *Jane's delivery for Seth had become even slower toward the end of the session.)*

NOTES: SESSION 821

1. Actually, the second Seven book named itself quite effortlessly as Jane worked on its first chapters: *The Further Education of Oversoul Seven.*

2. I underlined the word story (like this) in Seth's material just to remind the reader that the Christ figure *symbolizes* our idea of God and his relationships. According to Seth, the man we call Jesus Christ was actually composed of three individuals who were the physical manifestations of the same nonphysical entity: John the Baptist, St. Paul, and a man historically known as Christ. None of these were crucified. Their roles became blended and distorted in history. Seth discussed the Christ story in various passages in *The Seth Material* and *Seth Speaks*, and has at least touched upon it in all of his succeeding books.

3. Seth referred to the latest scientific ideas concerning "selfish genes" — a subject Jane and I had been talking about today. (Genes are units found on the chromosomes of the cell nucleus; they carry hereditary characteristics, and consist mainly of protein and DNA, or deoxyribonucleic acid.)

A number of scientists — biologists, zoologists, and psychologists, among others — have recently published highly praised books in which they claim to show how our genes manipulate our individual behavior with only their own genetic survival at stake, even when we think we are displaying subjective qualities like altruism. Jane and I think the idea of such self-centered genetic behavior is much too limited, simple, and "mechanistic," to use another term that's currently in scientific vogue. The idea of selfish genes also implies *plan* on the part of such entities — and so comes dangerously close to contradicting several basic tenets of science itself: among them that life arose by chance, that it perpetuates itself through random mutations and the struggle for existence (or natural selection), and that basically life has no meaning.

As I occasionally do in my notes, I'm anthropomorphosizing "science" by casting a multifaceted discipline in simple human or individual terms. But now it seems that when science claims to understand the workings of a molecule of DNA, for example — the "master molecule" of life, as it's often called — science then states that it's stripped away the mystery of DNA and reduced our functions to easily understood mechanistic ones. But Jane and I maintain that grasping the marvelous workings of DNA should instead *increase* our sense of the wonder and mystery of life. The DNA lies exposed in all of its parts, but the questions about the life within it remain unanswered. Why does science want us to live thinking that we're creatures programmed only for the survival of our selfish genes? Even the biologists (and other scientists) who insist upon our mechanistic bases do so with *feeling!*

SESSION 822, FEBRUARY 22, 1978
9:27 P.M. WEDNESDAY

Now: Good evening.

(*"Good evening. Seth."*)

Dictation: In the terms of our discussion, Framework 2 is the medium in which your world exists. It represents the vaster psychological reality in which your own subjective life resides.

That framework has been glimpsed throughout history by many individuals, and given many names. If you visit a foreign country, however, you have a tendency to describe the entire nation in terms of the small area you have visited, though other portions may be quite different in geography, culture, and climate.

The individuals who have to one extent or another perceived Framework 2 have, then, described it according to their own brief visits, taking it for granted "that the part was a representative sample of the whole." Plato conceived [of] it as the world of ideals, seeing within it the perfect model behind each imperfect physical phenomenon.

He thought of that realm as eternal and unchanging, a perfect but frozen composite that must indeed inspire men toward achievement on the one hand, and on the other reproach them for their failure, since their achievements must necessarily seem puny in contrast. Plato then saw Framework 2 as a splendid, absolute model in which all the works of man had their initial source. Man himself, according to this concept, could not affect that ideal world one whit. He could, however, use it as a source of inspiration.

Some ancient religions put the existence of gods there, and saw the spirits of each living thing as existing primarily in that invisible medium of reality. Therefore, Framework 2 has always been represented in one way or another as a source of your world. Christianity saw it as heaven, inhabited by God the Father, His angels, the saints, and [the] deceased faithful.

Once scientists theorized the ether as the medium in which the physical universe existed.[1] Framework 2 is the psychological medium in which the consciousness of the world exists. The word "ego" is much bandied about, and in many circles it has a poor reputation. It is, however, as I use it, a term meant to express the ordinarily conscious directive portion of the self. It is your conscious version of what you are — an excellent description, if I do say so myself *(with amusement)*. It is directed outward into the physical world. It is also aware, however, of some of your "unconscious" activities. It is the you you identify with, so it is as aware of your dreams, for example, as you are, and it is quite conscious of the fact that its existence rests upon knowledge that it does not itself possess.

As you have an ego, fully conscious, directed toward the physical world, you also have what I call an inner ego, directed toward inner reality. You have, in other words, a portion of yourself that is fully conscious in Framework 2. The ego in your ordinary world, which again we will call Framework 1, is uniquely equipped to deal with that environment. It manipulates with rules of cause and effect and consecutive moments. It deals with an objectified reality. It can stretch its capacities, becoming far more aware of inner events than it is normally allowed to do, but its main purpose is to deal with the world of effects, to <u>encounter</u> events.

The inner ego is fully conscious. It is a portion of you, however, that deals with the formation of events, that glories in a rather rambunctious and creative activity that your specifications of time and place physically preclude. The unconscious, so-called, <u>is</u> — and I have said this before[2] — quite conscious, but in another realm of activity. There must be a psychological chamber between these two portions of the self, however — these seemingly undifferentiated areas, in which back-and-forth translations can occur. Dream periods provide that service, of course, so that in dreams the two egos can meet and merge to some extent, comparing notes like strangers who perhaps meet on a train at night, and are amazed to discover, after some conversation, that they are indeed close relatives, each embarked upon the same journey though seemingly they travelled alone.

(10:14.) In those terms the undifferentiated area is actually filled with motion as psychological transitions and translations are made, until in dreams the two egos often merge into each other — so that sometimes you waken briefly with a sense of elation, or a feeling that in dreams you have met an old and valued friend.

Your world is populated by individuals concentrating upon physical activities, dealing with events that are "finished products" — at least in usual terms. Your inner egos populate Framework 2, and deal with the actual creation of those events that are then objectified. Since "the rules" of Framework 2 are different, that reality is not at all bound by your physical assumptions. It contains, therefore, the inner ego of each individual who has lived or will <u>ever</u> live upon the earth.

I am speaking of that framework now only as it applies to your world — not in its relationship to other realities. Earlier in his own experience Ruburt described that framework (in *Psychic Politics*) as the heroic dimension. He saw quite correctly that there was a great give-and-take between the two frameworks — your regular working one, Framework 1, and this other more comprehensive reality. He did not thoroughly understand, however, the creative ramifications involved, for it did not occur to him at the time that the prime work of your world was actually done by you in that other wider aspect of your existence.

Physically you have at your fingertips certain accumulations of knowledge, objectified through the passage of information verbally through the ages, in records or books, and through television. [Now] you use computers to help you process information, and you have a more or less direct access to physical knowledge. You acquired it through the use of your senses. There is systematized knowledge, where men have accumulated facts in one particular field, processing it in one way or another. Your own senses bring you information each moment, and that information is in a way already invisibly processed according to your own beliefs, desires, and intents.

You will ignore as information certain stimuli that another person, for example, will latch on to immediately. Even in your own world, then, your interests and desires serve as organizational processes that screen out certain information. The information available in Framework 2 is in your terms infinite.

(Long pause, one of many, at 10:28.) It is the source of your world, so therefore it contains not only all knowledge physically available, but far more. Give us a moment. . . . I do not want to compare the inner ego with a computer in any way, for a computer is not creative, nor is it alive. You think of course of the life that you know as LIFE, in capitals. It is, however, only the manifestation of what in those terms can only be called the greater life out of which your life springs. This is not to compare the reality that you know in derogative terms to the other-source existence, either, for your own world contains, as each other world does, a uniqueness and an originality that in those terms exists nowhere else — for no world of existence is like any other.

The inner ego is a portion of the self, for example — is the portion of your self — that is aware of your reincarnational activities. It is the part of you that exists outside of time, yet simultaneously lives in time. You form your own reality. The ego that you are aware of obviously could not form your body for you, however, or grow your bones. It knows how to assess the conditions of the world. It makes deductions. Your reasoning is highly important, yet alone it cannot pump your blood or tell your eyes how to see.

The inner ego does the actual work that brings about the events you have decided upon. In very simple terms, if you want to pick up a book, and then do so, you experience that event consciously, though you are quite unaware of all of the inner events that occurred to bring the motion about. The inner ego directs those activities.

If you want to change your job, and hold that desire, a new job will come into your experience in precisely the same fashion, in that the inner events will be arranged by the inner ego. A body event involves the working of numerous muscles and joints and so forth. An event involving a job change concerns motion on the part of many people, and implies a network of communication on the part of all of the inner egos involved. Obviously, then, a mass physical event implies an inner system of communications of proportions that would put your technological communications to shame.

Take your break.

(10:47 to 11:02.)

Dictation: You may then, again, unknowingly acquire an illness and recover, never aware of your malady, being healed because of a series of events that would seemingly have nothing to do with the illness itself — because in Framework 2 the inner ego, knowing both the reason for the illness, and its cure, brought about those precise situations that remedied the condition. Such events happen automatically, when nothing hampers recovery at your end.

The communication between the inner and outer egos should obviously be as clear and open as possible. As a general rule, the inner ego depends upon your assessment of physical events. Your involvement in the private aspects of your living, and your participation in mass events, has much to do with your estimation of the physical situation, and with your beliefs and desires regarding it. Give us a moment . . . A very simple example (colon): If you want to write a letter you do so. There is no conflict between your desires, beliefs, and the execution of the act, so the action itself flows smoothly. If for some reason or another, through a poor assessment of your reality, you believe that such an act is dangerous, then you will hamper the flow between the desire and the execution. The flow of creativity begun by the inner ego will be impeded.

End of dictation, and give us a moment. . . .

(11:13. After presenting some material for both Jane and a friend of ours, Seth ended the session at 11:42 P.M.)

NOTES: SESSION 822

1. Jane rather surprised me: I knew she had an interested if generalized awareness of the old theory of the ether (or the luminiferous ether), but I hadn't realized she was well-enough acquainted with the idea to be able to verbalize it that succinctly for Seth. In several texts I have, the authors wrote about the ether, and Jane may have read those passages. I may have discussed the theory with her, but I don't remember doing so.

The idea of the ether, or something like it, had been around since the time of the ancient Greeks. By the last decades of the 19th century, and in line with Newtonian physics, the ether was postulated as an invisible, tasteless, odorless substance that pervaded all unoccupied space, and served as the medium for the passage of electromagnetic waves of light and other kinds of radiant energy, like heat — just as the earth itself serves as the medium for the transmission of seismic waves, for instance.

Late in the last century some very ingenious experiments failed to scientifically prove the existence of the ether, however, and the theory was finally dispensed with for good following Albert Einstein's publication of his special theory of relativity in 1905.

I think the idea of the ether is an excellent example of how man has always attempted to posit or visualize in physical reality his innate knowledge of Framework 2.

2. Note 13, for Appendix 18 in Volume 2 of *"Unknown" Reality,* contains excerpts from one of the sessions Seth has given on the inner self-conscious self.

SESSION 823, FEBRUARY 27, 1978
9:43 P.M. MONDAY

(A week has passed, and I'm still surprised: Not only has Jane helped me considerably in planning the notes for Psyche, *but the other day she switched over to my Introductory Notes for Volume 2 of* "Unknown" Reality *and began organizing them in the same loose way.*

(Not long ago I reached an impasse with both the Introductory Notes and the Epilogue for Volume 2, as I tried to give order to the mass of notes, excerpts, and jotted-down ideas that I've assembled for them since finishing work on Volume 1 in September 1976. That was some 18 months ago, but actually

to one degree or another I've been involved with "Unknown" Reality *for four years now; I think that temporarily I've simply grown tired and overly concerned about the whole project, even while I still have a considerable way to go to finish certain notes and appendixes for Volume 2. Not that I haven't worked on a number of other things at the same time, of course — but my labors on those two books represent the prolonged, intense focus I always search for in my creative life, and without which I feel incomplete. Jane knows all too well what I mean, for her own attitudes here follow mine very closely.*

(So in one day Jane was able to mentally sort out my material and start to delineate the flow necessary to make the Introductory Notes successful, and she intends to do the same thing with the Epilogue. It'll still be up to me to add my kind of detail to each of those works, but there's no doubt that she's enjoying the challenge of playing with the Seth books from the "other side" — my viewpoint — for a change. I told her that I'd never envisioned her showing that kind of interest in my approach to the sessions and books.)

Good evening.

("Good evening, Seth.")

Dictation. *(With many pauses:)* The main myth through which you interpret your experiences, however, is the one that tells you that all perception and knowledge must come to you through the physical senses.

This is the myth of the exteriorized consciousness — a consciousness that you are told is open-ended only so far as objective reality is concerned. It seems to be closed "at the other end," which in those terms would represent your birth.

The consciousness of that myth can indeed have no origin, for the myth precludes anything but a physically-oriented and physically-mechanized consciousness. Not only could that consciousness have no existence before or after death, but obviously it could have no access to knowledge that was not physically acquired. It is this myth that hampers your understanding most of all, and that closes you off from the greater nature of those events with which you are most intimately concerned. That myth also makes your own involvement with mass events sometimes appear incomprehensible.

There seems to be no reason for many of them, simply because the intricate inner communication systems of consciousness go utterly unrecognized, generally speaking.

I am speaking largely to a Western audience, and so here I am using terms for a particular reason, to explain concepts in a way that will be understood. The inner ego *(see the last session)* is perfect as a term to suit my purposes. Let me stress again that the "unconscious" is indeed conscious — and by conscious I mean that its reasoning is not irrational. Its methods are not chaotic, and its characteristics are not only equal to those of the known ego, but indeed are more resilient and knowledgeable.

Frameworks 1 and 2 obviously represent not only different kinds of reality in normal terms, but two different kinds of consciousness. To make this discussion as simple as possible for now, at least, think of these two frameworks or states of consciousness as being connected by "undifferentiated areas" in which sleep, dreaming, and certain trance states have their activity. Those undifferentiated areas are involved in the constant translation of one kind of consciousness into the other, and with energy transferences. You constantly process those data that come to you in your private life, and that information includes bulletins from all over the world, through your news broadcasts and so forth.

The inner ego has access, again, to a much vaster amount of knowledge. It is aware not only of its own private position, as you are of yours, but it is also familiar with the mass events of its reality. It is intimately involved in the creation of your own private experience.

I said that the inner ego reasons, but its reasoning is not restricted to the cause-and-effect limitations that you apply to the reasoning process. The action of the inner ego within the wider sphere of Framework 2 explains many events and seeming coincidences that otherwise seem to make no sense within your world. Many realities within Framework 2 cannot suitably be explained as facts to you in Framework 1, simply because they involve psychological thicknesses that cannot be translated into facts as you think of them. These often appear in the symbolic language of the arts instead, and many of your dreams are translations in which the events of Framework 2 appear in symbolic form.

(A one-minute pause at 10:14.) Give us a moment . . . On any given day the events of your private lives fit within the larger pattern of world events, in which they have their context. On any given night

the intimate events of your dream lives also exist in the greater context of the world's dreams — in which <u>they</u> have their reality.

Give us a moment . . . The consciousness that you have, as generally described in psychology, is in a strange fashion like the bright shiny skin of a fruit — but with no fruit inside; a consciousness with a shiny surface that responds to sun or rain or temperature, and to its surroundings; but for all of that a psychological fruit that has no pulp or pits, but contains at its heart a vacancy. In those terms you experience only one half of your consciousness: the physically-attuned portion. Fruit trees have roots, but you assign no ground of being to this consciousness.

Jung's collective unconscious was an attempt to give your world its psychological roots, but Jung[1] could not perceive the clarity, organization, and deeper context in which that collective unconscious has its own existence. Reality as Framework 2 is organized in a different fashion than it is in the Framework 1 world, and the processes of reasoning are far quicker. In Framework 1 the reasoning processes work largely by deduction, and they must constantly check their own results against the seemingly concrete experience of physical events. The reasoning of the inner ego is involved with the creative <u>invention</u> of those experiences. It is involved with events in a context of a different kind, for it deals intimately with probabilities.

(Long pause.) [Each of] you, with your beliefs and intents, tell the inner ego which of an infinite number of probable events you want to encounter. In the dream state events from both frameworks are processed. The dream state involves not only a state of consciousness that exists between the two frameworks of reality, but also involves, in those terms, a connecting reality of its own. Here I would like to emphasize that to one degree or another all species of plant and animal life "dream." The same applies to the "psychological activity" of atoms and molecules, and any "particle."[2] Period.

(10:40.) There are intensities of behavior, then, in which the activity, the inside activity, of any being or particle is directed toward [the] physical force [that is] involved in the cooperative venture that causes your reality. There are variances, however, when such activity is directed instead into the interior nature of reality. You have an inner system of communication, then, in which the cells of all

living things are connected. In those terms there is a continuum of consciousness.

Take your break.

(10:45. Before the session, Jane told me now, she'd known "that Seth would talk about some of that stuff." As it had been in the last session, her delivery tonight was quite slow; the difference this evening, though, was that she'd sensed many of those pauses. But this was the kind of session she liked, and when she came out of trance she felt that more time should have passed. Jane added that "you get a deeper subjective flow" of material when the delivery lasted without a break for an hour, or thereabouts, instead of for the old half-hour periods.

(Resume in the same slow manner at 11:01.)

To really understand your own connection with the events you encounter privately, and in relationship to others, you must first become acquainted with that medium in which events themselves are formed.

What part, for example, does chance play in your life? Is it chance if you arrive too late to board a plane, for example — to find later that the plane crashed? Perhaps your late arrival was caused by "a chance meeting" with a friend at the last moment, or by a misplaced ticket, or by a traffic jam that seemingly had nothing to do with you at all.

You may have become a part of the drama of a natural disaster, or avoided it as a result of other seemingly chance occurrences. What appears to you as chance or coincidence, however, is actually the result of the amazing organizations and communications active in the psychological reality of Framework 2. Again, you form your reality — but how? And how do private existences touch each other, resulting in world events? Before we go any further, then, we must look into the nature of Framework 2.

This will not be a dry, intellectual exploration, because the intent itself will begin to trigger within your lives the emergence of hints and clues as to your own immersion in Framework 2's creativity.

End of chapter.

CHAPTER 4

THE CHARACTERISTICS OF FRAMEWORK 2.
A CREATIVE ANALYSIS OF THE MEDIUM IN WHICH
PHYSICALLY-ORIENTED CONSCIOUSNESS RESIDES,
AND THE SOURCE OF EVENTS

(11:13.) Next chapter *(4)*: "The Characteristics of Framework 2." *(Long pause.)* "A Creative Analysis of the Medium in Which Physically-Oriented Consciousness Resides, and the Source of Events."

Give us a moment . . . No chance encounter of physical elements alone, under any circumstances, could produce consciousness — or the conditions that would then make consciousness possible.

If you think of your world with all of its great natural splendors as coming about initially through the auspices of chance — through an accident of cosmic proportions — then it certainly often seems that such a world can have no greater meaning. Its animation is seen as having no source outside itself. The myth of the great CHANCE ENCOUNTER, in caps, that is supposed to have brought forth life on your planet then presupposes, of course, an individual consciousness that is, in certain terms, alive by chance alone.

It is somewhat humorous that such a vital consciousness could even suppose itself to be the end product of inert elements that were themselves lifeless, but somehow managed to combine in such a way that your species attained fantasy, logic, vast organizational power, technologies, and civilizations. Your myths tell you that nature itself has no intent except survival. It cares little for the individual — only insofar as the individual helps the species to endure. In its workings, nature then appears to be impersonal, even though it so consists of individuals that it cannot be regarded otherwise.

Without the particular plants, animals, people, or even individual cells or viruses, nature has no meaning. Your physical universe, then, had a nonphysical origin, in which it is still couched. In the same manner your individual consciousness has an origin in which it is still couched.

(11:35.) Give us a moment . . . Framework 2 represents the inner sphere of reality, the inner dimensions of existence, that gives your world its own characteristics. The energy and power that keeps you alive, that fuels your thoughts — and also the energy that lights your cities — all have their origins in Framework 2. The same energy that leaps into practical use when you turn on your television sets also allows you to tune into the daily experienced events of your lives.

End of session. End of dictation, unless you have questions.

(I paused, tired. "I don't know what to say. . . .")

To parallel these sessions, it would be nice if the two of you kept Framework 2 in mind, and utilized it with a bit more confidence, and became alert again to those "coincidences" that always appear in current experience.

I bid you a fine good evening.

("Thank you very much, Seth. Good night.")

(End at 11:42 P.M.)

NOTES: SESSION 823

1. Volume 2 of *"Unknown" Reality* contains a number of references to Carl Jung, the Swiss psychologist and psychiatrist who lived from 1875–1961.

2. For those who are interested: As soon as Seth mentioned the "psychological activity" of atoms and molecules, I was intuitively and strongly aware of connections between his statement and at least two principles of modern physics. Yet I hesitated. "I know my feelings are right," I told Jane, "but how do I explain them in a few words and make any sense?" I was also constrained by the limits of my own knowledge. Especially, though, I sensed relationships between Seth's idea on the one hand, and both the uncertainty principle of quantum mechanics and the principle of complementarity on the other.

The uncertainty principle, or the principle of indeterminacy (advanced by Heisenberg in 1927, and part of the theory of quantum mechanics), sets definite limits to the accuracy possible in measuring both the motion and position of atoms and elementary particles simultaneously; more importantly to my mind, for the purposes of this note, the uncertainty principle maintains that there is an interaction between the observer (with his instruments) and the object or quality being measured.

The complementarity principle (stated by Bohr in 1928) resolves the seeming paradox posed by contradictory experiments that show how light, for example, can be regarded as consisting of either waves or particles. Both experiments and conclusions are right — and mutually exclusive; whichever result is obtained is due to the nature of the particular experiment.

I doubt if physicists in the 1920s were concerned about the psychological activity of atoms, molecules, or particles, although it seems that Heisenberg came close to Seth's idea when he considered the free behavior of an electron emitted by a light ray. Albert Einstein, whose own work was rooted in strict causality, found a notion like the free will of an electron untenable, even though much earlier (in 1905) he had laid the foundation for quantum mechanics in his special theory of relativity.

Jane is largely unfamiliar with the details of the uncertainty principle and the principle of complementarity, although the general ideas fascinate her. Her feelings for these works of science, then, are the same as those she has for the ether; see Note 1 for Session 822.

SESSION 824, MARCH 1, 1978
9:40 P.M. WEDNESDAY

(After supper tonight Jane and I had a discussion about the theory of evolution. But before that. . . .)

Good evening.

("Good evening, Seth.")

Dictation: In connection with the creation of the universe, and with the creation of public and private events alike, let us for a moment consider a different kind of myth.

Tonight, during a pleasant supper time, our friends Ruburt and Joseph watched a television production based upon the Cinderella fairy tale. According to the definition I gave earlier, this fairy tale is a myth. Surely it may seem that such a children's tale has little to do with any serious adult discussion concerning anything so profound as the creation of the known world. And most certainly, it may appear, no scientifically pertinent data about the nature of events can possibly be uncovered from such a source.

For one thing, [the] Cinderella [tale] has a happy ending, of course, and is therefore highly unrealistic *(with irony),* according to many educators, since it does not properly prepare children for life's necessary disappointments. Fairy godmothers are definitely a thing of the storyteller's imagination, and many serious, earnest adults will tell you that daydreaming or wishing will get you nowhere.

In the Cinderella story, however, the heroine, though poor and of low estate, manages to attain a fulfilling and seemingly impossible goal. Her desire to attend a spectacular ball, and meet the prince, initiates a series of magical events, none following the dictates of logic. The fairy godmother, suddenly appearing, uses the normal objects of everyday life so that they are suddenly transformed, and we have a chariot[1] from a pumpkin, and other transformations of a like nature.

The tale has always appealed to children because they recognize the validity behind it.[2] The fairy godmother is a creative personification of the personalized elements in Framework 2 — a personification therefore of the inner ego, that rises to the aid of the mortal self to grant its desires, even when the intents of the mortal self may not seem to fit into the practical framework of normal life. When the inner ego responds in such a fashion, even the commonplace, ordinary, seemingly innocuous circumstances suddenly become charged with a new vitality, and appear to "work for" the individual involved. If you are reading this book you are already too old to clearly remember the constant fantasies of your early childhood. Children however know quite well, automatically, that they have a strong hand in the creation of the events that then seem to happen to them.

They experiment very often, and quite secretly, since their elders are at the same time trying to make the children conform to a given concrete reality that is more or less already mass-produced for them.

Children experiment with the creation of joyful and frightening events, trying to ascertain for themselves the nature of their <u>control over their own experience.</u> They imagine joyful and terrifying experiences. They are in fact fascinated by the effects that their thoughts, feelings, and purposes have upon daily events. This is a natural learning process. If they create "bogeymen," then they can cause them to disappear also. If their thoughts can cause them to become ill, then there is no real reason for them to fear illness, for it is their own creation. This learning process is nipped in the bud, however. By the time you are adults, it certainly seems that you are a subjective being in an objective universe, at the mercy of others, and with only the most superficial control over the events of your lives.[3]

(10:02.) The tale of Cinderella becomes a fantasy, a delusion, or even a story about sexual awakening, in Freudian terms. The disappointments you have faced indeed make such a tale seem to be a direct contradiction to life's realities. To some extent or another, however, the child in you remembers a certain sense of mastery only half realized, of power nearly grasped, then seemingly lost forever — and a dimension of existence in which dreams quite literally came true. The child in you sensed more, of course: It sensed its own greater reality in another framework entirely, from which it had only lately emerged — yet with which it was intimately connected. It felt itself surrounded, then, by the greater realities of Framework 2.

The child knew "that it came from somewhere else" — not by chance but by design. The child knew that in one way or another its most intimate thoughts, dreams, and gestures were as connected with the natural world as blades of grass are to a field. The child knew it was a unique and utterly original event or being that on the one hand was its own focus, and that on the other hand belonged to its own time and season. In fact, children let little escape them, so that, again, they experiment constantly in an effort to discover not only the effect of their thoughts and intents and wishes upon others, but the degree to which others influence their own behavior. To that extent, they deal rather directly with probabilities in a way quite foreign to adult behavior.

In a fashion, they make quicker deductions than adults, and often truer ones, because they are not conditioned by a past of structured memory. Their subjective experience then brings them in rather direct contact with the methods by which events are formed.

Will you open this *(beer)* for our friend. Do you want to rest your hand?

(10:28. "No. . . .")

Children understand the importance of symbols, and they use them constantly to protect themselves — not from their own reality but from the adult world. They constantly pretend, and they quickly learn that persistent pretending in any one area will result in a physically-experienced version of the imagined activity. They also realize that they do not possess full freedom, either, for certain pretended situations will later happen in less faithful versions than the imagined ones. Others will seem almost entirely blocked, and never materialize.

Before children are acquainted with conventional ideas of guilt and punishment, they realize that it is easier to bring about good events, through wishing, than it is to bring about unhappy ones. The child carries with him [or her] the impetus and supporting energy provided him at birth from Framework 2, and he knows intuitively that desires conducive to his development "happen" easier than those that are not. His natural impulses naturally lead him toward the development of his body and mind, and he is aware of a cushioning effect and support as he acts in accordance with those inner impulses. The child is innately honest. When he gets sick he intuitively knows the reason why, and he knows quite well that he brought about the illness.

Parents and physicians believe, instead, that the child is a victim, ill for no personal reason, but indisposed because of elements attacking him — either the outside environment, or [something] working against him from within. The child may be told: "You have a cold because you got your feet wet." Or: "You caught the cold from Johnny or Sally." He may be told that he has a virus, so that it seems his body itself was invaded despite his will. He learns that such beliefs are acceptable. It is easier to go along than to be honest, particularly when honesty would often involve a kind of communication his parents might frown upon, or the expression of emotions that are quite unacceptable.

(10:46.) Mother's little man or brave little girl can then stay at home, for example, courageously bearing up under an illness, with his or her behavior condoned. The child may know that the illness is the result of feelings that the parents would consider quite cowardly, or otherwise involves emotional realities that the parents simply would not understand. Gradually it becomes easier for the child to accept the parents' assessment of the situation. Little by little the fine relationship, the precise connections between psychological feelings and bodily reality, erode.

I do not want to oversimplify, and throughout this book we will add other elaborations upon such behavior. The child who gets the mumps with a large number of his classmates, however, knows he has his private reasons for joining into such a mass biological reality, and usually the adult who "falls prey" to a flu epidemic has little conscious awareness of his own reasons for such a situation. He does not understand the mass suggestions involved, or his own reasons for accepting them. He is usually convinced instead that his body has been invaded by a virus despite his own personal approval or disapproval — despite his own personal approval or disapproval *(most emphatically)*. He is therefore a victim, and his sense of personal power is eroded.

When a person recovers from such an ordeal, he [or she] usually grants his recovery to be the result of the medication he has been given. Or he may think that he was simply lucky — but he does not grant himself to have any real power in such an affair. The recovery seems to occur to him, as the illness seemed to happen to him. Usually the patient cannot see that he brought about his own recovery, and was responsible for it, because he cannot admit that his own intents were responsible for his own illness. He cannot learn from his own experience, then, and each bout of illness will appear largely incomprehensible.

Take your break.

(11:00. Jane's pace in trance had been considerably faster than in recent sessions. However, resume at a slower rate at 11:10.)

Dictation: Some years ago, before our sessions actually began (in late 1963) — though immediately previous — Ruburt *(Jane)* had an experience that he has described in his own books.

That event resulted in a scribbled manuscript, unpublished, called *The Physical Universe as Idea Construction.* His desire and intense intent to understand more of the nature of reality triggered the production of that fragmentary automatic manuscript. He found himself as a young adult, at the time of the President Kennedy assassination, in a world that seemed to have no meaning. At the same time, while conditioned by the beliefs of his generation — beliefs that still tinge your times — he held on to one supporting belief never completely lost from childhood.

His belief, illogical as it sounded when spoken, contradictory as it seemed when applied to daily life, stated that the individual somehow could perceive the nature of reality on his or her own by virtue of innate capacities that belonged to the individual by right — capacities that were a part of man's heritage. In other words, Ruburt felt that there was a slim chance of opening doors of knowledge that had been closed, and he decided to take that chance.

The results, appearing initially in that now-yellowed handwritten script, made him initially see that he had chosen the events of his life in one way or another, and that each person was not the victim but the creator of those events that were privately experienced or jointly encountered with others.

In that literally power-packed few hours, he also knew that the physical senses did not so much perceive concrete phenomena, but actually had a hand in the creation of events that were then perceived as actual.

End of dictation.

(11:26. Still in trance, Jane now came through with a few paragraphs of material for us. Among them was this insight, which Seth related to his discussion of the Cinderella fairy tale:)

Forgive the terminology, but you each believed in "magic," or the sessions never would have started. You believed that reality had more to it than the senses showed. You believed that together you could achieve what had not been achieved earlier — that you could some-how or other offer meaningful and real solutions to the world's problems. . . . *(End at 11:34 P.M.)*

NOTES: SESSION 824

1. At first Jane and I thought Seth was in error when he said "chariot" instead of "coach" or "carriage." But from the dictionary we learned that in archaic terms a chariot could be a four-wheeled lightweight carriage, used either for pleasure or on certain affairs of state.

2. Jane and I watched an adaptation of the Westernized Cinderella fairy tale, of course. I almost didn't bother looking it up, but I'm glad I did, for we learned that the power of Cinderella has been much longer-lasting and more pervasive than we'd realized: The Cinderella tale reaches back to China in the 9th century, and exists in hundreds of versions around the world.

3. The 806th session proper can be found in Chapter 2, but in the deleted portion of that session Seth came through with some comments relative to children that fit in well with his material this evening: "The point of power is in the present. Whenever possible, minimize the importance of a problem. Forget a problem and it will go away. Dumb advice, surely, or so it seems. Yet children know the truth of it. Minimize impediments in your mind and they do become minimized. Exaggerate impediments in your mind and in reality they will quickly adopt giant size."

SESSION 825, MARCH 6, 1978
9:31 P.M. MONDAY

(Happily refreshed by a few days' rest, I'm back working on my notes and appendixes for Volume 2 of "Unknown" Reality. *Over the weekend Jane began typing my Introductory Notes as she's put them together for the book. "And in a couple of days I'll get something done on the Epilogue," she said.)*

Good evening.

("Good evening, Seth."

(With many pauses:) Dictation: The physical universe is the result of idea construction, as Ruburt perceived in the experience mentioned in the last session *(at 11:10).*

That perception was not the sort of official sense data recognized by your sciences. Ruburt did not come to his recognition of the world's mental source through reasoning. Neither could any ordinary physical perception have given him that information. His consciousness left his body — an event not even considered possible by many educated people. Ruburt's consciousness merged, while still retaining its own individuality, with the consciousness of the leaves outside his window, and with the nail in the windowsill, and traveled outward and inward at the same time, so that like a mental wind his consciousness traveled through other psychological neighborhoods.

The origin of your universe is nonphysical, and each event, however grand or minute, has its birth in the Framework 2 environment. Your physical universe arose from that inner framework, then, and continues to do so.

The power that fuels your thoughts has the same source. In a manner of speaking the universe as you understand it, with all the events that it includes, functions "automatically" in its important processes, as your own body does. Your individual desires and intents direct that activity of your body's spontaneous processes — that is, your body walks across the floor at your command as a result of your wishes, even though the processes involved must happen "by themselves."

Your intents have a great effect upon your body's health. In the same fashion, jointly all of the people alive at any given time "direct" the events of the universe to behave in a certain fashion, even though the processes must happen by themselves, or automatically. Other species have a hand in this also, however, and in one way or another all of you direct the activity of the physical body of the world in much the same way that you [each] direct your own bodily behavior.

(9:50.) Give us a moment . . . You were born with the impetus toward growth built in — automatically provided with the inner blueprints that would lead to a developed adult form. Not only the cells, but the atoms and molecules that compose them contained a positive intent to cooperate in a bodily formation, to fulfill themselves, and they were then predisposed not only toward survival, but with an idealization leading toward the best possible development and maturity.

All of those characteristics have their sources in Framework 2, for the psychological medium in Framework 2 is automatically conducive to creativity. It is not simply a neutral dimension, therefore, but contains within itself an automatic predisposition toward the fulfillment of all patterns inherent within it. As James said in Ruburt's book,[1] "The universe *is* of good intent." It is automatically predisposed, again, toward the creation of "good" events. I put the word "good" in quotes for now because of your misconceptions about the nature of good and evil, which we will discuss somewhat later.[2]

To that extent then the physical universe, like each physical body, is "magical." I use the term purposefully, for it confounds the dictates of your adult reasoning, and perhaps by so confounding what you think of as reason, I may manage to arouse within you a hint of what I refer to as the higher intellect.

Reasoning by itself can only deal with deductions made about the known world. It cannot accept knowledge that comes from "elsewhere," for such information will not fit in reason's categories, and confounds its cause-and-effect patterning. The power to reason comes from Framework 2. In the terms of this discussion, you are able to reason as a result of "magical" events that make reason itself possible. The term "magic" has in one way or another been used to simply describe events for which reason has no answer — events that exist outside of the framework in which reason feels comfortable.

Your scientists consider themselves quite rational, yet many of them, at least, would be more honest when they tried to describe the beginning of the universe if they admitted that reason alone cannot provide any true insight. Each of you are as familiar with the so-called birth of the universe, as close to it or as distant [from it], as your own recognized consciousness is to your own physical birth, for the initiation of awareness and sensation in one infant really carries all of the same questions as those involved with the birth of the universe.

The mother could not consciously control the bodily processes that lead to birth. In the truest sense, the birth magically happens, as miraculous in those terms as the so-called initial emergence of life upon the planet itself. Scientific analysis of the brain will tell you nothing about the power that moves your thoughts, or hint at the source of the brain's abilities. However, the constant activity between Frameworks 1 and 2 is constantly apparent in the very existence of your world, and in the relationships involving your imagination, feelings, and beliefs, and those private and shared events that compose your experience.

Take your break.

(10:13. Break came a little early, after Jane had been in trance for just 42 minutes. "I didn't feel too much with it before the session," she said. "Maybe I got tired this afternoon, working on the Intro for 'Unknown.' *I've had messages from Seth the last few days about the book stuff for the session tonight, but what we got doesn't fit any of them . . . And I've got that feeling again, that more time should have passed while I was under: I think it should be a lot later now than it is. It's as though when the material's good I expect that it should take more time to get, or something like that . . . But the flow just ended, so break came."*

(Resume at 10:25.)

I do not mean to speak of reason in derogatory terms, for it is well suited to its purposes, which are vital in your reality. It is also true that in the deepest terms you have not developed your reasoning, so that your version of it is bound to result in some distortions.

Nor do I mean to agree with those who ask you to use your intuitions and feelings at the expense of your reason. Instead I will suggest other paths later in this book. Your reasoning as you now use it, however, deals primarily with reality by dividing it into categories, forming distinctions, following the "laws" of cause and effect — and largely its realm is the examination of events already perceived. In other words, it deals with the concrete nature of ascertained events that are already facts in your world.

On the other hand your intuitions follow a different kind of organization, as does your imagination — one involved with associations, an organization that unifies diverse elements and brings even known events together in a kind of unity that is often innocent of the limitations dictated by cause and effect. In those terms, then, Framework 2 deals with associations, so that within it the recognizable events of the physical world can be put together in an infinite number of ways, after which they appear in your private experience according to directions you have given them through those associations that you form mentally.

The coincidences that seem to happen, the chance encounters, the unexpected events — all of these come into your experience because in one way or another you have attracted them, even though their occurrences might seem to have insurmountable odds against them. Those odds — those impediments — do not exist in Framework 2.

(10:40.) To some extent or another, your intuitions acquaint you with the fact that you have your own place in the universe, and that the universe itself is well-disposed toward you. The intuitions speak of your unique and vital part in the fabric of that universe. The intuitions know that the universe bends in your direction. Your reasoning can deal only with results of your physical perception, however — at least with the training your societies have allowed it. You have in fact denied your reasoning the results of important data, for you have taught it to distrust the psychic faculties. Children's fairy tales still carry some of that ancient knowledge.

So far, I have been speaking of Frameworks 1 and 2 separately, and I will continue to do so for your convenience and understanding. Actually the two merge, of course, for your Framework 1 existence is immersed in Framework 2. Again, your body itself is constantly replenished in Framework 1 because of its simultaneous reality in Framework 2. Framework 2 is ever exteriorizing itself, appearing in your experience as Framework 1. You concentrate so thoroughly upon exterior reality, however, that you often ignore the quite apparent deeper sources of your own physical existence. As a result you deal with methods of division and categorization so completely that you lose sight of associative organizations, even though you use them constantly in your own most intimate thought processes.

End of session, unless you have questions.

(*"What do you think of Jane helping me with the Introductory Notes for Volume 2 of* 'Unknown' *?"*)

(*Emphatically:*) I think it is an excellent idea. I am letting events magically emerge as they grow beneath the surface of your lives — because Ruburt likes happy surprises. He is very active now on other levels, and is putting our material to good use. A fond good evening.

(*"Thank you, Seth. Good night."*)

(*11:56 P.M.*)

NOTES: SESSION 825

1. Jane's book (which is now being typeset) is *The Afterdeath Journal of an American Philosopher: The World View of William James.* See, for example, Note 2 for Session 801, and the opening notes for sessions 804 and 821.

2. Jane and I are really looking forward to Seth's material on man's "misconceptions about the nature of good and evil." Judging from our mail, we know that many others will also be very interested in it.

SESSION 826, MARCH 8, 1978
9:35 P.M. WEDNESDAY

Now, good evening.

(*"Good evening, Seth."*)

Dictation: You must understand that in a manner of speaking, Framework 2 is on the one hand an invisible version of the physical universe. On the other hand, however, it is far more than that, for it contains within it probable variations of that universe — from the most cosmic scale, say, down to probable versions of the most minute events of any given physical day.

In simple terms, your body has an invisible counterpart in Framework 2. During life that counterpart is so connected with your own physical tissues, however, that it can be misleading to say that the two — the visible and invisible bodies — are separate. In the same way that your thoughts have a reality in Framework 2, and only for the sake of a meaningful analogy, thoughts could be said to be the equivalent, now, of objects; for in Framework 2 thoughts and feelings are far more important even than objects are in physical reality.

In Framework 2 thoughts instantly form patterns. They are the "natural elements" in that psychological environment that mix, merge, and combine to form, if you will, the psychological cells, atoms, and molecules that compose events. In those terms, the physical events that you perceive or experience can be compared to "psychological objects" that appear to exist with a physical concreteness in space and time. Such events usually seem to begin somewhere in space and time, and clearly end there as well.

You can look at an object like a table and see its definitions in space. To some extent you are too close to psychological events to perceive them in the same fashion, of course, yet usual experience seems to have a starting point and a conclusion. Instead, experienced events usually involve only surface perceptions. You observe a table's surface as smooth and solid, even though you realize it is composed of atoms and molecules full of motion.

In the same way you experience a birthday party, an automobile accident, a bridge game, or any psychological event as psychologically solid, with a smooth experienced surface that holds together in space and time. Such events, however, consist of indivisible "particles" and faster-than-light perceptions[1] that never show. In other words, they contain psychic components that flow from Framework 2 into Framework 1.

(Long pause.) Any event, therefore, has an invisible thickness, a multidimensional basis. Your skies are filled with breezes, currents, clouds, sunlight, dust particles and so forth. The sky vaults above the entire planet. The invisible [vault of] Framework 2 contains endless patterns that change as, say, clouds do — that mix and merge to form your psychological climate. Thoughts have what we will for now term electromagnetic properties. In those terms your thoughts mix and match with others in Framework 2, creating mass patterns that form the overall psychological basis behind world events. Again, however, Framework 2 is not neutral, but automatically inclined toward what we will here term good or constructive developments. It is a growth medium. Constructive or "positive" feelings or thoughts are more easily materialized than "negative" ones, because they are in keeping with Framework 2's characteristics.[2]

(10:05.) If that were not the case, your own species would not have existed as long as it has. Nor would the constructs of civilization — art, commerce, or even technology — have been possible. Framework 2 combines order and spontaneity, but its order is of another kind. It is a circular, associative, "naturally ordering process," in which spontaneity automatically exists in the overall order that will best fulfill the potentials of consciousness.

At birth, each person is automatically equipped with the capacity toward natural growth that will most completely satisfy its own abilities — not at the expense of others, but in an overall context in which the fulfillment of each individual assures the fulfillment of each other individual.

In those terms there is "an ideal" psychological pattern to which you are yourself intimately connected. The inner ego constantly moves you in that direction. On the other hand, that pattern is not rigid, but flexible enough to take advantage of changing circumstances, even as a plant will turn toward the sun though you move it from room to room while the sunlight varies its directions. The inner ego does not exist in time as you do, however, so it relies upon your assessment of situations with which your reasoning is equipped to cope.

Obviously there are objects of all sizes, durability, and weight. There are private objects and public ones. There are also "vast psychological objects," then, sweeping mass events, for example, in which whole countries might be involved. There are also mass natural events of varying degrees, as say, the flooding of large areas. Such events involve psychological configurations on the part of all those involved, so that the inner individual patterns of those lives touched by each such event have in one way or another a common purpose that at the same time serves the overall reality on a natural planetary basis. In order to endure, the planet itself must be involved in constant change and instability. I know it is difficult to comprehend, but every object that you perceive — grass or rock or stone — even ocean waves or clouds — any physical phenomenon — has its own invisible consciousness, its own intent and emotional coloration. Each is also endowed with patterns toward growth and fulfillment — not at the expense of the rest of nature, but to the contrary, so that every other element of nature may also be completed (*all with much emphasis*).

At certain levels these intents of man and nature may merge. I am speaking in very simple terms now, and yet those involved in a flood, for example, want the past washed away, or want to be flooded by bursts of vital emotions such as disasters often bring. They want to feel a renewed sense of nature's power, and often, though devastated, they use the experience to start a new life.

Those with other intents will find excuses to leave such areas. There will be, perhaps, a chance meeting that will result in a hasty trip. On a hunch someone else might suddenly leave the area to find a new job, or decide to visit a friend in another state. Those whose experiences do not merge with nature's in that regard will not be part of that mass event. They will act on information that comes to them from Framework 2. Those who <u>stay</u> also act on the same information, by choosing to participate.

(*Long pause.*) When you enter time and physical life, you are already aware of its conditions. You are biologically and psychologically predisposed to grow within that rich environment, to contribute on all levels to the fulfillment of your species — but more than this, to add your own unique viewpoint and experience to the greater patterns of consciousness of which you are part.

You are beginning to understand the intimate connections that exist in your physical environment. The psychological connections, however, are far more complicated, so that each individual's dreams and thoughts interweave with every other person's, forming ever-changing patterns of desire and intent. Some of these emerge as physical events, and some do not.

Take your break.

(*10:37 to 10:55.*)

End of dictation.

(Even though he said he was through with Mass Events *for the evening, the first subject Seth touched upon now — my dream of early yesterday morning — certainly was related to statements he'd made just before break, like this one: "When you enter time and physical life, you are already aware of its conditions." I think my dream is an excellent example of that philosophy; I'd discussed the dream with Jane yesterday, and intended to ask Seth to comment upon it this evening if he didn't voluntarily do so. I'm not claiming the dream inspired his material for tonight's session, or that it was precognitive, in that I'd "picked up" on his subject matter for tonight, and constructed the dream around a portion of it in order to give myself that particular information. Perhaps I should have questioned Seth about such possibilities, but their implications escaped me while he was speaking and I was busy taking notes. From my dream notebook, with age data about all involved added for the reader's convenience:*

("Dream, Tuesday morning, March 7, 1978.

("Very vivid, and in color as usual: I dreamed that I was in the kitchen of our hill house in Elmira, preparing to go outside into the back yard. My mother, who died five years ago at the age of 81, was with me. She was of an indeterminate age in the dream, as I was, and I believe she was telling me what to expect out there. However, I also knew what to expect.

("Out on the grass, I saw them: my deceased father and his mother. My father had also been 81 at the time of his death seven years ago. I estimate that his very elderly mother had died in 1926, when I was seven years old [I'm almost 59 now].

("A very unusual dream. My father and his mother were waiting for me. The strange thing was that Grandmother Butts looked considerably younger than her son, my father. She was in her late 30's or early 40's, a beautiful woman with straight brown hair and striking blue-green eyes that had a strong magnetic quality.

("Now my grandmother was on her knees, kneeling upright in the grass. I dropped to my knees before her. We greeted each other like old friends, wrapping our arms around one another as we talked, and kissed very animatedly. We were so pleased to see each other! I remember my father's legs as he stood beside us. He was more shadowy all through the dream, however, not nearly as substantial and real as his mother was. Nor did I see my own mother — his wife — much more clearly. All of us were talking constantly, but I don't remember what any of us said, except that our meeting marked a joyous occasion.

("I don't recall having had any other dreams of this kind. I woke up as it ended — or faded out of my perception — with the certain feeling that it represented something quite unusual. Jane was sleepily stirring beside me, and I told her I'd had quite a dream. I described it in detail for her when we got up at about 7:00 A.M."

(Now here's what Seth had to say about the dream right after break ended:)

In your terms, your father's mother is ready to enter time again. Your father was pointing you out to her, and acquainting her with other such living members of the family as well, who are still in time. Many individuals do this, psychologically becoming aware of relatives still living, even though in life they may never meet.

You may feel alone in life if all of your relatives are dead, for example. In the same way, entering life, you often assure yourselves that past friends or relatives are there before you.

(The dream suggests numerous subjects that Seth didn't go into, and that I'll leave for the reader to consider: reincarnation, the shifting of ages and the independence of memory from time in the dream state, and so forth. I do have a few clear conscious memories of Grandmother Butts; the last time I saw her she was ill, a few months before her death 52 years ago. Yet, strangely, I can consciously accept that my grandmother passed away more than half a century ago easier than I can the fact that my own father and mother have already been dead for seven and five years, respectively.

(After briefly dealing with a couple of other matters following this dream material, Seth closed out the session at 11:05 P.M.)

NOTES: SESSION 826

1. See Note 2 for Session 803.

2. I think that tonight, when he started talking about the inclination of Framework 2 toward good or constructive development, Seth began to elaborate a bit on his statement after 9:50 in the last session, when he told us that the universe "is automatically predisposed . . . toward the creation of 'good' events."

I also think Seth's passages in this (826th) session bear upon his remarks in Session 821, concerning man's "true identification with nature," his "place in the context of his physical planet."

SESSION 827, MARCH 13, 1978
9:59 P.M. MONDAY

(In this noon's mail Jane received from her editor, Tam Mossman, an early printer's proof of the book jacket for The Afterdeath Journal of an American Philosopher: The World View of William James. *This is the first time we've seen the design, and we like it very much: The long title, along with Jane's name and* Introduction by Seth, *are well arranged in subtle pastel colors against a deep blue background. However, this proof doesn't contain the copy that Tam will prepare for the inside flaps and the back of the jacket.[1])*

Good evening.

("Good evening, Seth.")

A potpourri. Heredity plays far less a part in the so-called forma-tion of character than is generally supposed.

For that matter, [the same is true of] environment, as it is usually understood. Your cultural beliefs predispose you to interpret experi-ence in terms of heredity and environment, however, so that you focus primarily upon them as prime causes of behavior. This in turn results in much more structured experience than necessary. You do not concentrate upon the exceptions — the children who do not seem to fit the patterns of their families or environments, so of course no attempts are made to view those kinds of unofficial behavior.

Because of this, large organized patterns behind human activity often escape your notice almost completely. You read constantly of people who seem to have been most affected by fictional characters, for example, or by personalities from the past, or by complete strangers, more than they have been affected by their own families. Such situations are considered oddities.

The human personality is far more open to all kinds of stimuli than is supposed. If information is thought to come to the self only through physical means, then of course heredity and environment must be seen behind human motivation. When you realize that the personality can and does have access to other kinds of information than physical, then you must begin to wonder what effects those data have on the formation of character and individual growth. Children do already possess character at birth, and the entire probable intent of their lives exists then as surely as does the probable plan for the adult body they will later possess.

Consciousness forms the genes, and not the other way around, and the about-to-be-born infant is the agency that adds new material through the chromosomal structure.[2] The child is from birth far more aware of all kinds of physical events than is realized also. But beside that, the child uses the early years to explore — particularly in the dream state — other kinds of material that suit its own fancies and intents, and it constantly receives a stream of information that is not at all dependent upon its heredity or environment.

On these other levels the child knows, for example, of its contemporaries born at about the same time. Each person's "individual" life plan fits in somewhere with that of his or her contemporaries. Those plans are communicated one to the other, and probabilities instantly are set into motion in Framework 2. To some degree or another calculations are made so that, for instance, individual A will meet individual B at a marketplace 30 years later — if this fits in with the intents of both parties. There will be certain cornerstone encounters in each person's life that are set up as strong probabilities, or as plans to be grown into.

There are bodies of events, then, that in a certain fashion you will materialize almost in the same way that you will materialize your own adult body from the structure of the fetus. In those terms the body works with physical properties — though again these properties, as discussed often, have their own consciousnesses and realities.

Your mental life deals with psychological events, obviously, but beneath so-called normal awareness the child grows toward the mental body of events that will compose his or her life. Those unique intents that characterize each individual exist in Framework 2, then — and with birth, those intents immediately begin to impress the physical world of Framework 1.

Each child's birth changes the world, obviously, for it sets up an instant psychological momentum that begins to affect action in Framework 1 and Framework 2 alike.

(10:26) A child may be born with a strong talent for music, for example. Say the child is unusually gifted. Before he [or she] is old enough to begin any kind of training, he will know on other levels the probable direction that music will take during his lifetime. He will be acquainted in the dream state with other young budding musicians, though they are infants also. Again, probabilities will be

set into motion, so that each child's intent reaches out. There is great flexibility, however, and according to individual purposes many such children will also be acquainted with music of the past. To one extent or another this applies to every field of endeavor as each person adds to the world scene, and as the intents of each individual, added to those of each other person alive, multiply — so that the fulfillment of the individual results in the accomplishments of your world.[3] And the lack of fulfillment of course produces those lacks that are also so apparent.

Give us a moment . . . Some readers have brothers or sisters, or both. Others are only children. Your ideas of individuality hamper you to a large extent. To one extent or another, again, each portion of consciousness, while itself, contains [the] potentials of all consciousnesses. Your private information about the world is not nearly as private as you suppose, therefore, for behind the experience of any one event, each of you possesses information pertaining to other dimensions of that same event that you do not ordinarily perceive.

If you are involved in any kind of mass happening, from a concert to an avalanche, you are aware on other levels of all of the actions leading to that specific participation. If buildings are constructed of bricks quite visible, so mass events are formed by many small, invisible happenings — each, however, fitting together quite precisely in a kind of psychological masonry in which each of you has a mental hand. This applies to mass conversions and to natural disasters alike.

End of dictation — that was dictation.

(10:43. As he progressed with the session I began hoping that Seth meant it for Mass Events; *finally I decided to insert it in the book even if he didn't.*

(The following isn't dictation, of course, but concerns instead a very vivid dream Jane had the day before yesterday, and Seth's interpretation of it this evening. We're presenting that dream material here because it contains elements of general interest, and covers points some readers have touched upon in their letters to Jane [and Seth]. Jane's dream made me a little envious [even if an element of fear might be involved in such an event], since I don't recall ever having had one like it. She wrote:

("Dream, Saturday afternoon, March 11, 1978.

("I took a nap, and awakened remembering this dream experience: First I was in a room asking a group of people about 'the council' — I wanted to

know if there was such a thing. Instantly a white light came from the floor up through the ceiling, door width, with some symbols in or on it. I immediately whooshed up through the air into it, ascending out of the room at great speed. I became somewhat frightened and wished to return; I think I was afraid of being carried away too completely. I don't know what I saw. I returned to the room at once, but forget how or the circumstances.

("Later, I'm in some kind of spiritualistic reading room, telling a woman of my experience. When I say I'm the author of the Seth material she becomes upset, saying that they don't accept it. This doesn't bother me."

(Now from Seth:)

Ruburt, I understand, was looking for the council. He was looking for counsel of a most exalted kind, and so it became the council — an excellent term, by the way, standing for the most intimate and yet exalted counsel possible for any individual.

He was looking for a state of higher consciousness that would represent a unique and yet universal source of information and revelation. Such a source does exist for each individual, regardless of how it is interpreted. The white light is characteristically a symbol in such cases. He could not assimilate the information, and became frightened, to some extent at least, at the vastness of the experience involved, as if the ancient yet new knowledge that he sought for his individual reasons was so encompassing that his own individuality would have trouble handling it while retaining its own necessary frame of reference. A natural-enough reaction, simply because of the usual unfamiliarity of such experiences.

He was bathed in that light, however, filled with it, refreshed by it, and given new comprehensions that will now emerge in his experience in a piecemeal fashion that can be assimilated in his normal frame of reference. Translations, then, are even now being made. The contact will also be reestablished.

(After taking several minutes to cover some other material for Jane, Seth said good night at 11:10 P.M.)

NOTES: SESSION 827

1. Speaking of books: Even with all of the help Jane has given me lately on *Psyche* and Volume 2 of *"Unknown" Reality* (see the opening notes for sessions 821 and 823, respectively), I'm still only too conscious of the work I have to do to finish the notes and other material for both books, and put together their manuscripts for the publisher. I often discover the overall commitment, or plan, lingering in my mind on a distant conscious level — a pressure toward accomplishment that seems bound to accompany these long-range projects. At times this feeling can beset me, and I may find myself trying to estimate the number of weeks it'll take me to finish Volume 2 first, then *Psyche*.

But naturally, I told Jane recently — again — I *chose* to become involved with the whole Seth phenomenon in the most intimate ways. I did so because I knew from its very beginning (in late 1963) that this process of discovery with Seth was more than worth it. I still think so. I added that I'd certainly choose to do the same thing again, and that I hoped to stay involved with the Seth books indefinitely. Granted that Seth's material may "only" be bringing into our conscious awareness knowledge we already possess and use on other levels, still it's a fine thing that his material makes us *aware* of that inner comprehension — and so new dimensions of consciousness become available to us. I "drew" a rough analogy with painting (to make a pun): The artist may start working on a blank canvas, yet each physical brush stroke he or she delineates is built upon inner knowledge and experience; in the painting these qualities are objectified in new combinations, which in turn add further to the artist's conscious comprehension. And when the painting is finished, the artist contemplates a new reality of his or her own creation.

I mailed the last chapter of *Emir* to Prentice-Hall just a month ago (on February 8). Because of various delays, Jane is still waiting for news of the book's official acceptance, even though she knows that Tam and other executives there like it very much. *Emir*, however, is of an in-between length — shorter than a novel, far longer than most children's books — and she wonders: Is that fact going to complicate Prentice-Hall's presentation of *Emir* as a story for "readers of all ages"? There's talk of publishing it in two shorter volumes. Jane doesn't know what to think. In the meantime, see the opening notes for Session 814.

2. Chromosomes are rod-like bodies within the cell nucleus, and carry the genes that govern hereditary characteristics. They separate lengthwise to double in number during cell division. See Note 2 for Session 821.

3. Seth's material on individual creativity at once reminded me of a certain passage of his in the private, or deleted, portion of the 580th session for April 12, 1971. I came across it recently while looking for some other references he'd made to Jane, or Ruburt. (The regular part of the 580th session, incidentally, was for a book, too: Chapter 20 of *Seth Speaks*.) I like the following quotation so much that I've made copies of it for us to keep where we can refer to them — in my case, pinned up on a wall in my studio. This little affair is a typical example of how something good can get lost in the constantly growing mass of Seth material; even with our attempts at indexing, it's very difficult to keep track of single paragraphs like this:

"Ruburt is, as you know, highly creative. What most artists do not realize is that the self is the first creation. They do not think of themselves as products of their own creativity. Because of Ruburt's energy and creativity, he has always perfectly mirrored and even somewhat exaggerated the condition of the inner self, its activities and inner postures."

Obviously, then, Seth's observation doesn't apply to people in the arts alone, but to everyone.

SESSION 828, MARCH 15, 1978
9:53 P.M. WEDNESDAY

Good evening.

(Good evening, Seth.")

Now: In your terms, speaking more or less historically, early man was in a more conscious relationship with Framework 2 than you are now.

As Ruburt mentioned in *Psychic Politics,* there are many gradations of consciousness, and as I mentioned in *The Nature of the Psyche,* early man used his consciousness in other ways than those you are familiar with. He often perceived what you would call the products of the imagination as sense data, for example, more or less objectified in the physical world.

The imagination has always dealt with creativity, and as man began to settle upon a kind of consciousness that dealt with cause and effect, he no longer physically perceived the products of his imagination directly in the old manner. He realized in those earlier times that illness, for instance, was initially as much the result of the imagination as health was, for he experienced far more directly the brilliant character of his own imagination. The lines between imaginative and physical experience have blurred for you, and of course they have also become tempered by other beliefs and the experiences that those beliefs then engender.

I am putting this very simply here. It is far more complicated — and yet early man, for example, became aware of the fact that no man was injured without that event first being imagined to one extent or another. Therefore, imagined healings were utilized, in which a physical illness was imaginatively cured — and in those days the cures worked.

Regardless of your histories, those early men and women were quite healthy. They had strong teeth and bones. They dealt with the physical world through the purposeful use of the imagination, however, in a way now most difficult to understand. They realized they were mortal, and must die, but their greater awareness of Framework 2 allowed them a larger identification, so they understood that death was not only a natural necessity, but also an opportunity for other kinds of experience and development *(see Note 1 for Session 803).*

(Long pause at 10:10.) They felt their relationship with nature acutely, experiencing it in a far different fashion than you do yours. They felt that it was the larger expression of their own moods and temperament, the materialization of self-events that were too vast to be contained within the flesh of any one individual or any group of individuals. They wondered where their thoughts went after they had them, and they imagined that in one way or another those thoughts turned into the birds and rocks, the animals and trees that were themselves ever-changing.

They also felt that they were themselves, however; that as humans [they were] the manifestation of the larger expression of nature that was too splendid to be contained alone within nature's framework, that nature needed them — that is, men — to give it another kind of voice. When men spoke they spoke for themselves; yet because they felt so a part of the natural environment they spoke for nature also, and for all of its creatures.

Much is not understood in your interpretations. In that world men knew that nature was balanced. Both animals and men must die. If a man was caught and eaten by animals, as sometimes happened, [his fellows] did not begrudge that animal its prey — at least, not in the deepest of terms. And when they slayed other animals themselves and ate the heart, for example, it was not only to obtain the animals' "stout hearts," or fearlessness; but also the intent was to preserve those characteristics so that through men's experiences each animal would continue to live to some extent.

Men in those times protected themselves against storms, and yet in the same way they did not begrudge the storm its victims. They

simply changed the alliances of their consciousnesses from the identification of self-within-the-flesh to self-within-the-storm. Man's and
nature's intents were largely the same, and understood as such. Man
did not fear the elements in those early times, as is now supposed.

(10:25.) Some of the experiences known by early man would
seem quite foreign to you now. Yet in certain forms they come down
through the centuries. Early man, again, perceived himself as himself, an individual. He felt that nature expressed for him the vast
power of his own emotions. He projected himself out into nature,
into the heavens, and imagined there were great personified forms
that later turned into the gods of Olympus, for example. He was
also aware of the life-force within nature's smallest parts, however,
and before sense data became so standardized he perceived his own
version of those individualized consciousnesses which much later
became the elementals, or small spirits. But above all he was aware of
nature's source.

He was filled with wonder as his own consciousness ever-newly
came into being. He had not yet covered over that process with the
kind of smooth continuity that your own consciousness has now
achieved — so when he thought a thought he was filled with curiosity: Where had it come from? His own consciousness, then, was forever a source of delight, its changing qualities as <u>noticeable</u> and
apparent as the changing sky. The relative smoothness of your own
consciousness — in those terms, at least — was gained at the
expense of certain other experiences, therefore, that were possible
otherwise. You could not live in your present world of time if your
consciousness was as playful, curious, and creative as it <u>was</u>, for
[then] time was also experienced far differently.

It may be difficult for you to understand, but the events that you
now recognize are as much the result of the realm of the imagination, as those experienced by early man when he perceived as real
happenings that now <u>you</u> would consider hallucinatory, or purely
imaginative.

It seems quite clear to you that the mass events of nature are
completely outside of your domain. You feel you have no part in
nature except as you exert control over it through technology, or
harm it, again through technology. You grant that the weather has

an effect upon your moods, but any deeper psychic or psychological connections between you and the elements strikes most of you as quite impossible.

(10:40.) Give us a moment . . . You use terms like "being flooded by emotion," however, and other very intuitive statements showing your own deeper recognition of events that quite escape you when you examine them through reason alone. Man actually courts storms. He seeks them out, for emotionally he understands quite well their part in his own private life, and their necessity on a physical level. Through nature's manifestations, particularly through its power, man senses nature's source and his own, and knows that the power can carry him to emotional realizations that are required for his own greater spiritual and psychic development.

Death is not an end, but a transformation of consciousness. Nature, with its changing seasons, constantly brings you that message. In that light, and with that understanding, nature's disasters do not claim victims: Nature and man together act out their necessary parts in the larger framework of reality.

Your concepts about death and nature, however, force you to see man and nature as adversaries, and also program your experience of such events so that they seem to only confirm what you already believe. As I mentioned earlier *(in Session 821)*, each person caught in either an epidemic or a natural disaster will have private reasons for choosing those circumstances. Such conditions also often involve events in which the individual senses a larger identification, however — even sometimes a renewed sense of purpose that makes no sense in ordinary terms.

End of dictation.

(10:51. After giving half a page of notes for Jane, Seth ended the session at 10:58 P.M.)

SESSION 829, MARCH 22, 1978
9:30 P.M. WEDNESDAY

(Last Monday evening Seth gave a very short private session for Jane; it turned out to consist of just one page of double-spaced typewritten information. During the session Seth said that he was "preparing some special

material for Ruburt," but except for the excellent relaxation effects Jane has experienced since then, we have yet to learn what else may be involved.

(In Jane's case, I mean something different by "relaxation" than might be expected. Just recently I quoted her in Volume 2 of "Unknown" Reality; from Note 6 for Appendix 19, in part:

("It's a sort of superrelaxation; almost profound, and mental and physical at once. A completely different thing than just yawning, even though I might be yawning. It involves a curious sense of dropping down inwardly, of going slowly beneath the realities we usually perceive . . . Such a relaxation, then, is almost an extension of biological insight."

(Even while immersed in her most enjoyable state, Jane still wanted to hold the session. "I think I know his subject matter for tonight," she said, "but I don't know if it'll be dictation or not. . . ." Then she took off her glasses as she went into trance:)

Good evening.

("Good evening, Seth.")

Now: The animals do have imagination, regardless of your current thought. Yet man is so gifted that he directs his experience and forms his civilizations largely through the use of his imaginative abilities.

You do not understand this point clearly at all, but your social organizations, your governments — these are based upon imaginative principles. The basis of your most intimate experience, the framework behind all of your organized structures, rests upon a reality that is not considered valid by the very institutions that are formed through its auspices.

It is now nearing Easter *(on March 26),* and the yearly commemoration of what is considered historic fact: the [resurrection and] ascension of Christ into heaven.[1] Untold millions have in one way or another commemorated that occasion through the centuries. Private lives have merged with public sentiment and religious fervor. There have been numberless village festivals, or intimate family gatherings, and church services performed on Easter Sundays now forgotten. There have been bloody wars fought on the same account, and private persecutions in which those who did not agree with one or another's religious dogmas were quite simply killed "for the good of their souls."

There have been spiritual rebirths and regenerations — and ungodly slaughter as well, as a result of the meaning of Easter. Blood and flesh have certainly been touched, then, and lives changed in that regard.

All of those religious and political structures that you certainly recognize as valid, arising from the "event" of Christ's ascension, existed — and do exist — because of an idea. The idea was the result of a spectacular act of the imagination that then leapt upon the historical landscape, highlighting all of the events of the time, so that they became illuminated indeed with a blessed and unearthly light.

The idea of man's survival of death was not new. The idea of a god's "descent" to earth was ancient. The old religious myths fit a different kind of people, however, and lasted for as many centuries in the past as Christianity has reached into the future.[2] The miraculous merging of imagination with historical time, however, became less and less synchronized, so that only r-i-t-e-s *(spelled)* remained and the old gods seized the imagination no longer. The time was ripe for Christianity.

(9:49.) Because man has not understood the characteristics of the world of imagination, he has thus far always insisted upon turning his myths into historical fact, for he considers the factual world alone as the real one. A man, literally of flesh and blood, must then prove beyond all doubt that each and every other [human being] survives death — by dying, of course, and then by rising, physically-perceived, into heaven. Each man does survive death, and each woman *(with quiet amusement),* but only such a literal-minded species would insist upon the physical death of a god-man as "proof of the pudding."

(Intently:) Again, Christ was not crucified. The historical Christ,[3] as he is thought of, was a man illuminated by psychic realities, touched with the infinite realization that any one given individual was, by virtue of his or her existence, a contact between All That Is and mankind.

Christ saw that in each person divinity and humanity met — and that man survived death by virtue of his existence within the divine. Without exception, all of the horrors connected with Christianity's name came from "following the letter rather than the spirit of the law," or by insistence upon literal interpretations — while the spiritual, imaginative concepts beneath were ignored.

Again, man directs his existence through the use of his imagination — a feat that <u>does</u> distinguish him from the animals. What connects people and separates them is the power of idea and the force of imagination. Patriotism, family loyalty, political affiliations — the ideas behind these have the greatest practical applications in your world. You project yourselves into time like children through freely imagining your growth. You instantly color physical experience and nature itself with the tints of your unique imaginative processes. Unless you think quite consistently — and deeply — the importance of the imagination quite escapes you, and yet it literally forms the world that you experience and the mass world in which you live.

The theory of evolution,[4] for instance, is an imaginative construct, and yet through its lights some generations now have viewed their world. It is not only that you think of yourselves differently, <u>but you actually experience a different kind of self.</u> Your institutions change their aspects accordingly, so that experience fits the beliefs that you have about it. You act in certain ways. You view the entire universe in a fashion that did not exist before, so that imagination and belief intangibly structure your subjective experience and your objective circumstances.

(10:10.) In all of the other imaginative constructs, for example, whatever their merits and disadvantages, man felt himself to be a part of a plan. The planner might be God, or nature itself, or man within nature or nature within man. There might be many gods or one, but there was a meaning in the universe. Even the idea of fate gave man something to act against, and roused him to action.

(All with much emphasis and irony:) The idea of a meaningless universe, however, is in itself a highly creative imaginative act. Animals, for example, could not imagine such an idiocy, so that the theory shows the incredible accomplishment of an obviously ordered mind and intellect that can <u>imagine</u> itself to be the result of nonorder, or chaos — [you have] a creature who is capable of "mapping" its own brain, imagining that the brain's fantastic regulated order could emerge from a reality that itself has no meaning. Indeed, then, the theory actually says that the ordered universe <u>magically</u> emerged —

and evolutionists must certainly believe in a God of Chance some-where, or in Coincidence with a capital C, for their theories would make no sense at all otherwise.

The world of the imagination is indeed your contact with your own source. Its characteristics are the closest to those in Framework 2 that you can presently encounter.

Your experience of history, of the days of your life, is invisibly formed by those ideas that exist in the imagination only, and then are projected upon the physical world. This applies to your individ-ual beliefs about yourself and the way you see yourself in your imag-ination. You are having wars between the Jews and the Arabs and the Christians once again, because emphasis is put upon literal interpre-tations of spiritual truths.

In each person the imaginative world, its force and power, merges into historical reality. In each person, the ultimate and unassailable and unquenchable power of All That Is is individualized, and dwells in time. Man's imagination can carry him into those other realms — but when he tries to squeeze those truths into frameworks too small, he distorts and bends inner realities so that they become jagged dogmas.

Take your break.

(10:26 to 10:40.)

Now: The latest growth of fundamentalist religion has arisen as a countermeasure against the theories of evolution. You have, then, an overcompensation, for in the Darwinian[5] world there was no mean-ing and no laws. There were no standards of right or wrong, so that large portions of the people felt rootless.

The [fundamentalists] returned to an authoritarian religion in which the slightest act must be regulated. They gave release, and they are giving release, to the emotions, and are thus rebelling against scientific intellectualism. They will see the world in black-and-white terms again, with good and evil clearly delineated in the most simplistic terms, and thus escape a slippery, thematic universe, in which man's feelings seemed to give him no foothold at all.

Unfortunately, the fundamentalists accept literal interpretations of intuitive realities in such a way that they further narrow the chan-nels through which their psychic abilities can flow. The fundamental framework, in this period of time, for all of its fervor, is not rich — as for example Christianity was in the past, with its numerous saints. It is instead a fanatical Puritan vein, peculiarly American in character, and restrictive rather than expansive, for the bursts of emotion are highly structured — that is, the emotions are limited in most areas of life, permitted only an explosive religious expression under certain conditions, when they are not so much spontaneously expressed as suddenly released from the dam of usual repression.

The imagination always seeks expression. It is always creative, and underneath the frameworks of society it provides fresh incentives and new avenues for fulfillment, that can become harnessed through fanatical belief. When this happens your institutions become more repressive, and violence often emerges as a result.

If you look for signs of God's vengeance you will find them everywhere. An avalanche or a flood or an earthquake will not be seen as a natural act of the earth's natural creativity, but instead as a punishment from God for sin.

In evolution man's nature is amoral, and anything goes for survival's sake. There is no possibility of any spiritual survival as far as most evolutionists are concerned. The fundamentalists would rather believe in man's inherent sinful nature, for at least their belief system provides for a framework in which he can be saved. Christ's message was that each man is good inherently, and is an individualized portion of the divine — and yet a civilization based upon that precept has never been attempted. The vast social structures of Christianity were instead based upon man's "sinful" nature — not the organizations and structures that might allow him to become good, or to obtain the goodness that Christ quite clearly perceived man already possessed.

(11:01.) It seems almost a sacrilege to say that man is good, when everywhere you meet contradictions, for too often man certainly appears to act as if his motives were instead those of a born killer. You have been taught not to trust the very fabric of your being. You cannot expect yourselves to act rationally or altruistically in any consistent manner if you believe that you are automatically degraded, or that your nature is so flawed that such performance is uncharacteristic.

Give us a moment . . . You are a part of nature that has learned to make choices, a part of nature that naturally and automatically produces dreams and beliefs about which you then organize your reality. There are many effects which you do not like, but you possess a unique kind of consciousness, in which each individual has a hand in the overall formation of a world reality, and you are participating at a level of existence in which you are learning how to transform the imaginative realm of probabilities into a more or less specific, physically experienced world.

In a way you choose from an infinite, endless, <u>uncomputable</u> number of ideas, and sculpt these into the physical fragments that compose normal experience. You do this in such a way that the timeless events are experienced <u>in</u> time, and so that they mix and merge to conform to the dimensions of your reality. Along the way there are accomplishments that are as <u>precious</u> as any creatures of any kind could produce. There are also great failures — but these are failures only in comparison with the glittering inner knowledge of the imagination that holds for you those ideals against which you judge your acts.

Those ideals are present in each individual. They are natural inclinations toward growth and fulfillment.

That was dictation. That was also the end of the chapter — and I bid you a fond good evening.

("Thank you very much, Seth. Good night.")

(11:16 P.M. I'd say that much of Seth's excellent delivery since break is related to some of his material in the 825th session, including this passage: "I put the word 'good' in quotes for now because of your misconceptions about the nature of good and evil, which we will discuss somewhat later.")

NOTES: SESSION 829

1. I added "[resurrection and]" to Seth's passage because Jane told me that according to ordinary teaching Christ's resurrection from the dead took place on Easter Sunday, the third day following his crucifixion (on Friday), while his ascension into heaven transpired at an indefinite later time — up to 40 days later, as stated in the writings of St. Luke in the Acts of the Apostles (AA 1:10). As far as we know, Seth's inference that Christ's resurrection and ascension took place on the same day is contrary to popular belief.

"Here Seth seemed to telescope the two events into one, "Jane wrote, "or refer to them together, as if the distinction didn't exist for him . . . Seth may be implying that the *ascension* was the main issue in the Christ story, rather than the resurrection, or telling us that the two events are so intertwined thematically as to be treated as one." Since we do not arbitrarily change Seth's copy, his reference here to the ascension rather than the resurrection, and a similar one that soon follows, stand as they were given. But, obviously, we did decide to add this note.

At the same time, Jane and I checked a number of biblical references on the New Testament — and discovered that Seth's passage seems to be a case where he shows a knowledge we don't consciously possess. For we learned that of the four Gospels (according to Mark, Matthew, Luke, and John, in that order), some scholars believe that Luke and John can be read as stating that Christ's resurrection and ascension took place on the same day. Yet in Acts, Luke postulates the 40-day interval between the two events. (Originally Luke composed his Gospel and Acts as one treatise; the two were separated early in the second century.) Out of such contradictions as those implied in Luke's case, however, confusion and opposing opinions reign when one studies the Gospels and related material. Christ himself left no written records, nor are there any eyewitness or contemporary accounts of his life.

In the 591st session for *Seth Speaks,* I noted claims for an earlier date for the origin of the first Gospel, that according to Mark; nevertheless, most authorities still believe that the Gospels were written between A.D. 65 and 110. Since Christ was presumably crucified around A.D. 30, this means that some 35–40 years passed before the advent of Mark's account. There are many consistencies in the Gospels, but also inconsistencies that cannot be resolved. Even the authorships of the Gospels according to Matthew and John are now being questioned. A study of the New Testament books alone can quickly lead one into a maze of questions: Why isn't the resurrection itself described? Why are there so few references to the ascension? Matthew doesn't mention it at all in his Gospel, for example; and Paul alludes to it only once (1 Timothy 3:16) in his writings. Is the Gospel according to Luke merely schematic, rather than chronological? If time (as much as 40 days) *did* elapse between Christ's resurrection and ascension, where was he physically during all of that period, other than on the few occasions cited in the Gospels and in Acts, when on various occasions he revealed himself to the women who discovered his empty tomb, to the apostles, and to some others? Sometimes Christ appeared as an apparition — but as Seth commented in a private session: "You could not have a world in which the newly risen dead mixed with the living. An existence in a spiritual realm had to follow such a resurrection."

I'd say that in this 829th session Seth spoke out of a knowledge of biblical tradition and history; that is, he wasn't saying that Christ *did* rise from the dead or ascend into heaven, but referring to Christianity's *interpretation* of its own creative Christ story. Seth has always maintained that Christ wasn't crucified to begin with — indeed, he told us in the same private session that ". . . in the facts of history, there was no crucifixion, resurrection, or ascension. In the terms of history, there was no biblical Christ. In the terms of the biblical drama (underlined), however, Christ was crucified.

"It was the Jewish tradition that nourished the new religion in its early stages. Christ, as you know, was a common name, so when I say that there was a man named Christ involved in those events, I do not mean to say that he was the biblical Christ. His life was one of those that were finally used to compose the composite image of the biblical Christ." (In Chapter 20 of *Seth Speaks,* see Session 586 for July 24, 1971.)

And finally, here's an answer to a number of inquiries from readers. The 647th session for Chapter 21 of *Personal Reality* was held on July 2, 1973, and in it I quoted a remark Seth made to me the following September: "You can have more material on Jerusalem or Christ now, or when you want it. You can have *The Christ Book* when you want it. . . ."

So far, we've done nothing about producing *The Christ Book,* except to talk about it once in a while. "Well, it's true that I have ambiguous feelings about doing a book on religion," Jane said as we discussed this note. "But for all that, if Seth started dictating it tomorrow, I'd do it. Many issues would be involved — maybe even current national events. I guess I think Seth would know the best time for such a book to be done and publicly introduced.

"When he said, 'You can have *The Christ Book* when you want it,' I think he was just stating his *willingness* to comply. Maybe he knows that really *wanting* it might take a while, at least on my part. But I do know my attitude about getting such a book has improved a lot in the last year or two."

Neither of us has any doubt that *The Christ Book* would be controversial indeed.

2. According to Seth, then, those old religious myths lasted for about 20 centuries, dating from 2000 B.C.

3. See Note 2 for Session 821.

4. Once again: See my material on evolution in Appendix 12 for Volume 2 of *"Unknown" Reality,* when that book is published. In *Mass Events,* see Note 2 for Session 821.

5. See Note 4 for Session 802.

CHAPTER 5

THE MECHANICS OF EXPERIENCE

SESSION 830, MARCH 27, 1978
9:15 P.M. MONDAY

*(S*ince Jane began dictating *Mass Events* 11 months ago, I've mentioned our checking the printer's page proofs for two of her other books: Volume 1 of "Unknown" Reality, and Cézanne. Now I can add a third book, James, to the list. The uncorrected proofs, typeset in the actual page format in which the book will be published, arrived last Thursday. So now we're spending much of our working time checking — and double-checking — the proofs against our carbon copy of the copyedited James manuscript. Our scrutiny will include spelling, punctuation, and all of the other indicia that people take for granted when they read the finished work. We must also make sure that no words, sentences, or paragraphs have been inadvertently duplicated or omitted. We estimate that we should have the whole job finished and in the mail to Prentice-Hall in about 10 days.*

(Five weeks ago [in the notes leading off Session 821], I wrote that Jane could resume work on The Further Education of Oversoul Seven — *or* Seven Two — *at any time. She finished her first novel about Seven in July 1972, and within a month, long before it was published, she wrote the first five chapters for* Seven Two. *Then we became involved in so many other projects that she laid it aside until August 1976, when she wrote two more chapters. The book has hovered in the back of her consciousness ever since,*

waiting until she focused her attention upon it once again. "Seven's got all the time in the world," she laughed more than once. But now that her editor, Tam Mossman, has scheduled a visit to us at the hill house in a couple of weeks [on April 10, to be exact], Jane feels that she wants to study what she's done on Seven Two, *go over it with Tam, and perhaps take up work on it again.)*

Good evening.

("Good evening, Seth.")

To begin with, dictation. New chapter *(5):* "The Mechanics of Experience."

Your world and everything in it exists first in the imagination, then. You have been taught to focus all of your attention upon physical events, so that they carry the authenticity of reality for you. Thoughts, feelings, or beliefs appear to be secondary, subjective — or somehow not real — and they seem to rise in response to an already established field of physical data.

You usually think, for example, that your feelings about a given event are primarily reactions to the event itself. It seldom occurs to you that the feelings themselves might be primary, and that the particular event was somehow a response to your emotions, rather than the other way around. The all-important matter of your focus is largely responsible for your interpretation of any event.

For an exercise, then, imagine for a while that the subjective world of your thoughts, feelings, inner images and fantasies represent the "rockbed reality" from which individual physical events emerge. Look at the world for a change from the inside out, so to speak. Imagine that physical experience is somehow the materialization of your own subjective reality. Forget what you have learned about reactions and stimuli. Ignore for a time everything you have believed and see your thoughts as the real events. Try to view normal physical occurrences as the concrete physical reactions in space and time to your own feelings and beliefs. For indeed your subjective world causes your physical experience.

In titling this chapter I used the word "mechanics," because mechanisms suggest smooth technological workings. While the world is not a machine — its inner workings are such that no technology could ever copy them — this involves a natural mechanics in which the inner dimensions of consciousness everywhere emerge to

form a materialized, cohesive, physical existence. Again, your interpretations of identity teach you to focus awareness in such a way that
you cannot follow the strands of consciousness that connect you with
all portions of nature. In a way, the world is like a multidimensional,
exotic plant growing in space and time, each thought, dream, imaginative encounter, hope or fear, growing naturally into its own bloom
— a plant of incredible variety, never for a moment the same, in
which each smallest root, leaf, stem, or flower has a part to play and
is connected with the whole.

Even those of you who intellectually agree that you form your own
reality find it difficult to accept emotionally in certain areas. You are,
of course, literally hypnotized into believing that your feelings arise
in response to events. Your feelings, however, cause the events you
perceive. Secondarily, you do of course then react to those events.

(9:45.) You have been taught that your feelings must necessarily
be tied to specific physical happenings. You may be sad because a relative has died, for example, or because you have lost a job, or
because you have been rebuffed by a lover, or for any number of
other accepted reasons. You are told that your feelings must be in
response to events that are happening, or have happened. Often, of
course, your feelings "happen ahead of time," because those feelings
are the initial realities from which events flow.

A relative might be ready to die, though no exterior sign has
been given. The relative's feelings might well be mixed, containing
portions of relief and sadness, which you might then perceive — but
the primary events are subjective.

It is somewhat of a psychological trick, in your day and age, to
come to the realization that you do in fact form your experience and
your world, simply because the weight of evidence seems (underlined twice) to be so loaded at the other end, because of your habits
of perception. The realization is like one that comes at one time or
another to many people in the dream state, when suddenly they
"awaken" while still in the dream, realizing first of all that they are
dreaming, and secondarily that they are themselves creating the
experienced drama.

To understand that you create your own reality requires that
same kind of "awakening" from the normal awake state — at least for
many people. Some of course have this knack more than others. The

realization itself does indeed change "the rules of the game" as far as you are concerned *(louder)* to a rather considerable degree. There are reasons why I am mentioning this now rather than in earlier books. Indeed, our books follow their own rhythms, and this one is in a way a further elaboration upon *The Nature of Personal Reality.*[1]

As long as you believe that either good events or bad ones are meted out by a personified God as the reward or punishment for your actions, or on the other hand that events are largely meaningless, chaotic, subjective knots in the tangled web of an accidental Darwinian world, then you cannot consciously understand your own creativity, or play the role in the universe that you are capable of playing as individuals or as a species. You will instead live in a world where events happen to you, in which you must do sacrifice to the gods of one kind or another, or see yourselves as victims of an uncaring nature.

While still preserving the integrity of physical events as you understand them, [each of] you must alter the focus of your attention to some extent, so that you begin to perceive the connections between your subjective reality at any given time, and those events that you perceive at any given time. You are the initiator of those events.

This recognition does indeed involve a new performance on the part of your own consciousness, a mental and imaginative leap that gives you control and direction over achievements that you have always performed, though without your conscious awareness.

As mentioned before *(in Session 828)*, early man had such an identification of subjective and objective realities. As a species, however, you have developed what can almost be called a secondary nature — a world of technology in which you also now have your existence, and complicated social structures have emerged from it. To develop that kind of structure necessitated a division between subjective and objective worlds. Now, however, it is highly important that you realize your position, and accomplish the manipulation of consciousness that will allow you to take true conscious responsibility for your actions and your experience.

You can "come awake" from your normal waking state, and that is the natural next step for consciousness to follow — one for which your biology has already equipped you. Indeed, each person <u>does</u> attain that recognition now and then. It brings triumphs and challenges as well. In those areas of life where you are satisfied, give yourselves credit, and in those areas where you are not, remind yourselves that you are involved in a learning process; you are daring enough to accept the responsibility for your actions.

Let us look more clearly, however, at the ways in which your private world causes your daily experience, and how it merges with the experience of others.

Take your break.

(10:25. Seth returned at 10:37 with a good bit of personal material for Jane and me, then ended the session at 11:06 P.M.

(His delivery just above, about accepting the responsibility for one's actions, reminded us of the personal challenges that have accompanied the roles we've chosen in our own physical lives. Jane and I try to keep in mind these passages of Seth's from the private session for June 25, 1977:

("Because of your individual and joint intuitive understanding and intellectual discrimination, you were able from an early age to clearly perceive the difficulties of your fellows. This helped incite stimuli that made you question the entire framework of your civilization. You were able to do something few people can: leap intuitively and mentally above your own period — to discard intellectually and mentally, and sometimes emotionally, the shortsighted, unfortunate religious, scientific, and social beliefs of your fellows.

("Many of those old beliefs still have an emotional hold, however, and some helpful beliefs have also been overdone, or carried on too long. Because you can see so clearly the failings of your age, you each have a tendency to exaggerate them, or rather to concentrate upon them, so that you do not have an emotional feeling of safety. You react by setting up defenses. . . . ")

NOTES: SESSION 830

1. Jane and I have also been thinking of *Mass Events* as an extension of Seth's second book, *Personal Reality*. It seems incredible to us, so fast has the time passed, but counting *Mass Events* Seth produced *Personal Reality* five books ago — and some five to six years ago from this moment; he dictated it during 1972–73.

SESSION 831, JANUARY 15, 1979
9:22 P.M. MONDAY

(The roses seemed to linger particularly late last fall. On September 28, 1978, Jane wrote this little poem when I brought in a few blooms from the climber growing up the trellis at the northeast corner of our hill house, near the kitchen windows:

The temporal rose
Contains
Eternal seeds
In which
The entire universe
(and you and I)
Are all implied.

(Jane's poem can also serve as a symbol to show that she hasn't held a session for Mass Events *for 42 weeks, or since giving the 830th session last March; indeed, the summer, fall, and winter of 1978 have passed, and we're into the next year [and a very cold and stormy one it is, so far]. We accomplished many things during those nine and a half months, however, including the holding of 56 nonbook sessions. Those sessions, whether private or not, are of course more than double in number the 22 sessions Jane has given for* Mass Events *[not counting tonight's]. In connection with our feelings about the long intervals that have materialized several times during the production of this book, see my opening notes for the 815th session — especially those concerning simultaneous time, and my statement that "We do not plan to ask Seth when the book will be done." I'll continue our chronology here, then, by describing many of our professional activities since last March, and follow it with Jane's own account of at least some of the reasons for the long interruption in book work.*

(Although each of us had looked over Mass Events *occasionally, still it seemed strange to hear Seth come through with new material for it after all of that time had passed, and equally strange to resume work on these notes. I rechecked my opening notes for the last session: Yes, we did finish correcting the page proofs for* James *early in April 1978. Tam Mossman did visit later that month, and at his urging Jane did go back to work on* Seven Two *with her old enthusiasm.*

(Then in May 1978 Sue Watkins began helping me by typing the final manuscript for the session notes for Volume 2 of "Unknown" Reality. In June, with no hard feelings involved on anybody's part, Jane withdrew Emir *from consideration at Prentice-Hall when the decision was made there to publish the story in two volumes; on July 12, Eleanor Friede at Delacorte Press accepted* Emir *for publication as a single book. Later in July Sue finished typing the notes and started in on the appendixes for Volume 2, just as we received the first books for* James. *Jane completed* Seven Two *in August, and set to work preparing the manuscript for Tam. Late that month — unbelievably to me — I finished my own work on Volume 2 of "Unknown" Reality, and immediately began to type the final draft of the sessions; as I finished groups of sessions I mailed them to Tam every few days, while at the same time collaborating with Jane on the table of contents for the book. On September 23 Sue delivered the completed appendix material for Volume 2, and I sent Tam each appendix, with its notes, as I checked it. Jane finished typing her manuscript for* Seven Two *on October 3, and I helped her correct that book for mailing on October 9. My own mailings for Volume 2 continued until the 21st of the month, when at last that very long project was completed and out of the house in its entirety for the first time. I felt like celebrating!*

(Now another event took place in October 1978 that is most important to Jane and me: Sue Watkins received the go-ahead from Tam Mossman to write a book on the ESP classes that Jane had conducted for some seven and a half years, from the fall of 1967 to February 1975. It's to be called Conversations With Seth. *This is great news for the three of us, of course. It's a project that Jane herself never figured she'd do, but wanted done — and Sue, who was a class member, is talented psychically herself, has a newspaper and reporting background, and is ideally qualified for the job.[1]*

(Conversations, *we think, is sure to be published before* Mass Events, *since Tam is supposed to have Sue's manuscript in hand by January 1980, for publication in the fall of that year. Even assuming that Seth will finish dictating* Mass Events *later this year [1979], Jane and I will still have too much work to do on it for publication in 1980.*

(Resuming our chronology: On October 24, 1978, Jane worked out the Table of Contents for Seth's Psyche, *and started her Introduction for it on the 26th; we mailed* Psyche *to Tam in sections as we put the manuscript together, and finished with that endeavor on November 9. On November 14*

Eleanor Friede visited us to renew an old friendship and to go over Emir *with Jane. No sooner had she left than Tam arrived, two days later, bringing with him the copyedited manuscript[2] of* Seven Two *for us to check; on the 20th, our work completed on it, I sent it back to him at Prentice-Hall. We received the printer's sample pages for* Seven Two *on December 4 [we see these for each book, and they show us just how the work will look when published]. On December 7 the copyedited manuscript for Volume 2 of* "Unknown" Reality *came; it's more than 900 pages long, and painstakingly checking every word on every page of that book kept us busy until Christmas Eve; I mailed it to Tam on December 26. Next, on January 13, 1979, the copyedited manuscript for* Psyche *arrived. Jane and I are still going over it.*

(Since last March, then, we've been holding our private, or nonbook, sessions twice a week usually: Their regular production came to be a steady, reassuring flow of creativity in back of all of the other, often hectic activities I've listed here. Those 56 sessions are too numerous to quote in any meaningful way, and even difficult to briefly summarize. Jane did review them for me while I was working on this note, however, and here's a slightly edited version of what she wrote as a result of her study:

("Looking over those nine-and-a-half months of sessions now, it's fairly obvious what Seth was up to. He'd initially given us the material on Frameworks 1 and 2 in private sessions not long after starting Mass Events, *as Rob explained in his notes for Session 814. Yet even though Seth also discussed those psychic frameworks to some degree in a dozen sessions for the book, still he finally took that break in dictation to 're-educate' us, looking at our own previous beliefs and those of the world at large in the light of Frameworks 1 and 2.*

("In an important fashion those private sessions parallel his material for Mass Events . . . *material that did make us view the world and current events quite differently than we had earlier. Several times we asked about local fatal accidents we read about, for instance, wondering how such events fit in Frameworks-1-and-2 activity. Some of those sessions were devoted to our private beliefs, but usually Seth put such beliefs into the larger social context. Four days after they took place, he began discussing the disastrous events at Jonestown, Guyana, involving the murder or suicide of more than 900 Americans in that South American settlement last November 18, 1978. Since then, we've voiced our hopes often that Seth will go into the entire Jonestown affair in* Mass Events; *he can't but help be aware of our wishes! So interspersed*

in all of that private material are some excellent — and lively — discussions of events current in the world at that time, as well as discourses on connections between creativity and Framework 2, and topics as diverse as psychotic behavior and early civilizations. It was as though Seth were trying to help us break up old associations for once and for all. Certainly he tried his best, and any failings are on our parts.

("We have our hassles like everyone else, of course. Seth 'never promised us a rose garden,' and we have our good days and our bad days as we encounter life's daily challenges, joys, adventures, and misadventures. In this large group of sessions, Seth addressed himself to several of our individual problems: Rob's occasional bouts of indisposition when he felt 'under the weather' generally, or was bothered by a variety of minor but annoying symptoms; and my own long-standing troubles with severe stiffness. If Seth didn't give us a rose garden, he certainly did — and does — try to tell us where the weeds come from! This personal material did help give us a much larger perspective on our various challenges, and we've made some inroads in overcoming them. Like anyone else, we have to put Seth's material to use for ourselves. The thing is, often we're so busy getting the material and preparing it for publication that we don't have the time to really study it as our readers do. Perhaps Seth was trying to compensate for that in those private sessions, by taking time out from dictation to help us put the material to greater personal use.")

(We held our first session for 1979 — a private one — on the evening of New Year's Day. During it Seth remarked that he'd "begin book sessions again next Wednesday," but that didn't quite work out; he still had a few more nonbook sessions to go. Jane has been looking over his material on Mass Events *every so often lately, though, with the idea of going back to work on it. And then, on the very night when she told me that she thought Seth would resume book dictation, Sue Watkins called with news that it was all official now: Today she'd signed her contract with Prentice-Hall for the publication of* Conversations With Seth.*)*

Good evening.

("Good evening, Seth.")

Dictation: This is a continuation of the chapter begun (5): "The Mechanics of Experience."

Organized religion has committed many important blunders, yet for centuries Christianity provided a context accepted by large portions of the known world, in which experience could be judged against very definite "rules" — experience once focused, chiselled, and yet allowed some rich expression as long as it stayed within the boundaries set by religious dogma.

If a man was a sinner, still there was a way of redemption, and the immortality of the soul went largely unquestioned, of course. There were set rules for almost all kinds of social encounters and religious experiences. There were set ceremonies accepted by nearly all for death and birth, and the important stages in between. Church was the authority, and the individual lived out his or her life almost automatically structuring personal experience so that it fit within the accepted norm.

Within those boundaries, certain kinds of experience flourished, and of course others did not. In your society there is no such overall authority. The individual must make his or her own way through a barrage of different value systems, making decisions that were largely unthought of when a son followed his father's trade automatically, for example, or when marriages were made largely for economic reasons.

So your present experience is quite different than that of those forefathers who lived in the medieval world, say, and you cannot appreciate the differences in your [present] subjective attitudes, and in the quality, as well as the kind of, social intercourse that exists now. For all its many errors, at its best Christianity proclaimed the ultimate meaning for each person's life. There was no question but that life had meaning, whether or not you might agree as to the particular meaning assigned to it.

(9:35.) Men's dreams were also different in those times, filled far more with metaphysical images, for example, more alive with saints and demons — but overall one framework of belief existed, and all experience was judged in its light. Now, you have far more decisions to make, and in a world of conflicting beliefs, brought into your living room through newspapers and television, you must try to find the meaning of your life, or the meaning of life.

(Pause.) You can think in terms of experiments. You may try this or that. You may run from one religion to another, or from religion to science, or vice versa. This is true in a way that was impossible for the masses of the people in medieval times. The improved methods of communication alone mean that you are everywhere surrounded by varying theories, cultures, cults, and schools. In some important

areas this means that the mechanics of experience are actually becoming more apparent, for they are no longer hidden beneath one belief system.

(9:43.) Give us a moment ... Your subjective options are far greater, and yet so of course is the necessity to place that subjective experience into meaningful terms. If you believe that you do indeed form your own reality, then you instantly come up against a whole new group of questions. If you actually construct your own experience, individually and en masse, why does so much of it seem negative? You create your own reality, or it is created for you. It is an accidental universe, or it is not.

(Pause.) Now in medieval times organized religion, or organized Christianity, presented each individual with a screen of beliefs through which the personal self was perceived. Portions of the self that were not perceivable through that screen were almost invisible to the private person. Problems were sent by God as punishment or warning. The mechanics of experience were hidden behind that screen.

Now: The beliefs of [Charles] Darwin and of [Sigmund] Freud[3] alike have formed together to give you a different screen. Experience is accepted and perceived only as it is sieved through that screen. If Christendom saw man as blighted by original sin, Darwinian and Freudian views see him as part of a flawed species in which individual life rests precariously, ever at the beck and call of the species' needs, and with survival as the prime goal — a survival, however, without meaning. The psyche's grandeur is ignored, the individual's sense of belonging with nature eroded, for it is at nature's expense, it seems, that he must survive. One's greatest dreams and worst fears alike become the result of glandular imbalance, or of neuroses from childhood traumas.

Yet in the midst of these beliefs each individual seeks to find a context in which his or her life has meaning, a purpose which will rouse the self to action, a drama in whose theme private actions will have significance.

There are intellectual values and emotional ones, and sometimes there are needs of an emotional nature that must be met regardless of intellectual judgments. The church provided a cosmic drama in which even the life of the sinner had value, even if only to show God's compassion. In your society, however, the sterile psychic environment often leads to rebellion: People take steps to bring meaning and drama into their lives, even if intellectually they refuse to make the connection.

Take your break.

(9:59. Jane wasn't too surprised that Seth had returned to his book, since before the session she'd thought he would. Yet, she'd been "a bit nervous, even if it is dumb or stupid: I still wonder if I can do it after a layoff. The stuff isn't anything like I thought I'd get, though. . . ." It seemed incredible to us now that the last book session had been held over nine months ago.

(I told her it was fun to get the dictation, that it reminded me that there are other things in life besides personal sessions. It also reminded me of how good the material could be in its more generalized context, and that there were available from Seth reservoirs of information that we'd never be able to fully explore, simply because of our ages and other time-related limitations. My thoughts brought up feelings of regret, of course, but Jane suggested that instead we concentrate upon what we could do. Good advice.

(Resume at 10:07.)

When God went out the window for large masses of people, fate took His place *(long pause),* and volition also became eroded.

A person could neither be proud of personal achievement nor blamed for failure, since in large measure his characteristics, potentials, and lacks were seen as the result of chance, heredity, and of unconscious mechanisms over which he seemingly had little control. The devil went underground, figuratively speaking, so that many of his mischievous qualities and devious characteristics were assigned to the unconscious. Man was seen as divided against himself — a conscious figurehead, resting uneasily above the mighty haunches of unconscious beastliness. He believed himself to be programmed by his heredity and early environment, so that it seemed he must be forever unaware of his own true motives.[4]

Not only was he set against himself, but he saw himself as a part of an uncaring mechanistic universe, devoid of purpose, intent, and certainly a universe that cared not a whit for the individual, but only for the species. Indeed, a strange world.

(Pause.) It was in many respects a new world, for it was the first one in which large portions of humanity believed that they were

isolated from nature and God, and in which no grandeur was acknowledged as a characteristic of the soul. Indeed, for many people the idea of the soul itself became unfashionable, embarrassing, and out of date. Here I use the words "soul" and "psyche" synonymously. That psyche has been emerging more and more in whatever guise it is allowed to as it seeks to express its vitality, its purpose and exuberance, and as it seeks out new contexts in which to express a subjective reality that finally spills over the edges of sterile beliefs.

The psyche expresses itself through action, of course, but it carries behind it the thrust from which life springs, and it seeks the fulfillment of the individual — and it automatically attempts to produce a social climate or civilization that is productive and creative. It projects its desires outward onto the physical world, seeking through private experience and social contact to actualize its potentials, and in such a way that the potentials of others are also encouraged. It seeks to flesh out its dreams, and when these find no response in social life, it will nevertheless take personal expression in a kind of private religion of its own.

Give us a moment . . . Basically, religion is an activity through which man attempts to see the meaning of his life. It is a construction based on deep psychic knowledge. No matter what the name it might go by, it represents man's connection with the universe.

End of dictation. For now, a few notes.

(10:27. Seth came through with half a page of information for Jane — personal material that's deleted here — then ended the session at 10:34 P.M. "I'm so unsure of myself it must be terrible," Jane said as soon as she came out of trance. "I'm so glad he's back on the book again. I keep asking: 'Is it good, is it good?' I know it is, but I've got that empty feeling again, because of the suspense. . . .")

NOTES: SESSION 831

1. Jane and I had suggested to Sue last month (September) that she write a book on ESP class, although at various times previously the three of us have discussed such a project. Sue took us up on the idea this time, though — and was both exhilarated and terrified when Tam, who was instantly enthusiastic, asked her for an outline and a couple of chapters. "Doing the outline for the book came easily," Sue wrote for this note, later, "but then I spent the next four weeks in hell. The writing of the first chapter was agonizing and slow. . . ." After that initial plunge, though, she's been doing very well.

2. My brief description of the copyediting process can be found in the last paragraph of Note 2 for Session 801.

3. A reminder: Sigmund Freud (1856–1939) was the Austrian physician who founded psychoanalysis.

4. Once again, see my comments on "selfish genes" in Note 3 for Session 821.

SESSION 832, JANUARY 29, 1979
9:11 P.M. MONDAY

(Jane and I have been attending to the mechanics of publishing affairs more than ever since she held the 831st session two weeks ago [on January 15]. During the first week of that time off from sessions we worked steadily at checking the copyedited manuscript for Psyche. *In the meantime, the copyedited manuscript for* Emir *arrived on the 18th, sent to us by Eleanor Friede at Delacorte Press; and since* Emir *is a short book, we were able to go over it during one evening and get it in the mail back to Eleanor late the next day. I sent* Psyche *to Tam Mossman at Prentice-Hall on the 22nd, and on the same day we received from him the page proofs for* Seven Two. *We spent two days of concentrated labor studying those, and I returned them to Tam on the 24th. Then Jane, in a typical burst of inspiration the next day, began writing her third Seven book:* Oversoul Seven and the Museum of Time.

(This evening's session was of average length for recent ones — lasting about an hour and a half, including break — but Seth devoted only the first short portion of it to Mass Events.*)*

Now: Good evening. Dictation.

("Good evening, Seth.")

In your society, it is generally thought that a person must have a decent livelihood, a family or other close relationships, good health, and a sense of belonging if the individual is to be at all productive, happy, or content.

Better social programming, greater job opportunities, health plans or urban projects, are often considered the means that will bring fulfillment "to the masses." Little if anything is said about the personality's innate need to feel that his life has purpose and meaning. Little is said about the personality's innate desire for drama, the kind of inner spiritual drama in which an individual can feel part of a purpose that is his own, and yet is greater than himself.

There is a need within man to feel and express heroic impulses. His true instincts lead him spontaneously toward the desire to better the quality of his own life and that of others. He must see himself as a force in the world.

Animals also dramatize. They possess emotions. They feel a part of the drama of the seasons. They are fully alive, in those terms. Nature in all of its varieties is so richly encountered by the animals that it becomes their equivalent of your structures of culture and civilization. They respond to its rich nuances in ways impossible to describe, so that their "civilizations" are built up through the inter-weavings of sense data that you cannot possibly perceive.

They know, the animals, in a way that you cannot, that their private existences have a direct impact upon the nature of reality. They are engaged, then. An individual can possess wealth and health, can enjoy satisfying relationships, and even fulfilling work, and yet live a life devoid of the kind of drama of which I speak — for unless you feel that life itself has meaning, then each life must necessarily seem meaningless, and all love and beauty end only in decay.

When you believe in a universe accidentally formed, and when you think you are a member of a species accidentally spawned, then private life seems devoid of meaning, and events can seem chaotic. Disastrous events thought to originate in a god's wrath could at least be understood in that context, but many of you live in a subjective world in which the events of your lives appear to have no particular reason — or indeed sometimes seem to happen in direct opposition to your wishes. . . .

What kind of events can people form when they feel powerless, when their lives seem robbed of meaning — and what mechanics lie behind those events?

End of dictation for now. I have a few notes. . . .

(*9:34. Those "notes," however, dealing with other matters, ran for several more pages before Seth said good night at 10:38* P.M.

(*I told Jane that I think Seth's material on the animals' sense equivalents of human civilizations is the best of its kind I've ever heard — most evocative indeed. I hope Seth comes through with more on the subject before he finishes* Mass Events.)

SESSION 833, JANUARY 31, 1979
9:21 P.M. WEDNESDAY

(Jane has been having great fun in recent days, working on her new [and third] novel about the adventures of Oversoul Seven.)

Now: Dictation.

People die for "a cause" only when they have found no cause to live by. And when it seems that the world is devoid of meaning, then some people will make a certain kind of statement through the circumstances connected with their own deaths.

We will shortly return to a discussion of such "causes," and their relationship with the person's feeling that life has or does not have a meaning.

For now, consider a very simple act. You want to walk across the room and pick up a paper, for example. That purpose is simple and direct enough. It automatically propels your body in the proper fashions, even though you are not consciously aware of the inner mechanisms involved. You do not imagine the existence of blocks or impediments in your way, in the form of additional furniture placed in your path by accident, fate, or design. You make a simple straight path in the proper direction. The act has meaning because it is something you want to do.

There are purposes not nearly as easy to describe, however, intents of a psychological nature, yearnings toward satisfactions not so easily categorized. Man experiences ambitions, desires, likes and dislikes of a highly emotional nature — and at the same time he has intellectual beliefs about himself, his feelings, and the world. These are the result of training, for you use your mind as you have been taught.

One person may desire fame, and even possess certain abilities that he or she wants to use, and that will indeed lead to that claim. Such a person may also believe that fortune or fame leads to unhappiness, licentiousness, or in some other way brings about disastrous conditions. Here we have a clear purpose to use abilities and receive acclaim. We also have another quite opposing clear purpose: to avoid fame.

There are people who want children and mates, and have those excellent qualities that would serve them well as parents. Some of those same individuals may be convinced that love is wrong, however, or that sex is debasing, or that children mean the end of youth. Such persons may then find themselves breaking off good relationships with those of the other sex for no apparent reason, or forcing the other party to break with them. Here again we have two clear purposes, but they oppose each other.

Those who believe in the ultimate meaning of their lives can withstand such pressures, and often such dilemmas, and others like them, are resolved in an adequate-enough fashion. Disappointments, conflicts, and feelings of powerlessness can begin to make unfortunate inroads in the personalities of those who believe that life itself has little meaning. Such people begin to imagine impediments in their paths as surely as anyone would who imagined that physical barriers were suddenly put up between them and a table they wanted to reach at the end of the room.

(9:40.) When you simply want to reach a destination in space, there are maps to explain the nature of the land and waterways. When we are speaking of the psychological role of destinations, however, there is more to consider.

Once more — *(humorously:)* that will save you from scratching out another "again," "however," or whatever — your body is mobilized when you want to move. It responds to your intent and purpose. It is your private inner environment, psychically speaking. Your psychological intents instantly mobilize your energies on a psychic level. You have what I will call for now "a body of thought," and it is that "body" that constantly springs into action at your intent.

When you want to go downtown, you know that destination exists, though you may be miles away from it. When you want to find a mate you take it for granted that a potential mate exists, though where in space and time you do not know. Your intent to find a mate sends out "strands of consciousness," however, composed of desire and intent. Like detectives, these search the world, looking in a completely different way than a physical sleuth. The world is probed with your characteristics in mind, seeking for someone else with characteristics that will best suit your own. And whatever your purpose is, the same procedure on a psychic level is involved.

The organization of your feelings, beliefs, and intents directs the focus about which your physical reality is built. This follows with impeccable spontaneity and order. If you believe in the sinfulness of the world, for instance, then you will search out from normal sense data those facts that confirm your belief. But beyond that, at other levels you also organize your mental world in such a way that you attract to yourself events that — again — will confirm your beliefs.

Death is a part of you, even as birth is. Its import varies according to the individual — and in a certain fashion, death is your last chance to make a statement of import in any given life, if you feel you have not done so earlier.

Some people's deaths are quiet periods. Some others' are exclamation points, so that later it can be said that the person's death loomed almost greater in importance than the life itself. Some people die in adolescence, filled with the flush of life's possibilities, still half-dazzled by the glory of childhood, and ready to step with elation upon the threshold of adulthood — or so it seems. Many such young persons prefer to die at that time, where they feel the possibilities for fulfillment are intricate and endless. They are often idealists, who beneath it all — beneath the enthusiasm, the intelligence, and sometimes beneath extraordinary ability — still feel that life could no more than sully those abilities, dampen those spiritual winds, and darken that promise that could never be fulfilled.

This is not the reason for all such deaths by any means, but there is usually an implied statement in them so that the death seems to have an additional meaning that makes parents and contemporaries question. Such individuals usually choose deaths with a high dramatic content, because regardless of appearances they have not been able to express the dramatic contents of their psyches in the world as it seems to be to them. They turn their deaths into lessons for other people, forcing them to ask questions that would not be asked before. There are also mass statements of the same kind for people come together to die, however, to seek company in death as they do in life. People who feel powerless, and who find no cause for living, can come together then and "die for a cause" that did not give them the will or reason to live. They will seek out others of their kind.

(10:05.) The inner mechanics of emotions and beliefs are complicated, but these are individuals who feel that physical life has failed them. They are powerless in society. They think in black and white, and conflicts between their emotions, and their beliefs about their emotions, lead them to seek some kind of shelter in a rigid

belief system that will give them rules to go by. Such systems lead to the formation of cults, and the potential members seek out a leader who will serve their purposes as surely as they seem to serve his — through an inner mechanics of which each member is at least somewhat aware.

End of dictation. A few remarks.

(10:10. After giving a couple of paragraphs of material for Jane, Seth brought the session to a close at 10:15 P.M. Jane was more than a little surprised at its quick end; her delivery had been steady and forceful. "Gee, I felt like there were reams of material in there — just reams," she exclaimed. "I also felt like I was getting into the Guyana thing, without mentioning it by name. At least I thought I was." We agreed — and hoped — that Seth did seem to be preparing to discuss the Jonestown tragedy for Mass Events.*)*

SESSION 834, FEBRUARY 5, 1979
8:59 P.M. MONDAY

(After supper this evening Jane read some notes I'd written recently, in which I speculated about why I paint portraits — my "heads," as I call them — out of my "imagination," instead of using live models of "real people." I've often wondered if at least some of my motivations for working this way have reincarnational or counterpart[1] inspirations. I remarked tonight that it would be nice if Seth would discuss the subject, and Jane replied that she thought he'd do so.

(That statement, in fact, plus her desire for material from Seth on a question of her own, made her wonder whether we'd even receive any book dictation tonight. Then, no sooner had we sat for the session than Jane asked me to write down what she was about to say, since she had the material available whether or not Seth got to it: "A new part, or chapter heading: 'People Who Are Afraid of Themselves. Controlled Environments, and Positive and Negative Mass Behavior.'" I told her I thought Seth would not only have plenty of time to cover our respective questions, but would come through with some book work too, and this was the case.

(We're presenting his material for me because it has good general application: If Seth deals with my own painted images without even mentioning the words reincarnation or counterparts, still he does reveal how such "residents of the mind" make up part of each person's innate knowledge of his or her own greater — or larger — self.

(Whispering:) Good evening.

("Good evening, Seth.")

About your material, and allied matters.

As I have often said, there are concepts most difficult to explain, particularly concerning the nature of consciousness, for often in your frame of reference certain concepts, quite valid, can appear contradictory so that one will seem to invalidate the other.

I try to strongly state the pristine uniqueness of the individual. I also say that there are no limitations to the self. The two statements can appear to be contradictory. When you are a child, your sense of identity does not include old age in usual experience. When you are an old person, you do not identify yourself as a child. Your sense of identity, then, changes physically through the years. In a way it seems that you add on to yourself through experience, becoming "more than you were before." You move in and out of probable selfhoods, while at the same time — usually with the greatest of ease — you maintain an identity of yourself. The mosaics of consciousness are brilliant to behold.

When I speak of mosaics, you might think of small segments, shining and of different shapes and sizes. Yet the mosaics of consciousness are more like lights, radiating through themselves and through a million spectrums.

The infant sees mental images before birth, before the eyes are open. Your memory, it seems, is your own — yet I have told you that you have a history of other existences. You remember other faces, even though the mind you call the conscious one may not recognize the images from that deep inner memory. It must often clothe them in fantasy. You are yourself. Your self is secure in its own identity, unique in its characteristics, meeting life and the seasons in a way that has never happened before, and will never happen again — yet still you are a unique version of your greater self. You share in certain overall patterns that are in themselves original.

It is as if you shared, say, a psychological planet, populated by people who had the same roots, the same ground of being — as if you shared the same continents, mountains, and oceans. Instead you share certain patterns of development, images, memories, and desires. These are reflected in your physical life, and in one way or another elements of your life are shared in the same fashion.

(9:15.) Your [painted] faces represent such a recognition. You always thought (underlined twice) that your artistic talent should be enough. You thought (underlined twice) that it should be your consuming passion, but you never felt that it was — for if it was you would have followed it undeviatingly. *(Long pause.)* For you, painting had to be wedded to a deeper kind of understanding. Painting was even to be a teacher, leading you through and beyond images, and back to them again.

Your painting was meant to bring out from the recesses of your being the accumulation of your knowledge in the form of images — not of people you might meet now on the street, but portraits of the residents of the mind. The residents of the mind are very real. In a certain fashion, they are your parents more than your parents were, and when you express their realities, they are also expressing yours. All time is simultaneous. Only the illusion of time on each of your parts keeps you from greeting each other. To some extent, when you paint such portraits you are forming psychic bridges between yourself and those other selves: Your own identity as yourself grows.

Only in a manner of speaking (repeated twice), there are certain — *(humorously:)* a necessary qualifying word — "power selves," or personalities; parts of your greater identity who utilized fairly extraordinary amounts of energy in very constructive ways. That energy is also a part of your personality — and as you paint such images you will undoubtedly feel some considerable bursts of ambition, and even exuberance. The feelings will allow you to identify the images of such personalities.

(*"Well, I think I felt that way last week, when I was working on my latest head. That's why I wrote those notes — but I didn't take the time to discuss them with Jane."*)

That is why I mentioned it. I knew you did not tell Ruburt. The paint brush can indeed be a key to other worlds, or course. Your own emotional feelings carry over in such paintings.

(9:29.) Give us a moment . . . By all means encourage the dream activity, and there will be a correspondence between your dreams, your painting and your writing.[2] Each one encourages the others. Your writing gains vitality from your painting, your painting from your writing — and the dreaming self at one time or another is in contact with all other Aspects — capital "A" — of your reality.

(9:31. Now Seth came through with some material in answer to Jane's question, before calling for a break at 9:38. Resume at 9:56.)

Dictation: If you cannot trust your private self, then you will not trust yourself in your relationships with others or in society.

If you do not trust your private self, you will be afraid of power, for you will fear that you are bound to misuse it. You may then <u>purposefully</u> *(leaning forward, quietly emphatic but with some amusement)* put yourself in a position of weakness, while all of the time claiming that you seek influence. Not understanding yourself, you will be in a quandary, and the mechanics of experience will appear mysterious and capricious.

There are certain situations, however, in which those mechanics can be clearly seen, and so let us examine some such circumstances. *(Pause.)* A few that I discuss may be exaggerated, in that they are not "normal" conditions in most people's lives. Their rather bizarre nature, however, throws a giant spotlight upon intents, purposes, and cross-purposes, that too often appear in the lives of quite normal men and women.

When people are convinced that the self is untrustworthy, for whatever reasons, or that the universe is not safe, then instead of luxuriating in the use of their abilities, exploring the physical and mental environments, they begin to pull in their realities — to contract their abilities, to overcontrol their environments. They become frightened people — and frightened people do not want freedom, mental or physical. They want shelter, a definite set of rules. They want to be told what is good and bad. They lean toward compulsive behavior patterns. They seek out leaders — political, scientific *(humorously)*, or religious — who will order their lives for them.

In the next portion of this book we will discuss people who are frightened of themselves, then, and the roles that they seek in private and social behavior. To some extent we will be discussing closed environments, whether mental or physical, in which questioning becomes taboo and dangerous. Such environments may be private, as in the case of persons with what are generally called mental disorders, or they may be shared by many, in — for example — mass paranoia.

There are religious cults, and there are also scientific ones. There are people who follow a cult that is purely private, with rules and regulations as rigorous as any sent down to a group of frightened followers by a despot of whatever kind. Such conditions exist, and I hope that such a discussion will lead to greater understanding. A large portion of this book will be devoted, of course, to the introduction of concepts that will privately encourage greater productivity and creativity, and therefore automatically contribute to more healthy and sane social ways.

Now: The headings Ruburt gave: This [next] will be Part 3: "People Who are Frightened of Themselves."

Part 2 should go after Chapter 2, [and should be] called: "Framework 1 and Framework 2."

The other heading he gave helps make up the title for the next chapter *(6)*. Add to it: "Religious and Scientific Cults, and Private Paranoias."

End of session.

("Okay.")

Do you have questions?

("No, I guess not.")

Then I bid you a fond good evening.

("Thank you, Seth."

(End at 10:15 P.M.)

NOTES: SESSION 834

1. In Volume 2 of *"Unknown" Reality* Seth began developing his theory of counterparts — that the larger psychological self, or entity, of each of us manifests not just one physical life in any given century, say, but several, so as to gain that much more experience in a variety of roles involving different ages, nationalities and languages, sexual orientations, family roles, and so forth. As I understand the counterparts thesis, the individual may or may not meet at least some of his or her counterparts, scattered as they can be among earth's different countries and cultures. Jane and I have encountered a few of our respective counterparts, however, principally through her now-defunct ESP class.

2. Seth mentioned a "correspondence" among my dreams, painting, and writing because just lately I've been doing small oil paintings of a few of my more vivid dream images. I've discovered that this is great fun — and much more challenging than I'd anticipated, as I try to reduce the shifting, brilliant dream elements to the motionless painted surfaces we're so used to in waking reality. Each little painting becomes a unique adventure both technically and emotionally, and I hardly succeed in solving every attempt I make. Now, futilely, I wonder why I didn't try painting images from my dreams at a much earlier age; and why one so seldom hears about other artists doing the same thing. I don't personally know any other artist working with dreams this way.

PART THREE

PEOPLE WHO ARE FRIGHTENED OF THEMSELVES

CHAPTER 6

CONTROLLED ENVIRONMENTS, AND
POSITIVE AND NEGATIVE MASS BEHAVIOR.
RELIGIOUS AND SCIENTIFIC CULTS,
AND PRIVATE PARANOIAS

SESSION 812, OCTOBER 1, 1977
9:33 P.M. SATURDAY

(W*hen he originally gave us the 812th session some 16 months ago, Seth told us it would "be part of a chapter later in the book. . . ." [See my opening notes for Session 814.] The 812th session was held following an encounter Jane and I had with an unexpected visitor, although these excerpts aren't personal at all. They fit in well with material in* Mass Events, *however — indeed, as soon as Seth confirmed Jane's headings for Part 3 and Chapter 6, we knew that we'd found the place to present this material. We made our decision without consulting Seth, by the way.*

(Whispering:) Good evening.

("Good evening, Seth.")

Now: Subject: Paranoia, and its manifestations.

Paranoia is extremely interesting because it shows the ways in which private beliefs can distort events that connect the individual with other people. The events are "distorted," yet while the paranoid is convinced that those events are valid, this does not change other people's perception of the same happenings. . . .

What I want to emphasize here is the paranoid's misinterpretation of innocuous personal or mass events, and to stress the ways in which physical events can be put together symbolically, so that from them a reality can be created that is almost part physical and part dream.

You must of course interpret events in a personal manner. You create them. Yet there is also a meeting ground of more or less shared physical encounters, a sense plateau that offers firm-enough footing for the agreement of a mass-shared world. With most mental aberrations, you are dealing with people whose private symbols are so heavily thrust over prime sense data that even those data sometimes become almost invisible. These individuals often use the physical world in the way that most people use the dream world, so that for them it is difficult to distinguish between a private and a publicly-shared reality.

Many such people are highly creative and imaginative. Often, however, they have less of a solid foundation than others in dealing with a mass-shared reality, and so they attempt to impose their own private symbols upon the world, or to form a completely private world. I am speaking in general terms now, and in those terms such people are leery of human relationships. Each person forms his or her own reality, and yet that personal reality must also be shared with others, and must be affected by the reality of others . . .

Now give us a moment . . . As creatures dwelling in time and space, your senses provide you with highly specific data, and with a cohesive-enough physical reality. Each person may react to the seasons in a very personalized manner, and yet you all share those natural events. They provide a framework for experience. It is up to the conscious mind to interpret sense events as clearly and concisely as possible. This allows for the necessary freedom of action for psychological and physical mobility. You are an imaginative species, and so the physical world is colored, charged, by your own imaginative projections, and powered by the great sweep of the emotions. But when you are confused or upset, it is an excellent idea to return your attention to the natural world as it appears at any given moment — to sense its effect upon you as separate from your own projections.

You form your own reality. Yet if you are in the Northeast in the wintertime, you had better be experiencing a physical winter *(humorously)*, or you are far divorced from primary sense data.

The paranoid has certain other beliefs. Let us take a hypothetical individual — one who is convinced he has a healthy body, and is proud of mental stability. Let us call this friend Peter.

Peter [for his own reasons] may decide that his body is out to get him and punish him, rather than, say, the FBI. He may symbolically pick out an organ or a function, and he will misinterpret many body events in the same way that another may misinterpret mass events. Any public service announcements, so-called, publicizing symptoms connected with his sensitive area, will immediately alarm him. He will consciously and unconsciously focus upon that part of the body, anticipating its malfunction. Our friend can indeed alter the reality of his body.

Peter will interpret such body events in a negative fashion, and as threatening, so that some quite normal sensations will serve the same functions as a fear of policemen, for example. If he keeps this up long enough, he will indeed strain a portion of the body, and by telling others about it he will gradually begin to affect not only his personal world, but that part of the mass world with which he has contact: It will be known that he has an ulcer, or whatever. In each case we are dealing with a misinterpretation of basic sense data.

When I say that a person misinterprets sense data, I mean that the fine balance between mind and matter becomes overstrained in one direction. There are, then, certain events that connect the world. Though when everything is said and done these events come from outside of the world's order, nevertheless they appear as constants within it. Their reality is the result of the most precise balancing of forces so that certain mental events appear quite real, and others are peripheral. You have dusk and dawn. If in the middle of the night, and fully awake, you believe it is sunrise in physical terms, and cannot differentiate between your personal reality and the physical one, then that balance is disturbed.

The paranoid organizes the psychological world about his obsession, for such it is, and he cuts everything out that does not apply, until all conforms to his beliefs. An examination of unprejudiced sense data at any point would at any time bring him relief.

Take your break. A note: This will be part of a chapter, later in the book, on mass events.

(10:31. Now Seth left this material to go into a discourse for Jane. He ended the session at 11:30 P.M.)

SESSION 835, FEBRUARY 7, 1979
9:11 P.M. WEDNESDAY

(Jane was very relaxed before the session — and for a better understanding of her special kind of relaxation, see the opening notes for the 829th session.)

Good evening.

("Good evening, Seth.")

Chapter 6 — headings as given last time *(in Session 834).*

There is an enchanting suggestion, solemnly repeated many times, particularly after the turn of the century: "Every day, in every way, I am getting better and better."[1]

This might sound like a bit of overly optimistic, though maybe delightful, nonsense. To a degree, however, that suggestion worked for millions of people. It was not a cure-all. It did not help those who believed in the basic untrustworthiness of their own natures. The suggestion was far from a bit of fluff, however, for it could serve — and it did — as a framework about which new beliefs could rally.

We often have in your society the opposite suggestion, however, given quite regularly: "Every day, in every way, I am growing worse, and so is the world." You have meditations for disaster, beliefs that invite private and mass tragedies. They are usually masked by the polite clothing of conventional acceptance. *(Pause.)* Many thousands may die in a particular battle or war, for example. The deaths are accepted almost as a matter of course. These are victims of war, without question. It seldom occurs to anyone that these are victims of beliefs *(emphatically)* — since the guns are quite real, and the bombs and the combat.

The enemy is obvious. His intentions are evil. Wars are basically examples of mass suicide — embarked upon, however, with all of the battle's paraphernalia, carried out through mass suggestion, and through the nation's greatest resources, by men who are convinced that the universe is unsafe, that the self cannot be trusted, and that strangers are always hostile. You take it for granted that the species is aggressively combative. You must out-think the enemy nation before you yourself are destroyed. These paranoiac tendencies are largely hidden beneath man's nationalistic banners.

"The end justifies the means." This is another belief, most damaging. Religious wars always have paranoiac tendencies, for the fanatic always fears conflicting beliefs, and systems that embrace them.

(Pause.) You have occasional epidemics that flare up, with victims left dead. Partially, these are also victims of beliefs, for you believe that the natural body is the natural prey of viruses and diseases over which you have no personal control, except as it is medically provided. In the medical profession, the overall suggestion that operates is one that emphasizes and exaggerates the body's vulnerability, and plays down its natural healing abilities. People die when they are ready to die, for reasons that are their own. No person dies without a reason.[2] You are not taught that, however, so people do not recognize their own reasons for dying, and they are not taught to recognize their own reasons for living — because you are told that life itself is an accident in a cosmic game of chance.

(9:33.) Therefore, you cannot trust your own intuitions. You think that your purpose in life must be to be something else, or someone else, than you are. In such a situation many people seek out causes, and hope to merge the purposes of the cause with their own unrecognized one.

There have been many great men and women involved in causes, to which they gave their energies, resources, and support. Those people, however, recognized the importance of their own beings, and added that vitality to causes in which they believed. They did not submerge their individuality to causes. Instead, they asserted their individuality, and became more themselves. They extended their horizons, pushed beyond the conventional mental landscapes — driven by zest and vitality, by curiosity and love, and not by fear (*all of the above with much emphasis*).

Many people lost their lives recently in the tragedy of [Jonestown] Guyana. People willingly took poison at the command of their leader. No armies stood outside the grounds. No bombs fell. There was no physical virus that spread through the multitude. There was no clothing to decorate the mechanisms of events. Those people succumbed to an epidemic of beliefs, to an environment [that was] closed mentally and physically. The villains consisted of the following ideas: that the world is unsafe, and growing deadly; that the species itself is tainted by a deadly intent; that the individual has no power over his or her reality; that society or social conditions exist as things in themselves, and that their purposes run directly counter to the fulfillment of the individual; and lastly, that the end justifies the means, and that the action of any kind of god is powerless in the world.

The people who died were idealists — perfectionists of exaggerated quality, whose very desire for the good was tainted and distorted by those beliefs just mentioned. For those beliefs must gradually shut out perception of good from experience.[3]

Man is of good intent. When you see evil everywhere in man's intent — in your own actions and those of others — then you set yourself up against your own existence, and that of your kind. You focus upon the gulf between your ideals and your experience, until the gulf is all that is real. You will not see man's good intent, or you will do so ironically — for in comparison with your ideals, good in the world appears to be so minute as to be a mockery.

(9:56.) To this extent experience becomes closed. Such people are frightened of themselves, and of the nature of their existence. They may be intelligent or stupid, gifted or mundane, but they are frightened of experiencing themselves as themselves, or of acting according to their own wishes. They help create the dogma or system or cult to which they "fall prey." They expect their leader to act for them. To a certain extent he soaks up their paranoia, until it becomes an unquenchable force in him, and he is their "victim" as much as his followers are his "victims."

In the Guyana affair, you had "red-blooded Americans" dying on a foreign shore *(in South America),* but not under a banner of war, which under certain circumstances would have been acceptable. You did not have Americans dying in a bloody revolution, caught among terrorists. You had instead Americans succumbing in a foreign land to some beliefs that are peculiarly American, and home-grown.

Beside the list given earlier [tonight], you have the American belief that money will solve almost any social problem, that the middle-class way of life is the correct "democratic" one, and that the difficulty between blacks and whites in particular can be erased by applying social bandages, rather than by attacking the basic beliefs behind the problem.

Many young men and women have come to adulthood in fine ranch houses in good neighborhoods. They would seem to be at the peak of life, the product of the best America has to offer. They never had to work for a living, perhaps. They may have attended colleges — but they are the first to realize that such advantages do not necessarily add to the quality of life, for they are the first to arrive at such an enviable position.

The parents have worked to give their children such advantages, and the parents themselves are somewhat confused by their children's attitudes. The money and position, however, have often been attained as a result of the belief in man's competitive nature — and that belief itself erodes the very prizes it produces: The fruit is bitter in the mouth. Many of the parents believed, quite simply, that the purpose of life was to make more money. Virtue consisted of the best car, or house or swimming pool — proof that one could survive in a tooth-and-claw world. But the children wondered: What about those other feelings that stirred in their consciousnesses? What about those purposes they sensed? The hearts of some of them were like vacuums, waiting to be filled. They looked for values, but at the same time they felt that they were themselves sons and daughters of a species tainted, at loose ends, with no clear destinations.

They tried various religions, and in the light of their opinions of themselves their earlier advantages seemed only to damn them further. They tried social programs, and found a curious sense of belonging with the disadvantaged, for they were also rootless. The disadvantaged and the advantaged alike then joined in a bond of hopelessness, endowing a leader with a power they felt they did not possess.

(Long pause at 10:14.) They finally retreated into isolation from the world that they knew, and the voice of their leader at the microphone was a magnified merging of their own voices. In death they fulfilled their purposes, making a mass statement. It would make Americans question the nature of their society, of their religions, their politics, and their beliefs.

(Long pause in an intent delivery.) Each person decided to go along on that course.

End of session unless you have questions.

(10:17. "Do you want to say something about Jane?" I asked. Seth promptly came through with two lines of encouraging material for her. Then:)

End of session.

(With a laugh: "Okay."

(10:19 P.M. "I'm still that way, quite a bit," Jane said as soon as she came out of trance; she referred to her very beneficial and relaxed condition. "Right now my right temple, my right knee and my right foot are all going whooosh, whooosh, whooosh. . . ." And I can add that her relaxed state enhances her session material each time.)

NOTES: SESSION 835

1. Seth cited the same famous autosuggestion from the work of the French psychotherapist, Emile Coué (1857–1926), in Chapter 4 of *Personal Reality,* and then as now, he was correct except for the first two words. He should have said: "Day by day, in every way, I am getting better and better." In a note for *Personal Reality* I wrote that "Coué was a pioneer in the study of suggestion, and wrote a book on the subject in the 1920s. His ideas were well received in Europe at the time, but weren't in this country to any large degree. In fact, his lecture tour of the United States turned out to be a failure because of the hostile press reaction."

2. See Note 3 for Session 802, and Note 2 for Session 805.

3. After this session, I was rather surprised when Jane told me that the Jonestown tragedy was an emotionally charged subject for her, and that Seth knew it. I should have known it, too. She explained that it was disturbing for her "because the whole thing is an example of how a mad visionary can lead his people to destruction in the name of religion." Involved in her feelings, of course, are her own youthful conflicts with the Roman Catholic Church; these led to her abandoning organized religion by the time she was 18. Involved also are her adamant feelings against having the Seth material used as the basis for any kind of cult, with herself as its leader. Hence, she's continually examining Seth's revelatory material — and her own — with very critical eyes to make sure she isn't "a self-deluded nut leading people astray." Religious fanaticism frightens her because she regards it as being but a short step beyond fundamentalism, which is on the upsurge in this country. See Seth's material on evolution and fundamentalism in Session 829.

Jane laughed when I asked her why she hadn't told me of her feelings about Jonestown before: "You never asked me." She hadn't meant to be secretive, she added, but had simply accepted her attitudes as being based upon her own strong beliefs. The mass deaths at Jonestown (in November 1978) took place during our long layoff from book dictation, but Seth began discussing the affair almost at once in our private material, as Jane described in her own portion of the opening notes for Session 831. Now she told me that Seth introduced the subject in that manner so that later she'd be more at ease dealing with it for *Mass Events*.

SESSION 840, MARCH 12, 1979
9:28 P.M. MONDAY

(Almost five weeks have passed since Seth gave the 835th session. He's come through with four more sessions since then, too — the last three of them growing out of the unexpected death of our young cat, Billy, on February 28. Let me try to put that unhappy event in perspective now, in the continuing chronology of our lives as they're enmeshed in the Seth material in general and in Mass Events *in particular.*

(First, on February 12, five days after the 835th session was held, Jane and I received from Prentice-Hall the page proofs for Volume 2 of "Unknown" Reality. *Checking those 499 pages, word for word against our carbon copy of the original manuscript, called for the most demanding concentration on our parts for the next 13 days.*

(When I arose early on the 26th so that I could wrap the proofs for mailing, however, I noticed that Billy didn't appear to feel well. Jane watched him while I went to the post office. He was no better when I returned, and as the morning passed we came to realize that he had a urinary problem. That afternoon I took him to the veterinarian, who kept him for treatment; the problem was serious; by then the cat was in great pain. Jane and I both wondered: Why Billy? Why should such a seemingly perfect young creature suddenly become that sick, for no observable reason? "We were shocked,[1] no doubt about it," I wrote in my notes for the 836th session, a private or non-book one which Jane gave that evening. During the session Seth discussed Billy's illness to some extent, while also giving the first "installment" of an answer to a longstanding question of mine: I was curious about the relationship between the host — whether human, animal, or plant — and a disease it might contract, one that was "caused," say, by a virus. I'll return to the question at the end of these notes.

(On Tuesday the veterinarian told us by telephone that Billy was better, that "probably" we could take him home the following afternoon; I was to

call before making the drive across town, though. Wednesday afternoon, then, an hour before I was due to check, the phone rang. The thought of our vet flashed into my mind, naturally enough. And it was he, regretfully explaining that Billy had died an hour or so before. The doctor had left the office to make a call. When he returned he found Billy dead in his cage. He didn't know why the cat had died. . . . We felt badly indeed — yet that night Jane insisted upon holding the 837th session.[2]

(The events of our lives kept on unfolding. On the next day, March 1, the page proofs for Seth's Psyche *arrived from the publisher, but we could see that going over that much shorter book would be easy compared to our protracted labors for Volume 2 of "Unknown" Reality. The day after that, a dear friend brought us two six-week-old kittens, littermates fresh from a nearby farm. At once Jane and I named them Billy Two and Mitzi: Billy Two, obviously, because he was also a tiger cat and bore a strong resemblance to the dead Billy; Mitzi because with her longer, black and white fur she at once reminded me of the Mitzi who'd belonged to the Butts's next-door neighbors when I was a child. The two cats had lived only in a gloomy barn so far, and were so shy they hid under our living-room couch for several days.*

(On March 5 the frontmatter proofs for Volume 2 — consisting of items like the table of contents, a poem of Jane's, the titles of her previous books, and so forth — arrived for checking; we expect to see the proofs for Volume 2's index in a couple of weeks. That night Jane gave the 838th session. Wednesday, I mailed to Prentice-Hall the corrected page proofs for Psyche, *and Jane held the 839th session that evening.*

(Now for my question about viruses, referred to earlier in these notes.

("What," I wrote for the 836th session, "is the real *relationship between the host organism and disease?" Recently Jane and I talked about the evident worldwide eradication of smallpox, as announced earlier this month by WHO — the World Health Organization — and wondered if the disease has truly been eliminated. [WHO won't officially declare smallpox done away with for a year or so, while waiting to see if any new cases surface.] Or would smallpox appear again, say 10 years from now? Obviously, I said to Jane more than once, if as an entity smallpox could "think" as we do, it would hardly consider itself bad, or such an awful disease or scourge. If it was so terrible, why did it ever exist within nature's framework to begin with? What was its role in the whole panoply of life forms? Could the "disease" ever move from whatever probability it now occupies back into our own*

reality some day, thus appearing to have regenerated itself? What would we humans say if that happened? Smallpox's reappearance would undoubt-edly be rationalized: It had lain hidden or dormant in some uninvestigated pocket of humanity; or it was a mutation, somehow "evolving" into small-pox from one of the closely related animal poxes.

(In that same session, Seth gave these responses — among others — to my question:

("All viruses of any kind are important to the stability of your planetary life. They are a part of the planet's biological heritage and <u>memory</u>. *You cannot eradicate a virus, though at any given time you destroy every member alive of any given strain. They exist in the earth's memory, to be recreated, <u>as they were before, whenever the need arises.</u>*

("The same applies of course to any animal or plant considered extinct. Only an objectively tuned consciousness like man's would imagine that the physical eradication of a species destroyed its existence."

(Seth also touched upon the question while dealing mainly with Billy's death in the next three sessions, which are also private, but this evening he was more specific. Even though he didn't call this 840th session book dicta-tion, we're presenting part of it here because the material fits in so well with his themes for Mass Events.)

Now: Good evening.

("Good evening, Seth.")

(Vigorously:) You could not live without viruses, nor could your biological reality as you know it now exist.

(Pause.) Viruses appear to be "the bad guys," and as a rule you think of them separately, as for example the smallpox virus. There are overall affiliations in which viruses take part, however, in which delicate balances are maintained biologically. Each body contains countless viruses that could be deadly at any given time and under certain conditions. These — and I am putting it as simply as possible — take turns being active or inactive within the body, in accordance with the body's overall condition. Viruses that are "deadly" in certain stages are not in others, and in those later stages they react biologi-cally in quite beneficial ways, adding to the body's stability by bring-ing about necessary changes, say, in cellular activities that are helpful at given rates of action. These in turn trigger other cellular changes, again of a beneficial nature.

As an example from another field, consider poisons. Belladonna can be quite deadly, yet small doses of it were known to aid the body in disease conditions.[3]

(9:38.) Give us a moment ... The viruses in the body have a social, cooperative existence. Their effects become deadly only under certain conditions. The viruses must be triggered into destructive activity, and this happens only at a certain point, when the individual involved is actively seeking either death or a crisis situation biologically.

The initial contagion in such cases is always emotional and mental. Social conditions are usually involved, so that an individual is, say, at the lower end of a poor social environment (pause), a seeming victim of it, or in a situation where his individual value as a social member is severely weakened.

Now: In the same way that a member of such a society can go [askew], blow his stack, go overboard, commit antisocial acts, so in the same fashion such a person can instead trigger the viruses, wreck their biological social order, so that some of them suddenly become deadly, or run [amok]. So of course the resulting diseases are infectious. To that degree they are social diseases. It is not so much that a virus, say, suddenly turns destructive — though it does — as it is that the entire cooperative structure within which all the viruses are involved becomes insecure and threatened.

I told you (in the private 836th session) that viruses mutate. Such is often the case. It seems quite scientific to believe in inoculations against such dangerous diseases — and certainly, scientifically, inoculations seem to work: People in your time right now are not plagued by smallpox, for example. Some cultures have believed that illnesses were caused by demons. Medicine men, through certain ceremonies, would try to rid the body of the demons — and those methods worked also. The belief system was tight and accepted, and it only began to fail when those societies encountered "civilized views."

If you call the demons "negative beliefs," however, then you have taken strides forward. People continue to die of diseases. Many of your scientific procedures, including inoculations, of themselves "cause" new diseases. It does not help a patient inoculated against smallpox and polio if [eventually] he dies of cancer as a result of his negative beliefs.[4]

(9:55.) Give us a moment ... What I have said about viruses applies to all biological life. Viruses are "highly intelligent" — meaning that they react quickly to stimuli. They are responsive to emotional states. They are social. Their scale of life varies considerably, and some can be inactive for centuries, and revive. They have extensive memory patterns, biologically imprinted. Some can multiply in the tens of thousands within seconds. They are in many ways the basis of biological life, but you are aware of them only when they show "a deadly face."

You are not aware of the inner army of viruses within the body that protect it constantly. Host and virus both need each other, and both are part of the same life cycle.

Now give us a moment ... One brief note: Ruburt was momentarily upset before the session — cranky. He thought he did not feel like having a session at 9:30 P.M. to try to solve the world's problems. He just wanted to watch television and forget it all, and hidden in that crankiness is a good point: The sessions are an expression of your private and joint curiosity, a high and excellent curiosity about the nature of reality, a result of your desire to know; to know whether or not the knowledge can be held in your hands like a fruit, whether or not the knowledge can be dosed out to an ailing world as medicine.

I surely understand that you want to make the knowledge practical in the physical world, and to help people as much as you can, but that cannot be the only goal — for that goal must always be the high personal exploration of consciousness, the creative and artistic pursuit for which there may be no name. You do not make shoes to put on people's feet. You do not make deodorants to stop perspiration. If you did either of these things, you could see material results — material results — at once: people with shoes of your making, and people who did not sweat (*with some humor*). (In parentheses: Such deodorants are highly disadvantageous, incidentally.)

You are not dealing with material specifics, or even with the psychic specifics. You are dealing instead with the initiation of a framework of beliefs far better than those now current — a framework that is large enough to <u>contain</u> all specifics, through which people can indeed learn to understand themselves better. You are providing an overall aura of spiritual and intellectual light which would help people precisely because you are not <u>tied</u> to specifics, but engaged with the larger levels of reality from which the specifics emerge . . .

(*10:10.*) Give us a moment. . . .

(*After a long pause, Seth launched into a good bit of material that was outside of any related to his subject matter for* Mass Events. *He said good night at 10:26 P.M.*)

Notes: Session 840

1. We were shocked because Billy's unexpected — and serious — illness reminded us of the almost universally accepted view that life is terribly vulnerable. Any kind of life. Billy was a replacement for our previous cat, Willy (who'd died in November 1976 at the age of 16), and we'd found him at an animal shelter the next weekend after Willy's death; as far as having a pet to love went, we'd thought ourselves "set" for a number of years. At first we'd called the newcomer Willy Two, but soon automatically shortened that to Billy.

During the 836th session, Seth reminded us that "animals do not 'think' of long lives or short lives, but of a brilliant present, <u>which in a way</u>, compared to your framework, has no beginning or end . . . time, in your terms, does not exist for them — and in the <u>deepest of terms</u>, a life's quality on a human scale cannot be judged primarily in terms of its length, either."

I might add here another insight into the relationship between Jane and Seth — the kind of information we continue to search for. Before holding the 836th session, Jane had found herself mourning the possibility that Billy might die. From Seth she then picked up material to the effect that "time was in the present to the cat . . . in a way its life was eternal to it, whether it lived 10 months or 10 years, or whatever." At the time (she wrote later for me) emotionally she objected strenuously to that message of Seth's, since "it seemed too easy a way to sign off a cat's life — or any other life — even if it was true. And I did accept that it was true, or as close to the truth as we could get . . .

"Years ago such spontaneous objections of mine really bothered me," she continued, "and I'd sit and mentally argue with Seth so that the session didn't begin right away; it only started after I mentally shut up. Rob said I'd never told him this before, when I mentioned it as we got ready for the (836th) session. It just hadn't ever occurred to me, I guess."

2. In the 837th session Seth dealt mostly with Billy's death. It wasn't that the loss of "just a cat" was the only thing involved in our deep upsets (although Billy's death came first in our reactions); we also felt a host of emotional and intellectual ramifications arising from that event. We still couldn't believe Billy was gone for good. This effect was heightened because we had no body to "prove" his death to us. I hadn't gone after him: The ground was frozen so I couldn't bury him in the back yard beside Willy, and the veterinarian had agreed to dispose of the remains for us.

We'd felt the same way when Willy had died three years ago, and now — as she had then — Jane said sadly: "If I could answer our questions about that cat's death, maybe I could answer our questions about everything. . . ."

We're still trying to get answers, with the help of the Seth material. I don't mind noting that I think that with Seth, Jane *has* achieved some understanding of our species' larger questions about life and death. Seth went into those questions while talking about Billy in sessions 837–39, but his material is much too long to print in *Mass Events* — and even too long to touch upon the highlights in any adequate way. There follow a few quotations from the material he gave us in those private sessions, however. We hope they'll indicate some of the directions his answers took, about those intimate challenges that concern us all.

From Session 837 for February 28, held on the evening of the day Billy died: "My dear friends: Existence is larger than life or death. Life and death are both states of existence. An identity exists whether it is in the state of life or in the state of death. Your cat's consciousness never was dependent upon its physical form. Instead, the consciousness was itself choosing the experience of cathood. There was nothing that said: 'This consciousness must be a cat.'

"Billy belonged in another probability, and in a fashion you switched probabilities for him, though without his consent, when you took him from the animal shelter, where he would have soon been 'done away with.' His three years with you represented a grace period for him. . . . He did not make this probability his own because of what you may call 'other commitments' — or rather, other purposes.

"There is no such thing as a cat consciousness, basically speaking, or a bird consciousness. In those terms, there are instead simply consciousnesses that choose to take certain focuses. We have not touched upon some of these matters, and some are, again, most difficult to explain, as we wish to avoid distortions. These would have nothing to do with Ruburt *per se,* but simply the way you put concepts together at this stage of development."

From Session 838 for March 5: "I want to avoid tales of the transmigration of the souls of men to animals, say — a badly distorted version of something else entirely. If there is no consciousness 'tailored' to be a cat's or a dog's, then there is no prepackaged, predestined, particular consciousness that is meant to be human, either . . .

"You both knew Billy was about to die. So did the plants in your house, and the trees outside your door. The cellular announcement was made that the strong possibility existed, for the birth and death of each cell is known to all cells in the world. . . ." (For material on cellular communication, see Session 804 after 10:45.)

"Cellular communication is too fast for you to follow. The cat could have changed its mind, of course, but the signals were sent out, and ahead of time. [Several people who wrote to you] picked up on that probability. . . ." With some amazement Jane and I had noticed this in letters we received — from both friends and strangers — during the days immediately following Billy's death.

From Session 839 for March 7: "The quality of identity is far more mysterious than you understand, for you assign an identity in a blanket fashion, say, to each living thing. Now your dead cat, Billy, exists in the following manner:

"The units of consciousness that organized to form his identity as you knew it, still form that pattern — but not physically. The cat exists as itself in the greater living memory of its own 'larger' selfhood. Its organization — the cat's — exists inviolately, but as a part of the greater psychic organization from which it came.

"That identity of Billy's remains vital, known to itself whether or not it is reactivated in your terms. This is not necessarily always the case — and there is great variation — but Billy identified with 'the larger organization' of the litter [that is, with his brothers and sisters, all of whom are also dead], and the consciousnesses of that litter are now together. They are forming a gestalt, where the five consciousnesses will merge to form a new identity."

On separate days, both Jane and I had vivid psychic experiences involving our perceptions of Billy not long after his death: Each in our own way, we saw him "larger than life," performing with amazing vitality and grace. In my own case, the experience was so vivid as to be almost frightening. Jane hopes to use both events, plus some material she wrote on scientific experimentation with animals, in one of her own books.

And in closing: The index for Volume 2 of *"Unknown" Reality* will contain (when that book is published) a comprehensive list of references to Seth's discussions of his units of consciousness, or CU's, as presented in both volumes of that work.

3. Belladonna is a perennial herb native to Europe. Extracts made from it contain the alkaloid atropine (among others), which is used to relieve muscle spasms, and to dilate the pupil of the eye for optical surgery.

It's interesting to note, also, that in medieval Europe larger amounts of those extracts were used as hallucinogens by witches and the members of various other cults.

4. See Note 3 for Session 802, and Note 2 for Session 805.

SESSION 841, MARCH 14, 1979
9:08 P.M. WEDNESDAY

(*Seth hadn't called the last session book dictation, nor did he so desig-nate tonight's material. Just as we did with that 840th session, however, Jane and I are presenting portions of this evening's delivery in* Mass Events *because we think they should be published within that framework.*

(Whispering:) Good evening.

(Good evening, Seth.")

Now: I said, in book dictation, I believe *(in the 835th session),* that the people of Jonestown died of an epidemic of beliefs — or words to that effect. I used words to that effect.

The case was startling, again, because of the obvious suicidal acts. The poison was, after all, left as evidence. Had the same number of people been found dead *(pause)* of a vicious disease — smallpox or whatever — the virus involved would have been the villain. I want to discuss thoughts and viruses, along with the health of the body.

You think of viruses as physical, and of thoughts as mental. You should know that thoughts also have their physical aspects in the body, and that viruses have their mental aspects in the body. At times you have both asked why an ailing body does not simply assert itself and use its healing abilities, throwing off the negative influence of a given set of beliefs and thoughts.

When you think of thoughts as mental and viruses as physical, the question is understandable. It is not just that thoughts influence the body, as of course they do; but each one of them represents a triggering stimulus, bringing about hormonal changes and altering the entire physical situation at any given time.

(Pause at 9:16.) Your physical body . . . give us time . . . is, as an entity, the fleshed-out version — the physically alive version — of the body of your thoughts. It is not that your thoughts just trigger chem-ical reactions in the body, but that your thoughts have a chemical reality besides their recognizable mental aspects. I will have to use an analogy. It is not the best, but I hope it will get the point across: It is as if your thoughts turned into the various appendages of your body. *(Emphatically:)* They have an invisible existence within your body as surely as viruses do. Your body is composed not only of the stuff within it that, say, X-rays or autopsies can reveal, but it also involves

profound relationships, alliances and affiliations that nowhere physically show. Your thoughts are as physically pertinent to your body as viruses are, as alive and self-propagating, and they themselves form inner affiliations. Their vitality automatically triggers *(long pause, eyes open)* all of the body's inner responses. When you think thoughts, they are conscious. You think in sentences, or paragraphs, or perhaps in images. Those thoughts, as clearly as I can explain this, rise from inner components of which you are unaware.

When the thought is thought, it is, say, broken down again to those components. Your thoughts have an emotional basis, also. The smallest c-e-l-l *(spelled)* within your body contributes to that emotional reality, and reacts instantly to your thoughts.

(9:28.) Give us a moment . . . In those terms, thoughts move far quicker of course than viruses. The action of the virus follows the thought. Each thought is registered biologically. Basically (underlined), when you have an immunity to a disease you have a mental immunity.

You think of viruses as evil, spreading perhaps from country to country, to "invade" scores of physical mechanisms. Now thoughts are "contagious." You have a natural immunity against all thoughts that do not fit in with your own purposes and beliefs, and naturally *(pause, groping)*, you are "inoculated" with a wholesome trust and belief in your own thoughts above others. The old ideas of voodooism recognized some of these concepts, but complicated and distorted them with fears of evil, psychic invasion, psychic killing, and so forth. You cannot divide, say, mental and physical health, nor can you divide a person's philosophy from his bodily condition.

Give us a moment . . . While I say all of this about thoughts and viruses, remember the context of the discussion, for new information and insights are always available to an individual from Framework 2, and the body does indeed send its own signals.

Do you have any questions on that material?

("No, I'd like to study it first.")

The people who died at Jonestown believed that they must die. They wanted to die. How could their thoughts allow them to bring about their [bodily deaths]? Again, the question makes sense only if you do not realize that your thoughts are as physically a part of your body as viruses are *(intently)*.

(9:37. After discussing several other matters, Seth ended the session at 10:05 p.m. One of those "other matters," however, led to Note 1.)

NOTES: SESSION 841

1. In Note 1 for the 840th session I cited an insight we'd recently obtained into the relationship between Jane and Seth, and mentioned how we're always on the lookout for such clues. Jane had come up with that one, stressing her personal reactions. We're also eager to learn what we can about Jane or Seth *per se.* Tonight, then, in the deleted portion of the session, Seth gave us insights into his own personality. With humor, much power, and a touch of irony:

"I am not such a philosopher that I can compare my own thoughts and works with those of the noted professionals of whom [your correspondent writes]. I think I am — if you will forgive me — in my own way more earthy than those other gentlemen.

"I am — again in my way — more rambunctious and playful. The word 'truth' is a heavy one, and the more times it is repeated the more distant and inaccessible it seems. I do not put labels on my own theories, and I explain — or I try to explain — my most 'profound' statements by adding a dash of zest, a smidgen of humor, an egotistical touch of humility. I consider myself an exuberant psychological explorer, finding myself, at my own request, happily set adrift among universes, able to shout with a loud hearty voice from the hypothetical shore of one to another, news of what I have found and am still finding."

SESSION 844, APRIL 1, 1979
4:01 P.M. SUNDAY

(The last session we presented in Mass Events, *the 841st, was held on March 14. On the 19th we received from our publisher for checking the proofs of the index for Volume 2 of "*Unknown*" Reality, then two days later the proofs for the front matter of* Psyche *arrived. Going over these two sets of material was routine; nothing had to be returned, and in each case Jane called Tam Mossman at Prentice-Hall to give her approval and to make a few suggestions for changes. She's worked each day at her third novel on the adventures of* Oversoul Seven, *and has heard often from Sue Watkins about Sue's progress with her book on Jane's ESP class:* Conversations With Seth.[1] *And with all of her other activities, Jane has held four sessions since the 14th: two personal ones, and two [842–43] on matters other than book dictation.*

(Early last Wednesday an ominous development began unfolding at Three Mile Island, the nuclear power generating plant located on an island in the Susquehanna River below Harrisburg, Pennsylvania. It seems that through a combination of mechanical failures and human error, Unit No. 2, one of the plant's two nuclear reactors, overheated, discharging radioactive water into the river, and began releasing small amounts of radioactive gases into the atmosphere. [The entire plant is idle now, since Unit No. 1 had already been shut down for refueling.] By now the situation is much more serious, however: There's a chance of catastrophic "meltdown" of the uranium fuel rods in the damaged reactor's core — the worst possible accident that can occur in such circumstances short of an explosion, and a kind that proponents of nuclear power have long maintained "almost certainly cannot happen." If the meltdown takes place, spewing great clouds of radioactive materials into the atmosphere, several hundred thousand people could ultimately become casualties in one form or another.

(Now there's talk of evacuating up to a million people who live in the counties surrounding Three Mile Island. Some refugees have already reached the Elmira area, where we live, and upon checking a map Jane and I were surprised to see that we're only about 130 airline miles north of Harrisburg. We've driven the much longer road distance comfortably enough in one day. "Strange," I mused to Jane, "that of all the nuclear power plants in the world, we end up living that close to the one that goes wrong. . . ."

(Our region is supposed to be outside the danger zone — yet we see conflicting newspaper reports about whether the prevailing wind currents would make us vulnerable to the after-effects of a meltdown. Even now, local civil defense officials monitor the air several times daily with radiological survey meters — equipment similar to Geiger counters. Jonestown was far away, remote in another land, I said to Jane, but the potential mass tragedy at Three Mile Island hovers at the edges of our personal worlds. The whole affair has a sense of unreal immediacy, because there's nothing to see, and because I don't think most people really understand the probabilities involved. It would be hardly a coincidence, I added, that the mass events at Jonestown and Three Mile Island took place within less than six months of each other, and that they represented the two poles, or extremes, of mankind's present main belief systems: religion and science.

(Certainly we hope that as he continues with Mass Events *Seth will comment extensively on Three Mile Island, just as he's in the process of doing about Jonestown. In fact, material on Three Mile Island developed in*

the session held this afternoon, which is the main reason we decided to give these excerpts here.

(Actually, the session might better be called a Jane/Seth session, in that Jane's own consciousness was often uppermost, riding upon Seth's underlying and steadying influence. This rather unusual situation came about because after lunch today she wrote excellent analyses of two dreams I'd had recently. As we sat at the kitchen table discussing her work, Jane felt that she could go into a trance state that was her own for a change, instead of being in "just" a Seth trance. She began delivering the material at a measured pace in her usual voice. As soon as I realized that she wanted to have a session I asked her to wait until I found my pen and notebook. Then Jane proceeded to come through with much evocative material on dreams — our second reason for excerpting the session for Mass Events. *Some of the more generalized material is presented below, some of the more individualized portions [which, in fact, came at the start of the session] are given in Note 2.*

(After drinking half a glass of milk during a break, Jane resumed her delivery at 4:30:)

This is just loose now. But I've got a couple of points to make . . .

One is that because objects just originate in man's imagination anyway, there's always a strong connection between objects and man's dreams. They act as symbols of inner reality, so it's only natural that whether he's aware of it or not, man perceives objects in such a fashion that they also stand for symbols that first originate in his dreams.

This also has to do with large events, that you might for convenience's sake think of for now as psychological objects — that is, events seen and recognized by large numbers of people in the same way that objects are.

The Christ drama is a case in point, where private and mass dreams were then projected outward into the historical context of time, and then reacted to in such a way that various people became exterior participants — but in a far larger mass dream that was then interpreted in the most literal of physical terms. Even while it was, it also got the message across, though the inner drama itself was not recalled; and as the dream merged with historical events, and as it was interpreted by so many, its message also became distorted — or rather, it mixed and merged with other such dreams, whose messages were far different.

Look at your nuclear-reactor troubles at the plant by Harrisburg (Three Mile Island). The entire idea of nuclear power was first a dream — an act of the imagination on the part of private individuals — and then through fiction and the arts, a dream on the part of many people. Instantly, probabilities spun out from that dream in all directions, vast potentials and dangers.

It was hardly a coincidence that this particular situation arrived in the social climate first of all portrayed in a movie.

Nuclear power stands for power, plain and simple. Is it good or bad? It stands in man's dreams as belonging to God: the power of the universe *(intently)*. Man has always considered himself, in your terms, as set apart from nature, so he must feel set apart from nature's power — and there must be a great division in his dreams between the two. Nuclear energy in fact, then, comes as a dream symbol, and emerges into the world as something to be dealt with.

Fundamentalists think of nuclear power as a force that God might use, say, to destroy the world. That event in Harrisburg means one thing to them. Some of the scientists equate nuclear power with man's great curiosity, and feel that they wrest this great energy from nature because they are "smarter than" nature is — smarter than nature, smarter than their fellow men — so they read those events in their own way. The probabilities are still surging, of course, and in private and mass dreams people try out all kinds of endings for that particular story.

All in all, millions of people are involved, who will be affected of course to one extent or another.

(4:45. "I've learned something this afternoon," Jane said during a brief, unannounced break. "I've thought of it before, but finally I'm getting it through my head that the sessions are much better when I don't have any concern — and when I feel concern, I find it harder to get into it. I began to get cautious toward the end there, in some fashion . . . I think we'd have gotten more on the nuclear thing otherwise." She didn't think any fear of making predictions that might turn out to be wrong had anything to do with this concern.

("I remember he — Seth — even helped me out with stuff on the Christ drama in there," Jane said. "Oh-oh, there's more — " and she went back into "her" trance almost at once.)

There was a tie-in, and it's that the Christ drama happened as a result of man's dream, at least, of achieving brotherhood — a quiet, secure sense of consciousness, and a morality that would sustain him in the physical world.

The Christ drama did splash over into historical reality. Man's fears of not achieving brotherhood, of not achieving a secure state of consciousness, or a workable morality, result in his dreams of destruction, however they are expressed. And indeed, the present physical event as it exists now at the energy plant near Harrisburg can easily be likened to — and is — a warning dream to change man's actions.

(End at 4:47 P.M. "Okay," Jane said. "I knew there was some connection between the Christ thing and what's happening in the world today, and that was it. I like it when it's fun, and that was fun. That was a nice smooth state of consciousness.

("I should mention a couple more things, though. This happened at a time of day when I'm not usually at my best — around 4 in the afternoon. And I'll often get things like I did the first part of this session, when I was busy with the dishes. I'll notice it, then say to myself that I'll tell Rob later . . . So I wonder how often I've missed out on some good stuff by doing it that way. Especially when I even forget to tell you about it. . . .")

NOTES: SESSION 844

1. Sue has to do a considerable amount of research for *Conversations With Seth*, incidentally, especially locating, then interviewing — in person, by telephone or by mail, as the case may be — numerous class members. Many of them are scattered about the country by now, and some are abroad. Sue has also devised a questionnaire to be filled out by those cooperating in her study.

2. Much of Jane's trance material on how individuals use dreams personally came through in answer to a question of mine that we'd often speculated about lately: If most people do not remember their dreams most of the time, of what use can their dreams be to them? The question was really based upon our belief, indeed our certainty, that everything in nature is intentional and useful; therefore dreams must fulfill important roles in people's lives — but how, in ordinary terms? Here are quotations from the answers Jane gave while in trance today:

"Even if you don't consciously remember your dreams, you do get the message. Part of it will appear in your daily experience in one way or another — in your conversation or daily events.

"Because dreams are such a perfect combination of stimuli from the inner environment and the exterior environment, other events are often used to trigger inner dream messages, just as the opposite occurs. And in a gathering of three people watching the same TV drama, say, each of them might be interpreting different portions of the program so that those portions correlate with their individual dreams of the night before, and serve to bring them their dream messages in ways they can accept . . .

"Great discrimination is used to do that; for example, one newspaper item is noticed over others because a certain portion of that item represents some of the dream's message. Another portion might come from a neighbor — but from the dreamer's interpretation of the neighbor's remarks, that further brings home the dream message. In such cases the individual will scarcely be aware that a dream is involved . . .

"You might dream of going away on a long trip by car, only to find that a tire blew when you were driving too fast. You may never remember the dream. One way or another, however, you will hit upon some kind of situation — a portion of a TV drama, perhaps — in which a tire is blown. Or you will see an item of that nature in the newspaper, or you will hear a story, told directly or indirectly about the same kind of dilemma. The magnitude of the physical stimuli with which you are surrounded makes it possible, of course, for any number of like situations to come to your physical attention during any given day. Even then, you might not recall the dream, but the situation itself as it comes to your attention might make you check your tires, decide to put off your trip, or instead lead you to inner speculations about whether you are going too fast in a certain direction for your own good at this time. But you will get the dream's message."

SESSION 845, APRIL 2, 1979
9:25 P.M. MONDAY

(Although Seth didn't call this session book dictation, Jane and I decided to show portions of it in Mass Events for two reasons: 1. The material in Note 1 can be taken as an extension of the discussion on reasoning and the intuitions that Seth gave in the 825th session. 2. We want to offer his comments on Jonestown and Three Mile Island in the order received, even if they don't always come through within the context of "official" book sessions. This thinking also applies to anything Jane and I may want to add on either of those two mass events.

(Right now, a week after it began to manifest itself, the situation at the crippled nuclear power plant near Harrisburg is still very tense. Small amounts of radiation continue to leak into the atmosphere. Federal nuclear safety advisors call the dilemma "stable," and today the President visited Three Mile Island in an effort to reassure people — yet the chance of a meltdown of the overheated reactor core of Unit No. 2 still exists. We're told that a radioactive and potentially explosive bubble of hydrogen gas, which has been preventing cooling water from reaching the upper portions of the control rods within the reactor's fuel assembly, is now being very slowly and carefully vented into the atmosphere; this is a first step in the bubble's planned dissolution. On March 31, children and pregnant women were advised to evacuate an area within five miles of the plant, and today city and county civil defense directors in eastern Pennsylvania were given plans for a precautionary evacuation of everyone within a 25-mile radius of Three Mile Island. Protection is being planned against looting, which, it is estimated, would begin "two to three hours after the evacuees are gone." Local milk supplies are safe to drink, since dairy cattle are eating corn and hay that's been stored for months, but no one really knows the effects of radiation on the unborn calves being carried by many cows in the plant area. And so the entire country — indeed, the whole world — waits to see what will happen at Three Mile Island,[2] a place not far at all south of where I comfortably sit writing these notes.

(Seth actually delivered the material in Note 1 at the beginning of tonight's session. Then later, after Jane paused in trance at 10:12:)

Do you have questions?

("I haven't had too much time to think of questions, but today we were talking about the relationships between Jonestown and Three Mile Island — how those two events stand for the extremes of religion and science." [See my comments on this double polarity in the opening notes for yesterday's session.])

You are indeed correct, of course, and you are also dealing with the behavior of cults in both circumstances, each concerned with a closed system of belief, rigid attitudes, intense emotionally-charged states, and also with what amounts to compulsive behavior.

The Jonestown people thought that the world was against them, particularly the establishment, and the government of the country. They displayed paranoiac tendencies. The same applies to the scientists, who now feel that the cultural climate is turning against them, that people no longer trust them, so that they fear they will be pulled from high estate.

To some extent (underlined) — a qualified statement, now — the scientists have become somewhat contemptuous of all who do not understand their language: the non-elite. They resent having to get money from the government, from men who are not scientists, and they build up a false sense of comparative omnipotence in response — and that makes them less careful than they should be. They feel misunderstood by the public now.

None of them want any disaster, and yet some of them think it would serve the people right — for then the people might realize that politicians do not understand science, and that the scientists should after all be put in control: "We must have enough money, or who knows what can go wrong?"

The scientific elite could of course present a probability in which a world was created [where] the common man could have little knowledge of its workings. You actually have an excellent set of guards and balances in your country. Now your TV dramas, again, systematically show your old Frankenstein movies just when your scientists are contemplating all kinds of experiments supposed to bring forth life. Hardly a coincidence, for the mass minds of the people are able to make certain joint statements, and those statements are heard.

Do you have any questions?

("I guess not.")

End of session, and a fond good evening.

("Thank you very much."

(10:25 P.M. Now see Note 3 for material on an interesting aftermath to the session.)

NOTES: SESSION 845

1. "Now, for example," Seth told us this evening, "man deals with a kind of dual selfhood, in that he presently thinks of himself as an uneasy blend of body and mind. He identifies primarily with what I call a limited portion of his consciousness. That portion he equates with mind or intelligence. He identifies with events over which he is aware (underlined) of having some control.

"Man thinks of acts, for example, and acting and doing, but he does not identify himself with those inner processes that make acting and doing possible. He identifies with what he thinks of as his logical thought, and the abilities of reasoning. These seem to suggest that he possesses an elegant, cool separation from nature, that the animals for example do not. He does not identify, again, with the processes that make his logical thinking possible. Those processes are spontaneous and 'unconscious,' so it appears that anything outside of his conscious control must be undisciplined or chaotic, and lacking in all logic.

"Both religion and science are based upon such beliefs. Anything that happens spontaneously is looked upon with suspicion. The word seems to suggest elements out of control, or motion that goes from one extreme to another. Only the reasoning mind, it seems, has any idea of order, discipline, or control.

"Man is therefore set against his nature in his own mind, and he thinks he must control it. The fact is that man's consciousness can indeed become aware of — aware of — those spontaneous processes. But he himself has largely closed the door of comprehension, so that he only identifies with what he thinks of as his rational mind, and tries to forget as best he can those spontaneous processes upon which the mind rides so triumphantly.

"He has often become frightened of his own creativity, then, since he has not trusted its source."

2. Jane and I try to understand both the advocates of nuclear power and those who are against it. At the moment we're sure of but one thing: A nuclear reactor meltdown, like that threatened at Three Mile Island, is just not acceptable in our society under any circumstances. The devastation for many years of a large portion of a state like Pennsylvania, say, should not be risked because of economics, fuel shortages, convenience, apathy, or any other reason. Jane and I passionately believe that instead of concentrating primarily upon nuclear power the United States should be making massive efforts to utilize many other sources of energy — at least until the risks and technologies involved with generating nuclear power are understood much more thoroughly. And there are numerous other sources of energy that can be developed. Among them are: cogeneration, the use of waste heat from manufacturing processes to generate electricity; solar radiation; ocean waves; new, more sophisticated methods of burning coal so that it's much less polluting; subterranean heat; the production, from municipal solid wastes, of ethanol (alcohol) as an excellent substitute for gasoline; the burning of biomass — waste materials from the home and farm; various methods of deriving energy from the vast oil shale deposits in our western states; the establishment of "energy farms" of trees and hydrocarbon-generating plants; energy reservoirs of pumped water. We think such alternate sources should be pursued even if they cost *more* in economic terms than nuclear power, either initially or continually, for surely none of them could produce the horrendous results — and enormous costs — that would follow even one massive failure at a nuclear power plant.

Coupled with our reservations about the uncertain state of the art concerning nuclear power, Jane and I deeply mourn the shameful fact that for some 30 years now our country's government and industry have neglected to develop safe methods for the transportation and permanent storage of radioactive waste materials; some of these will remain highly toxic for hundreds of thousands of years, and thus pose potential threats to many many generations. As of now there are no solutions in sight for these extremely vexing scientific and political challenges. There may never be, and failure in these areas alone could ultimately dictate the demise of the entire nuclear endeavor for any peaceful (or even military) use at all.

Ideas about conservation enter in as a result of my comments about alternate sources of energy, of course, and these are related to a number of deep desires that Jane and I have. We want our nation to embark upon programs to cut, and eventually eliminate for all practical purposes, its continually growing dependence upon foreign oil, for we see great risks in an overreliance upon that course of action; we think those hazards should be obvious to everyone since the oil embargo declared against us in 1973 by the countries of the Middle East. This excessive dependence can be done away with eventually, but at considerable sacrifice. Jane and I are more than ready to make those sacrifices; indeed, we live very conservatively even now. We can't conceive of anything more worthwhile than to achieve an independence of spirit that's based upon an independence of means, whether on a personal or national scale. But once it's largely self-sufficient, the United States could really begin to fulfill its role of leadership in the world.

To coin a phrase, then, we see "fantastically great" lessons in the examples given us by Jonestown and Three Mile Island. We want our country and the world to benefit from those lessons, but at the same time we're terribly afraid and concerned that our species won't learn quickly enough. Jane and I want a sane world, in ordinary terms, and we want the freedom to explore every internal and external facet of that world. We want our world — our *living* world, the very planet itself — and every life form upon it, to exist in the greatest cooperative spirit possible, so that individually and collectively we can investigate what surely must be a myriad of still-unsuspected interior and exterior challenges.

3. "After last night's (845th) session," Jane wrote, "I watched television while Rob went for a walk. As I sat there I started to get more from Seth on one of the subjects mentioned in the session. The material came in ideas, though, not in Seth's 'finished copy.' I told Rob about it when he came back, and now this morning I'll see what I can recall for these notes.

"The idea is that the scientists' system of beliefs is bound to result in some destructive action; that is, the implied attitudes of today's scientists lead them to be less careful of life than they should be, and separate them from nature in a way that leads to some contempt on their parts of individual living things. The leaders of religious cults, like that of Jonestown, overexaggerate grandiose ideals of brotherhood and love, for example (as Seth has mentioned), while often forbidding the natural expression of love on the part of one individual for another — assaulting family affiliations and so forth. As a result, the idealized love becomes more and more inaccessible, with the growth of more guilt and despair.

"In the same way the scientific community speaks of grandiose ideals, of man's triumph over the planet and nature. At the same time these ideals further divorce the scientists from daily practical experience with their fellowman; and since they see animals as objects, they're bound to see human life in somewhat the same fashion. The sacrifice of, say, thousands of lives in a nuclear accident almost becomes justified in their minds if it is a means toward the grandiose goal of learning how to 'triumph over nature.' Again, this intent automatically turns them into mechanics.

"The scientist carries the burden of this alienation, and in his *heart* he must hope that his mission fails — for if it succeeds he will have effectively separated man from man's nature in the world of beliefs, philosophically casting man adrift as meaningless psychological debris. Therefore, the scientific community often sabotages its own efforts."

SESSION 846, APRIL 4, 1979
9:30 P.M. WEDNESDAY

(It's over! The crisis at Three Mile Island has passed — or so the governor of Pennsylvania announced on television this morning. That is, the threat of an "immediate catastrophe" from a meltdown in the plant's Unit No. 2 nuclear reactor has evidently passed; engineers have dissipated the hydrogen bubble in the reactor's core, but the core temperature is still considerably above normal, and children and pregnant women are still advised to stay out of the area.

(The challenges — and fears — created at Three Mile Island will last for years, however. Jane and I read that it will take up to four years and many millions of dollars to decontaminate, overhaul, and place the crippled reactor back in operation; the cost is given in incalculable estimates

ranging from $40 million to $400 million. Some government officials say that the reactor may never see service again, that it may end up junked, or as a sealed mausoleum, a mute symbol of our nuclear age. [Nor do we know what fate awaits the plant's undamaged Unit No. 1.] A current fear is that if and when cleanup operations are begun, the small and supposedly harmless amounts of radiation still seeping into the atmosphere may intensify. There's much debate already about the "cancer deaths" that may show up in the local populace, since no one really knows yet just what a "safe" dose of radiation could be in such a situation. And above all, our energy experts maintain that the United States has traveled too far along the nuclear path to turn back now.

(Regardless of whether the events at Three Mile Island have resulted in any significant radioactive fallout so far, they have *generated some disquieting fallout as far as Jane and I are personally concerned. I'll describe the latest of the many courses of action we've found ourselves considering over the years as we work with the Seth material, while trying to keep a balance between the realities we've created for ourselves and the possibilities we constantly encounter in the "outside" world.*

(Jane was quite upset before the session this evening, and I'm the one who was responsible for her state. Somehow, after supper, we got on the subject of Seth doing a "quick book" about Jonestown and Three Mile Island, something that could be offered to the public very soon, instead of material that would show up in a regular Seth book a couple of years from now. We already had the perfect title for the book, one we'd jokingly originated following last Monday night's session: Seth on Jonestown and Three Mile Island: Religious and Scientific Cults.

(I didn't get carried away by the idea this evening, but I was certainly taken with it as we talked. Yet I could see that I confused Jane, for to make such a venture possible we'd have to change certain beliefs and values that are deeply rooted within us; especially those about personal privacy and our reluctance to "go public" with such topical, immediate material, instead of trusting that the Seth material will exert a meaningful influence in society over the long run. Also involved would be the instant criticisms we'd encounter. But I think the main portion of my enthusiasm stemmed from the frustration I often feel because much of Seth's material will go unpublished at this time. This year alone, for instance, he's already given a good amount of excellent information upon a number of nonbook topics — among them the interpretation of dreams; human, animal, and plant consciousness,

and the interactions among them; human sexuality; viruses and inocula-
tion; other realities he himself inhabits, and so forth. We're sorry to think
that such material will be shelved indefinitely, but there's no room for most
of it in Mass Events, *and there probably won't be in future books either. I*
do try to give hints and clues to some of it in this book, though, as I've done
recently in sessions 841 and 844–45.

(At the same time, I told Jane tonight, I wasn't asking that she try for
a fast book because I didn't think she was ready for it, even though I knew
that she — and Seth — could do it. "I wish I had your confidence in me,"
she remarked at one point. "What would happen to Mass Events *in the*
meantime?"

("Nothing," I said. "It would just wait until the Jonestown–Three Mile
Island thing was done. Maybe we'd have sessions almost every night for a
few weeks, or whatever it took. Anyhow, we'd have to check to see whether
our publisher is set up to market a book that quickly, or would even want to."

(I sought to reassure her, but later when I went into her study to ask
about something else, I found her looking quite distressed as she sat at her
typewriter. My words had had more of an impact than I'd intended. I apol-
ogized. But Jane had written some chapter headings, which were very good,
and half a page of commentary for Seth's hypothetical book. Once again I
insisted that I wasn't suggesting she try for the project. Jane believed me,
finally, and in the course of the conversation I learned that she's also been
worrying about which of Seth's recent sessions should be presented in Mass
Events. *She agreed with the decisions I'd made in that area, but she also*
wanted Seth "to get back to the book per se, and call his sessions dictation.

("Well," she finally said after we'd sat for the session, "I guess I'm about
ready. . . ." Then Seth came through without his customary greeting:)

One remark: As far as your participation as of now in our books,
it might be better, Joseph *(as Seth calls me),* if you do not think in
terms of notes so much, but instead in terms of your writing contribution. Do you follow me?

("Yes.")

The change in attitude could be quite helpful to you in many
ways. It should be obvious to you that your own characteristics, interests, attributes, and directions also are partially responsible for the
form the material takes.

The Jonestown and Harrisburg incidents are indeed classic
examples of the meeting places between private and public realities.

I intend to deal with them in depth in *The Individual and the Nature of Mass Events,* where the background, particularly for Frameworks 1 and 2, has already been established.

I am quite willing to hold more sessions a week, and Ruburt *(Jane)* is very capable, particularly in rhythms. Do you follow me?

("Yes." Jane had also told me tonight that she'd particularly enjoyed last Sunday's unscheduled session — both the time of week it had been held, and the time of day. She'd felt free of worry or concern about what she had talked about, as well as from our usual routine.)

Now: Dictation. This is still part of Chapter 6.

(Pause.) The Jonestown disaster happened *(in November 1978)* long after we began this book *(in April 1977).* Just lately another event occurred — a breakdown and near disaster at a nuclear plant near Harrisburg, Pennsylvania. Now in my other books I have rarely commented upon public events of any nature. This manuscript, however, is devoted to the interplay that occurs between individual and mass experience, and so we must deal with your national dreams and fears, and their materializations in private and public life.

In scientific terms there was no fallout involved in the disaster at Jonestown. Yet there was of course a psychological fallout, and effects that will be felt throughout the land by people in all walks of life. The Jonestown situation definitely involved all of the characteristics that I have ascribed as belonging to a cult. There was fanaticism, a closed mental environment, the rousing of hopes toward an ideal that seemed unachievable because of the concentration upon all of the barriers that seemed to stand in its way.

Most cults have their own specialized language of one kind of another — particular phrases used repetitiously — and this special language further serves to divorce the devotees from the rest of the world. This practice was also followed by those at Jonestown. Loyalty to friends and family was discouraged, and so those in Jonestown had left strong bonds of intimacy behind. They felt threatened by the world, which was painted by their beliefs so that it presented a picture of unmitigated evil and corruption. *(Pause.)* All of this should be fairly well recognized by now. The situation led to the deaths of hundreds.

The Harrisburg situation potentially threatened the lives of many thousands, and in that circle of events the characteristics of a cult are less easy to discern. Yet they are present. You have scientific cults as well as religious ones.

Religion and science both loudly proclaim their search for truth, although they are seemingly involved in completely opposing systems. They both treat their beliefs as truths (underlined), with which no one should tamper. They search for beginnings and endings. The scientists have their own vocabulary, which is used to reinforce the exclusive nature of science. Now I am speaking of the body of science in general terms here, for there is in a way a body of science that exists as a result of each individual scientist's participation. A given scientist may act quite differently in his family life and as a scientist. He may love his family dog, for example, while at the same time think nothing of injecting other animals with diseased tissue in his professional capacity.

Granting that, however, cults interact, and so there is quite a relationship between the state of religion, when it operates as a cult, and the state of science when it operates as a cult. Right now your cultish religions exist in response to the cultish behavior of science. Science insists it does not deal with values, but leaves those to philosophers. In stating that the universe is an accidental creation, however, a meaningless chance conglomeration formed by an unfeeling cosmos, it states quite clearly its belief that the universe and man's existence has no value. All that remains is what pleasure or accomplishment can somehow be wrested from man's individual biological processes.

(9:58.) A recent article in a national magazine speaks "glowingly" about the latest direction of progress in the field of psychology, saying that man will realize that his moods, thoughts, and feelings are the result of the melody of chemicals that swirl in his brain. That statement devalues man's subjective world.

(Long pause.) The scientists claim a great idealism. They claim to have the way toward truth. Their "truth" is to be found by studying the objective world, the world of objects, including animals and stars, galaxies and mice — but by viewing these objects as if they are themselves without intrinsic value, as if their existences have no meaning (intently).

Now those beliefs separate man from his own nature.[1] He cannot trust himself — for who can rely upon the accidental bubblings of hormones and chemicals that somehow form a stew called consciousness *(louder and quite ironic)* — an unsavory brew at best, so the field of science will forever escape opening up into any great vision of the meaning of life. *(Long pause.)* It cannot value life, and so in its search for the ideal it can indeed justify in its philosophy the possibility of an accident that might kill many many people through direct or indirect means, and kill the unborn as well.[2]

That possibility is indeed written in the scientific program. There are plans, though faulty ones, of procedures to be taken in case of accident (underlined) — so in your world that probability exists, and is not secret. As a group the scientists rigorously oppose the existence of telepathy or clairvoyance, or of any philosophy that brings these into focus. Only lately have some begun to think in terms of mind affecting matter, and even such a possibility disturbs them profoundly, because it shatters the foundations of their philosophical stance.

(Pause.) The scientists have long stood on the side of "intelligence and reason," logical thought, and objectivity. They are trained to be unemotional, to stand apart from their experience, to separate themselves from nature, and to view any emotional characteristics of their own with an ironical eye. Again, they have stated that they are neutral in the world of values. They became, until recently, the new priests. All problems, it seemed, could be solved scientifically. This applied to every avenue of life: to health matters, social disorders, economics, even to war and peace.

(10:17.) How did such scientific gentlemen, with all of their precise paraphernalia, with all of their objective and reasonable viewpoints, end up with a nuclear plant that ran askew, that threatened present and future life? And what about the people who live nearby?

Give us a moment . . . End of chapter.

NOTES: SESSION 846

1. See sessions 825, 829 (especially at 10:10), and 832, among others.

2. Review the last session, along with Note 3, which Jane wrote.

CHAPTER 7

THE GOOD, THE BAD, AND THE CATASTROPHIC.
JONESTOWN, HARRISBURG, AND
WHEN IS AN IDEALIST A FANATIC?

(10:20.) Chapter 7: "The Good, the Bad, and the Catastrophic. Jonestown, Harrisburg, and When Is an Idealist a Fanatic?"

Give us a moment . . . (Long pause.) That is the end of dictation.

(10:22.) Now Seth came through with some material for Jane and me, including his interpretations — in his usual acute manner — of three of my recent dreams. End at 10:41 P.M.)

SESSION 848, APRIL 11, 1979
9:21 P.M. WEDNESDAY

(See Note 1 for my comments on TMI, or Three Mile Island.

(Jane had said before the 846th session, which she held a week ago, that she wanted Seth "to get back to" book dictation, and Seth had obligingly given the heading for Chapter 7 at the end of the session. Yet in Monday night's deleted 847th session that "energy personality essence," as he calls himself, digressed once again from work on Mass Events to give us more excellent material on plant and animal consciousness. He also discussed such divergent topics as the wide variety of responses that his material generates in correspondents — and not all of those reactions are so favorable, I might add.

(We were very busy with publishing affairs over the weekend. On Friday, April 6, we received from the production department at Prentice-Hall the printer's page proofs of the index for Seth's Psyche, *and on Saturday morning the proofs for* Emir *arrived from Eleanor Friede at Delacorte Press. We spent all of our waking hours checking everything, and on Monday Jane called certain people at Prentice-Hall to give her approval of the index while I mailed* Emir *back to Eleanor.*

(Through all of the mass and personal events referred to in the sessions and notes since she gave the 832nd session on January 29, Jane has occasionally written poetry and painted — and worked steadily at her third Seven *novel:* Oversoul Seven and the Museum of Time. *"I've done 16 chapters so far out of maybe 25 for the book," she said, "but some of them need more work."*

(While eating supper this evening Jane and I watched the television reports on the series of devastating tornadoes that had struck northern Texas and southern Oklahoma — an area known as "Tornado Alley" — late yesterday afternoon. Over 50 people have been counted dead so far, with hundreds injured and many thousands left homeless. We've driven through some of the communities that were damaged. We talked about why people would choose to live in a region where it's practically certain that such storms will materialize every year. Our questions would also apply to living in any dangerous environment on the planet, of course.

(Whispering:) Good evening.

("Good evening, Seth.")

Dictation. *(Loudly:)* Various — this is the beginning of the next chapter *(7)* — the headings were given — various kinds of governments represent the exercise of different aspects of consciousness.

(Pause.) The American experiment with democracy is heroic, bold, and innovative. In historic terms as you understand them, this is the first time that all of the inhabitants of a country were to be legally considered equal citizens one with the other. That was to be, and is, the ideal. In practical terms, of course, there often are inequalities. Treatment in the marketplace, or in society, often shows great divergence from that stated national ideal. Yet the dream is a vital portion of American national life, and even those who are unscrupulous must pay it at least lip service, or cast their plans in its light.

(Long pause.) In the past, and in large areas of the world now, many important decisions are not made by the individual, but by the

state, or religion, or society. In this century several issues came to the forefront of American culture: the exteriorization of organized religion, which became more of a social rather than a spiritual entity, and the joining of science with technology and moneyed interests. Ruburt's book on [William] James would be good background material here, particularly the sections dealing with democracy and spiritualism. In any case, on the one hand each individual was to be equal with each other person. Marriages, for example, were no longer arranged. A man no longer need follow his father's vocational footsteps. Young adults found themselves faced with a multitudinous number of personal decisions that in other cultures were made more or less automatically. The development of transportation opened up the country, so that an individual was no longer bound to his or her native town or region. All of this meant that man's conscious mind was about to expand its strengths, its abilities, and its reach. The country was — and still is — brimming with idealism.

(*Long pause at 9:37.*) That idealism, however, ran smack into the dark clouds of Freudian and Darwinian thought. How could a country be governed effectively by individuals who were after all chemicals run amok in images, with neuroticism built-in from childhood — children of a tainted species, thrown adrift by a meaningless cosmos in which no meaning could be found (*very intently*)?

Organized religion felt threatened; and if it could not prove that man had a soul, it could at least see to it that the needs of the body were taken care of through suitable social work, and so it abandoned many of the principles that might have added to its strength. Instead it settled for platitudes that equated cleanliness (*pause*) with virtue — hence, of course, your deodorant advertisements, and many other aspects of the marketplace (*amused*).

In the public mind, it made little difference whether the devil or tainted genes condemned the individual to a life in which it seemed he could have little control. He began to feel powerless. He began to feel that social action itself was of little value, for if man's evil were built-in, for whatever reasons, then where was there any hope?

There was some hope, at least, in looking for better living conditions personally. There was some hope in forgetting one's doubts in whatever exterior distractions could be found. Idealism is tough, and it is enduring, and no matter how many times it is seemingly slain, it comes back in a different form. So those who felt that religion had failed them looked anew to science, which promised — promised to — provide the closest approximation to heaven on earth: mass production of goods, two cars in every garage, potions for every ailment, solutions for every problem. And it seemed in the beginning that science delivered, for the world was changed from candlelight to electric light to neon in the flicker of an eye, and a man could travel in hours distances that to his father or grandfather took days on end.

And while science provided newer and newer comforts and conveniences, few questions were asked. There was, however, no doubt about it: Exterior conditions had improved (underlined), yet the individual did not seem any happier. By this time it was apparent that the discoveries of science could also have a darker side. Life's exterior conveniences would hardly matter if science's knowledge was used to undermine the very foundations of life itself.

(Pause.) The various potions taken faithfully by the public were now often found to have very unfortunate side effects. The chemicals used to protect agriculture had harmful effects upon people. Such situations bothered the individual far more than the threat of nuclear disaster, for they involved his contact with daily life: the products that he bought, the medicines that he took.

(9:55.) Some people looked, and are looking, for some authority — any authority — to make their decisions for them, for the world seems increasingly dangerous, and they, because of their beliefs, feel increasingly powerless. They yearn toward old ways, when the decisions of marriage were made for them, when they could safely follow in their father's footsteps, when they were unaware of the lure of different places, and forced to remain at home. They have become caught between science and religion. Their idealism finds no particular outlet. Their dreams seem betrayed.

Those people look to cults of various kinds, where decisions are made for them, where they are relieved of the burden of an individuality that has been robbed of its sense of power by conflicting beliefs. At one time the males might have been drafted into the army, and, secretly exultant, gone looking for the period before full adulthood — where decisions would be made for them, where they could mark time, and where those who were not fully committed to life could leave it with a sense of honor and dignity.

In the past also, even in your country, there were convents and monasteries for those who did not want to live in the world as other people did. They might pursue other goals, but the decisions of where to live, what to do, where to go, how to live, would be made for them. Usually such people were joined by common interests, a sense of honor, and there was no retaliation to be feared in this century.

Cults, however, deal primarily with fear, using it as a stimulus. They further erode the power of the individual, so that he is frightened to leave. The group has power. The individual has none, except that the power of the group is vested in its leader. Those who died in Guyana, for example, were suicidally inclined. They had no cause to live for, because their idealism became so separated from any particular actualization that they were left only with its ashes.

The leader of Jonestown was at heart an idealist. When does an idealist turn into a fanatic? *(Long pause.)* When can the search for the good have catastrophic results, and how can the idealism of science be equated with the near-disaster at Three Mile Island, and with the potential disasters that in your terms exist in the storage of nuclear wastes, or in the production of nuclear bombs?

Take your break.

(10:10 to 10:29.)

Now: People who live in tornado country carry the reality of a tornado in their minds and hearts as a psychological background.

To one extent or another, all of the events of their lives happen punctuated or accented by the possibility of disaster. They feel that at any time they might be caused to face the greatest challenge, to rely upon their strongest resources, their greatest forbearance, and faced by a test of endurance. They use — or they often use — such a psychological and physical backdrop to keep those qualities alive within themselves, for they are the kind of people who like to feel pitted against a challenge. Often the existence of probabilities and their acceptance does provide a kind of exterior crisis situation that individually and *en masse* is a symbol of independence and inner crisis. The crisis is met in the exterior situation, and as the people deal with that situation they symbolically deal with their own inner crises. In a way (underlined) those people trust such exterior confrontations, and even count upon a series of them *(intently),* of varying degrees of severity, that can be used throughout a lifetime for such purposes.

Those who survive feel that they have been given a new lease on life, regardless of their circumstances: They could have been killed and were not. Others use the same circumstances as excuses for no longer hanging on to a wish for life, and so it seems that while saving face they fall prey to the exterior circumstances.

I bid you a fond, and even a jolly good evening. And Ruburt's *(Jane's)* material on plants may lead him to some most creative extensions of his own consciousness, and new insights.

("Yes. Good night."

(10:42 P.M. Jane remembered that Seth had mentioned tornadoes, which we hadn't expected him to do. Her delivery in trance has been steady and often quite forceful.

(Seth's reference to her material on plants concerned some short humorous essays she'd started writing for her own amusement a couple of days ago, in response to some new ideas. Her heading for them is tentative: The Plants' Book of People. The Plants' Symposium: People. *I think the pieces are very well done. As she progresses with them Jane doesn't know whether they'll end up as a book, or even whether she'll do anything at all with them. If nothing else, she said now, the ideas could find their way into Seth's material — or else they'd originated in Seth material that was innate within her to start with.)*

NOTES: SESSION 848

1. A few miles below Harrisburg. Three Mile Island, with both of its nuclear reactors off line, or inoperative, sprawls on its island in the Susquehanna River like a wounded behemoth. Engineers are guiding the disabled reactor of Unit No. 2 toward a "cold shutdown," the state in which the temperature of the water in the reactor's primary cooling system drops below the boiling point, pressure is reduced, and the risk of a meltdown of the uranium fuel rods in the reactor core is eliminated. But it will be at least many months before the unit's highly radioactive containment building can be entered for an assessment of damage. In the meantime, Pennsylvania's governor has announced that it's safe for children and pregnant women to return to the area.

The severity of the "event" at Three Mile Island has spurred antinuclear protesters into action in many areas of the country; and the proliferating state, federal, and industry investigations into the accident promise to generate a collective fallout of a kind that's bound to have far more impact on the nuclear power industry, and society, than anything that's come from the crippled plant itself so far. Jane and I believe that eventually this worst accident yet will be seen as a most fortunate occurrence, emphasizing — indeed, as it already has — the great dangers inherent in the growing worldwide emphasis upon nuclear power at this time. We're following the whole affair involving Three Mile Island with the greatest interest, and my clipping file on it grows daily.

SESSION 850, MAY 2, 1979
9:49 P.M. WEDNESDAY

(See Note 1 for more on Three Mile Island.

(Since giving the 848th session for Mass Events, *on April 11, Seth has devoted three sessions to personal affairs that Jane and I have let go for a long time. Then he gave over last Monday night's "regular" 849th session to subjects he's not dealing with in this book.*

(Jane held the session later than usual this evening because at 9:00 we began watching the first half hour of a made-for-television movie that was aired on one of the major networks. Today — just in time — we'd received a letter from a young lady who played a supporting role in the film. We saw her in several scenes, and Jane will be writing to her.

(Whispering:) Good evening.

("Good evening, Seth.")

Dictation:

("Great.")

Give us a moment . . . Let us look at the many forms idealism can take. Sometimes it is difficult to identify idealists, because they wear such pessimistic clothing that all you can see are the patterns of a sardonic nature, or of irony. On the other hand, many who speak most glowingly, in the most idealistic fashions, underneath are filled with the darkest aspects of pessimism and despair. If you are idealists, and if you feel relatively powerless in the world at the same time, and if your idealism is general and grandiose, unrelated to any practical plans for its expression, then you can find yourself in difficulties indeed. Here are a few specific examples of what I mean.

One evening, in this very [living] room, a small group was assembled not too long ago. One visitor, a man from another part of the country, began to speak about the state of the nation, largely condemning all of his countrymen and women for their greed and stupidity. People would do anything at all for money, he said, and as his monologue continued, he expressed his opinion that the species itself would almost inevitably bring about its own destruction.

He cited many instances of nefarious acts committed for money's sake. A lively discussion resulted, but no countering opinion could enter this man's mind. Roger, let us call him, is an idealist at heart, but he believes that the individual has little power in the world, and so he did not pursue his personal idealism in the events of his own life. "Everyone is a slave to the system." That is his line of belief. He took a routine job in a local business and stayed with it for over 20 years, all of the time hating to go to work, or saying that he did, and at the same time refusing to try other areas of activity that were open to him — because he was afraid to try.

He feels he has betrayed himself, and he projects that betrayal outward until betrayal is all that he sees in the socio-political world. Had he begun the work of actualizing his ideals through his own private life, he would not be in such a situation. The expression of ideals brings about satisfaction, which then of course promotes the further expression of practical idealism.

Roger speaks the same way in any social group, and therefore to that extent spreads a negative and despairing aura. I do not want to define his existence by those attitudes alone, however, for when he forgets the great gulf between his idealism and practical life, and speaks about other activities, then he is full of charming energy. That energy could have sustained him far more than it has, however, had he counted on his natural interests and chosen one of those for his life's work. He could have been an excellent teacher. He had offers of other jobs that would have pleased him more, but he is so convinced of his lack of power that he did not dare take advantage of the opportunities. There are satisfactions in his life [however] that prevent him from narrowing his focus even further.

If you want to change the world for the better, then you are an idealist. If you want to change the world for the better, but you believe it cannot be changed one whit, then you are a pessimist, and your idealism will only haunt you. If you want to change the world for the better, but you believe that it will grow worse, despite everyone's efforts, then you are a truly despondent, perhaps misguided idealist. If you want to change the world for the better, and if you are determined to do so, no matter at what cost to yourself or others, no matter what the risk, and if you believe that those ends justify <u>any</u> means at your disposal, then you are a fanatic.

(10:14.) Fanatics are inverted idealists. Usually they are vague grandiose dreamers, whose plans almost completely ignore the full dimensions of normal living. They are unfulfilled idealists who are not content to express idealism in steps, one at a time, or indeed to wait for the practical workings of active expression. They demand immediate action. They want to make the world over <u>in their own images</u> *(louder)*. They cannot bear the expression of tolerance or opposing ideas. They are the most self-righteous of the self-righteous, and they will sacrifice almost anything — their own lives or the lives of others. They will justify almost any crime for the pursuit of those ends.

Two young women visited Ruburt lately. They were exuberant, energetic, and filled with youthful idealism. They want to change the world. Working with the Ouija board, they received messages telling them that they could indeed have a part in a great mission. One young lady wanted to quit her job, stay at home, and immerse herself in "psychic work," hoping that her part in changing the world could be accomplished in that manner. The other was an office worker.

There is nothing more stimulating, more worthy of actualization, than the desire to change the world for the better. That is indeed each person's mission *(intently)*. You begin by working in that area of activity that is your own unique one, with your own life and activities. You begin in the corner of an office, or on the assembly line, or in the advertising agency, or in the kitchen. You begin where you are.

If Roger, mentioned earlier, had begun where <u>he</u> was, he would be a different, happier, more fulfilled person today. And to some extent or other, his effect on all the other people he has met would have been far more beneficial.

When you fulfill your own abilities, when you express your personal idealism through acting it out to the best of your ability in your daily life, then you <u>are</u> changing the world for the better.

Our session is late this evening because Ruburt and Joseph watched the beginning of a *(television)* movie in which a young woman I will call Sarah appeared as an actress. Sarah wrote Ruburt a letter, telling him of the movie. Sarah has abilities, and she is banking on them, developing them in a practical way. She believes that she forms her own reality. She quenched doubts that she was not good enough to succeed, or that it was too difficult to get ahead in show business. The satisfaction of performance leads [her] to more expansive creativity, and to her natural sense of personal power. Through developing those abilities personally, she will contribute to the enjoyment of others. She is an idealist. She will try to bring a greater sense of values to the screen, for example, and she is willing to do the work necessary.

(10:30.) Get our friend some cigarettes. Is your [writing] hand tired?

("Nope.")

A young man from a nearby town came here recently — a highly gifted, intelligent young person. He had not gone to college. He attended a training school, however, and has a fairly technical position in a nearby factory. He is an idealist, given to great plans for developing novel mathematical and scientific systems, and he is highly gifted in that area. He wants to change the world for the better.

In the meantime, he looks with horror and disgust at the older men who have worked there for years, "getting drunk on Saturday nights, thinking only of the narrow world of their families," and he is determined that the same thing will not happen to him. He has been "called down" several times for "things that everyone else does," though he protests that no one else is caught. His mood was despondent. At the same time he did not consider trying to go to college, to get a scholarship or whatever, to better his knowledge in the field of his choice. He doesn't want to leave town, which is the place of his birth, to find a better job; nor does it occur to him to try and understand better the experiences of his fellow workers. He doesn't believe that he can change the world by beginning where he is, and yet he is afraid to count upon his own abilities by giving them a practical form of expression.

Youth is full of strength, however, so he very well may find a way to give his own abilities greater expression, and hence to increase his own sense of power. But in the meantime he is dealing with dark periods of despair.

Idealism also presupposes "the good" as opposed to "the bad," so how can the pursuit of "the good" often lead to the expression of "the bad?" For that, we will have to look further.

There is one commandment above all, in practical terms — a Christian commandment that can be used as a yardstick. It is good because it is something you can understand practically: "Thou shalt not kill." That is clear enough. Under <u>most</u> conditions you know when you have killed. That [commandment] is a much better road to follow, for example than: "You shall love your neighbor as yourself," for many of you <u>do not love yourselves to begin with</u>, and can scarcely love your neighbor as well. The idea is that if you love your neighbor you will not treat him poorly, much less kill him — but the commandment: "Thou shalt not kill," says you shall not kill your neighbor no matter <u>how</u> you feel about him. So let us say in a new commandment: "Thou shalt not kill even in the pursuit of your ideals."[2]

What does that mean? In practical terms it would mean that you would not wage war for the sake of peace. It would mean that you did not kill animals in experiments, taking their lives in order to protect the sacredness of <u>human</u> life. That would be a prime directive: "Thou shalt not kill even in the pursuit of your ideals" — for man has killed for the sake of his ideals as much as he has ever killed for greed, or lust, or even the pursuit of power on its own merits.

You are a fanatic if you <u>consider</u> (underlined) possible killing for the pursuit of your ideal. For example, your ideal may be — for ideals differ — the production of endless energy for the uses of mankind, and you may believe so fervently in that ideal — this added convenience to life — that you considered the hypothetical possibility of that convenience being achieved at the risk of losing some lives along the way. That is fanaticism.

(10:53.) It means that you are not willing to take the actual steps in physical reality to achieve the ideal, but that you believe that the end justifies the means: "Certainly some lives may be lost along the way, but overall, mankind will benefit." That is the usual argument. The sacredness of life cannot be sacrificed for life's convenience, or the quality of life itself will suffer. In the same manner, say, the ideal is to protect human life, and in the pursuit of that ideal you give generations of various animals deadly diseases, and sacrifice their lives.[3] Your justification may be that people have souls and animals do not, or that the quality of life is less in the animals, but regardless of those arguments this is fanaticism — and the quality of human life itself suffers as a result, for those who sacrifice any kind of life along the way lose some respect for all life, human life included. The ends do not justify the means *(all very emphatically).*

Take your break, for a moment.

(10:58. However, break didn't last long enough for me to even lay down my pen. Seth launched into a few paragraphs of material for Jane and me, then ended the session at 11:05 P.M.

(Jane's delivery had been good, almost driving, throughout the session; just about as fast as I could write most of the time. "I'm so glad to get back on the book," she said. "I know I've done it with every Seth book — wondering what he'll talk about, how he'll handle this or that . . . I remember those examples about the idealists, and the new commandment he gave. I didn't have any of that in mind before the session — but at my table tonight I did get some things from him that he never mentioned. . . .")

NOTES: SESSION 850

1. On April 20, technicians managed to lower below the boiling point the temperature of the cooling water in the damaged nuclear reactor at Three Mile Island; this success was achieved just 24 days after the accident began to unfold on March 28. The reactor hasn't reached an ideal "cold shutdown," however, when it will be on a natural circulation of water at atmospheric pressure; that situation will come about when an independent backup cooling system is completed several weeks from now.

Small amounts of radiation are still leaking from the plant, and Pennsylvania and federal health agencies have announced long-range studies of its effects upon the human and animal populations living nearby. At the same time, Jane and I hear and read conflicting and confusing reports on the whole business at TMI. True or false, we wonder: There never was any danger that the bubble of radioactive hydrogen gas in the core of the disabled reactor would explode; there never was any danger of a meltdown of the core's uranium fuel; an act of sabotage against the reactor's primary cooling system set in motion the whole chain of unfortunate events, with their national and worldwide repercussions. . . .

2. Here Seth probably referred to material that Jane and I recently came across concerning the views of a "radical" philosophy of change: Violence is permissible in order to bring about a revolution which, in turn, would lead to a new age. In that utopian society man would be free from restraints and could unify his intellect and intuitions. Many people have held such fashionable views in recent decades. Many still do. We speculated about the inevitable contradictions that would emerge should man ever manage to achieve such an "ideal" state, or society — for, given, his always restless and creative nature, he'd immediately start changing his supposed utopia. With some amusement we also considered the reactions of such radicals should they ever find themselves personally threatened or assaulted through the very "permissible" violence they advocate.

3. Seth referred to the way mice, rats, rabbits, and other animals are raised in laboratory captivity, to be sold to scientific researchers who conduct experiments with them that would be considered "unethical" to do in human beings. Mice, for example, are inbred in a sanitized environment for many generations until genetically "pure" strains are obtained; these ideal "models" for research into human defects may be born with — or develop — obesity, various cancers (including leukemia), epilepsy, different anemias, muscular dystrophy, and so forth. Some are born as dwarfs, or hairless, or with deformed or missing limbs. Inbred mice are also used now to test human environmental hazards.

SESSION 852, MAY 9, 1979
9:39 P.M. WEDNESDAY

(On May 3, the day after she'd delivered the last session, Jane was working on her third Seven novel when she received from Prentice-Hall a dozen complimentary copies of her second Seven: The Further Education of Oversoul Seven. *The book is just off the press.*

(It's almost as though there's an unspoken agreement among Jane, Seth and me — but starting with the 846th session, which was held over a month ago [on April 4], Seth has been dictating material for Mass Events *on Wednesday evenings only.)*

Good evening.

("Good evening, Seth.")

When you are discussing the nature of good and bad, you are on tricky ground indeed, for many — or most — of man's atrocities to man have been committed in misguided pursuit of "the good."

Whose good (question mark)? Is "good" an absolute (question mark)? In your arena of events, obviously, one man's good can be another's disaster. [Adolf] Hitler pursued his version of "the good" with undeviating fanatical intent. He believed in the superiority and moral rectitude of the Aryan race. In his grandiose, idealized version of reality, he saw that race "set in its proper place," as natural master of mankind.[1]

He believed in heroic characteristics, and became blinded by an idealized superman version of an Aryan strong in mind and body. To attain that end, Hitler was quite willing to sacrifice the rest of humanity. "The evil must be plucked out." That unfortunate chant is behind the beliefs of many cults — scientific and religious — and Hitler's Aryan kingdom was a curious interlocking of the worst aspects of religion and science alike, in which their cultish tendencies were encouraged and abetted.

The political arena was the practical working realm in which those ideals were to find fruition. Hitler's idea of good was hardly inclusive, therefore, and any actions, however atrocious, were justified.

How did Hitler's initially wishy-washy undefined ideals of nationalistic goodness turn into such a world catastrophe? The steps were the ones mentioned earlier *(in a number of sessions in Part 3),* as those involved with any cult. Hitler's daydreams became more and more grandiose, and in their light, the plight of his country seemed worsened with each day's events. He counted its humiliations over and over in his mind, until his mind became an almost completely closed environment, in which only certain ideas were allowed entry.

All that was not Aryan, really, became the enemy. The Jews took the brunt largely because of their financial successes and their cohesiveness, their devotion to a culture that was not basically Aryan. They would become the victims of Hitler's fanatical ideal of Germany's good.

Hitler preached on the great value of social action as opposed to individual action. He turned children into informers against their own parents. He behaved nationalistically, as any minor cult leader does in a smaller context. The Jews believed in martyrdom. *(Pause.)* Germany became the new Egypt, in which their people were set upon. I do not want to oversimplify here, and certainly I am nowhere justifying the cruelties the Jews encountered in Germany. You do each create your own reality, however *(intently),* and *en masse* you create the realities of your nationalities and your countries — so at that time the Germans saw themselves as victors, and the Jews saw themselves as victims.

(Pause at 10:00.) Both reacted as groups, rather than as individuals, generally speaking now. For all of their idealisms, both basically believed in a pessimistic view of the self. It was because Hitler was so convinced of the existence of evil in the individual psyche, that he set up all of his rules and regulations to build up and preserve "Aryan purity." The Jews' idea was also a dark one, in which their own rules and regulations were set to preserve the soul's purity against the forces of evil. And while in the Jewish books [of The Old Testament] Jehovah now and then came through with great majesty to save his chosen people, he also allowed them to suffer great indignities over long periods of time, seeming to save them only at the last moment — and this time, so it seemed, he did not save them at all. What happened?

(Long pause.) Despite himself, and despite his followers, Hitler brought to flower *(long pause)* a very important idea, and one that changed your history. *(Pause.)* All of the most morbid of nationalistic fantasies that had been growing for centuries, all of the most grandiose celebrations of war as a nation's inalienable right to seek domination, focused finally in Hitler's Germany.

The nation served as an example of what could happen in any country if the most fanatical nationalism was allowed to go unchecked, if the ideas of right were aligned with might, if any nation was justified in contemplating the destruction of others.

You must realize that Hitler believed that any atrocity was justified in the light of what he thought of as the greater good. To some extent or another, many of the ideals he held and advocated had long been accepted in world communities, though they had not been acted upon with such dispatch. The nations of the world saw their own worst tendencies personified in Hitler's Germany, ready to attack them. The Jews, for various reasons — and again, this is not the full story — the Jews acted as all of the victims of the world, both the Germans and the Jews basically agreeing upon "man's nefarious nature." For the first time the modern world realized its vulnerability to political events, and technology and communication accelerated all of war's dangers. Hitler brought many of man's most infamous tendencies to the surface. For the first time, again, the species understood that might alone did not mean right, and that in larger terms a world war could have no real victors. Hitler might well have exploded the world's first atomic bomb.

In a strange fashion, however, Hitler knew that he was doomed from the very beginning, and so did Germany as far as Hitler's hopes for it were concerned. He yearned for destruction, for in saner moments even he recognized the twisted distortions of his earlier ideals. This meant that he often sabotaged his own efforts, and several important Allied victories were the result of such sabotaging. In the same way *(pause)*, Germany did not have the [atomic] bomb for the same reasons.

Now, however, we come to Hiroshima, where this highly destructive bomb was exploded *(on August 6, 1945)* — and for what reason? To save life, to save American lives. The intent to save American lives was certainly "good" — at the expense of the Japanese this time. In that regard, America's good was not Japan's, and an act taken to "save life" was also designed to take individual lives.

(10:27.) At what expense is "the good" to be achieved — and whose idea of the good is to be the criterion? Man's pursuit of the good, to some extent now, fathered the Inquisition and the Salem witch hunts. Politically, many today believe that Russia is "the enemy," and that therefore any means may be taken to destroy that country. Some people within the United States believe fervently that "the establishment" is rotten to the core, and that any means is justified to destroy it. Some people believe that homosexuals and lesbians are "evil," that somehow they lack the true qualities of humanness [and therefore need not be treated with normal respect]. These are all value judgments involving your ideas of the good.

(Pause.) Very few people start out trying to be as bad as possible. At least some (underlined) criminals feel that in stealing they are simply righting society's wrongs. I am not saying that is their only motive, but in one way or another they manage to justify their activities by seeing them in their own version of the good and the right.

You must realize that fanatics always deal with grandiose ideals, while at the same time they believe in man's sinful nature, and the individual's lack of power. They cannot trust the expression of the self, for they are convinced of its duplicity. Their ideals then seem even more remote. Fanatics call others to social action. Since they do not believe that the individual is ever effective, their groups are not assemblies of private individuals come reasonably together, pooling individual resources. They are instead congregations of people who are afraid to assert their individuality, who hope to find it in the group, or hope to establish a joint individuality — and that is an impossibility *(emphatically)*.

True individuals can do much through social action, and the species is a social one, but people who are afraid of their individuality will never find it in a group, but only a caricature of their own powerlessness.

End of dictation. I have not forgotten the scientist's letter. We will work it in.

(10:41. Now Seth came through with a little information for Jane and me, then ended the session at 10:45 P.M. "When the session started I had no idea at all that he was going to talk about Hitler and Germany," Jane said. "None at all. But I did know he was going to go into the good and the bad."

(The scientist Seth referred to is a professor of physics Jane heard from early last month. He'd posed some intriguing questions about Seth's ideas of the "true" nature of the universe, and in the nonbook session for April 30 [the 849th], Seth had given a few paragraphs of material in a partial answer.)

NOTES: SESSION 852

1. Hitler's espousal of a German-Aryan superrace is an excellent example of how a leader can subvert history to his own ends. Anthropologists do not assign any validity to "Aryan" as a racial term. In Nazi eyes, Aryans were the non-Jewish, Caucasian, "Nordic" descendants of the prehistoric peoples who originally spoke the hypothetical parent language of the Indo-European language family. The Aryans flooded into India, the Middle East, and Europe from southern Russia and Turkestan. Hitler idealized their waves of conquest in his own racist philosophy, attempting to trace German origins back to Aryan ancestors.

SESSION 853, MAY 14, 1979
9:46 P.M. MONDAY

(Although this is a private session that Jane and I are filing separately from "regular" material, we're also presenting it in Mass Events *because of the many insights Seth offers into individual and mass events in general,*

and into our personal realities in particular. In fact, without those quali-
ties of ours that Seth touches upon this evening, I doubt that the Seth books
— indeed, even the sessions themselves — would exist. So in that sense this
session contains more of those insights into the how and why of the Seth
material that we're always searching for. See my comments in Note 1 for ses-
sions 840 and 841.

(The session really grew out of several insights that Jane herself has
voiced since giving last Wednesday night's book copy. Following several of
those verbal comprehensions, she experienced very pleasant relaxation effects
of the kind I described in the opening notes for the 829th session. "But right
now I'm just waiting," she said impatiently at 9:40, after we'd been ready
for Seth to come through since 9:25. "Actually, I'm mad. Here I was all set
to go earlier . . ." Then she amended her remarks: "It makes me mad because
I feel like I'm in an odd in-between subjective state. It isn't comfortable. I
want to be Seth or myself — one thing or the other, maybe. . . ."

(Then rather slowly — but, strangely, with emphasis:)

Good evening.

("Good evening, Seth.")

Dictation is for Wednesday.

I want to make a few comments. Generally speaking, creativity has
feminine connotations in your society, while power has masculine
connotations, and is largely thought of as destructive.

Your scientists are, generally now, intellectually oriented, believing in reason above the intuitions, taking it for granted that those
qualities are opposites. They cannot imagine *(pause)* life's "initial"
creative source, for in their terms it would remind them of creativity's
feminine basis.

In the framework of this discussion only, you have a male's universe. It is a universe endowed with male characteristics as these
appear in the male-female orientations of your history. The universe
seems to have no meaning because the male "intellect" alone cannot
discern meaning, since it must take nothing for granted. Even
though certain characteristics of the universe are most apparent, they
must be ignored.

(Pause.) You must understand, I know, that the terms "male" and
"female" here are being used as they are generally understood, and
have nothing to do with the basic characteristics of either sex. In
those terms, the male-oriented intellect wants to order the universe,

name its parts, and so forth. It wants to ignore the creative aspects of the universe, however, which are everywhere apparent, and it first of all believes that it must divorce itself from any evidence of feeling. You have in your history then a male god of power and vengeance, who killed your enemies for you. You have a prejudiced god, who will, for example, slay the Egyptians and half of the Jews to retaliate against previous Egyptian cruelty. The male god is a god of power. He is not a god of creativity.

Now, creativity has always been the species' closest connection with its own source, with the nature of its own being. Through creativity the species senses All That Is. Creativity goes by a different set of rules, however. It defies categories, and it insists upon the evidence of feeling. It is a source of revelation and inspiration — yet initially revelation and inspiration do not deal with power, but with knowing. So what often happens in your society when men and women have creative bents, and good minds to boot?

(10:03.) The Catholic Church taught that revelation was dangerous. Intellectual and psychic obedience was much the safer road, and even the saints were slightly suspect. Women were inferiors, and in matters of religion and philosophy most of all, for there their creativity could be most disruptive. Women were considered hysterics, aliens to the world of intellectual thought, swayed instead by incomprehensible womanish emotions. Women were to be handled by wearing down their energies through childbirth.

Ruburt *(Jane)* was highly creative, and so following the beliefs of his time, he believed that he must watch his creativity most carefully, for he was determined to use it. He decided early to have no children — but more, to fight any evidence of femininity that might taint his work, or jumble up his dedication to it. He loved you deeply and does, but he always felt he had to tread a slender line, so as to satisfy the various needs and beliefs that you both had to one extent or another, and those you felt society possessed. He was creative, and is. Yet he felt that women were inferior, and that his very abilities made him vulnerable, that he would be ridiculed by others, that women were not taken seriously as profound thinkers, or innovators in philosophical matters.

The trance itself had feminine connotations, though he conveniently forgot [several excellent male mediums]. And yet at the same time he was afraid of exerting power, for fear it would be thought that he was usurping male prerogatives.

Now *(to me):* You are creative, but you are a male — and one part of you considered creativity a feminine-like characteristic. If it were tied to moneymaking, as it once was, then painting became also powermaking, and hence acceptable to your American malehood; and I am quite aware of the fact that by the standards of your times both of you were quite liberal, more the pity. You would not take your art to the marketplace after you left commercial work, because then, in a manner of speaking, now, understand, you considered that the act of a prostitute — for your "feminine feelings" that you felt produced the paintings would then be sold for the sake of "the male's role as provider and bringer of power."

The art of the old masters escaped such connotations, largely because it involved so much physical labor — the making of colors, canvases, and so forth. That work, providing the artist's preparation, now belongs to the male-world manufacturer, you see, so as a male in your society the artist is often left with what he thinks of as art's feminine basis, where it must be confronted, of course.

(10:20.) I want to make it plain that such ideas are rampant in society, and are at the basis of many personal and national problems. They are behind large issues, involved in the [Three Mile Island] nuclear fiasco, for example, and in the scientist's idea of power and creation. Both of you, highly creative, find your creativity in conflict with your ideas of sexuality, privately and in your stances with the world. Much of this is involved with the unfortunate myths about the creative person, who is not supposed to be able to deal with the world as well as others, whose idiosyncrasies are exaggerated, and whose very creativity, it is sometimes said, leads to suicide or depression. No wonder few numbers of creative people persist in the face of such unfortunate beliefs!

Indeed, these are some of the reasons why Ruburt distrusted the spontaneous self: because it was feminine, he believed, and therefore more flawed than the spontaneous self of the male.

You run into many contradictions. God is supposed to be male. The soul is sometimes considered female. The angels are male. Now let us look at the Garden of Eden. The story says that Eve tempted the male, having him eat of the tree of good and evil, or the tree of knowledge. *(Pause.)* This represented a state of consciousness, the point at which the species began to think and feel for itself, when it approached a certain state of consciousness in which it dared exert its own creativity.

(Pause.) This is difficult to verbalize. *(Pause.)* It was a state when the species became aware of its own thoughts as its own thoughts, and became conscious of the self who thinks. That point released man's creativity. In your terms, it was the product of the feminine intuitions (though, as you know, such intuitions belong to both sexes). When the [Biblical] passages were written, the species had come to various states of order, achieving certain powers and organizations, and it wanted to maintain the status quo. No more intuitive visions, no more changes, were wanted. Creativity was to follow certain definite roads, so the woman became the villain.

I have given material on that before *(but in private sessions)*. To some extent, Ruburt became afraid of his own creativity, and so did you. In Ruburt's case the fear was greater, until it seemed sometimes that if he succeeded in his work he would do so at some peril: You might be put in an unpleasant light, or he might become a fanatic, displaying those despicable, feminine hysterical qualities.

(With much humor:) I hope this session benefits you both. End of session, and a fond good evening.

("Thank you, Seth. Good night."

(10:35 P.M. "I didn't know he was going to go into all of that," Jane said, after I'd told her she'd given an excellent session. "Maybe that's why I felt so uncomfortable before the session: Part of me knew Seth was going to talk about us. Now I feel exhausted. I could go right to bed, but I won't. . . ."

(She couldn't really describe them now, Jane said, but she'd had "great, hilarious, emotional feelings" when she delivered the part of the session about my thinking that selling paintings made me a prostitute. "Some gargantuan feelings there, full of humor," she added.

(She laughed. "You're so strange. Here you won't go to the marketplace, but you think of saving all of these private sessions for posterity, to give them to the world some day. You're very close-mouthed: You don't blab our personal business, but you'd do that . . . Instead, I see us when I'm 80 and you're 90, out in the back yard, burning it all."

(Yet she easily agreed that this evening's session, whether private or not, cast much light on the Seth material as a whole, adding depths of understanding and background information. And, incidentally, in spite of my feelings about the marketplace, I've sold a number of paintings over the years. . . .)

SESSION 854, MAY 16, 1979
9:35 P.M. WEDNESDAY

(Jane started a new book today, and she's exhilarated — intoxicated — by this development in her creative abilities. It came about because of a seemingly innocuous accident — an event that could hardly have been accidental at all.

(This morning, while working on Chapter 18 of Oversoul Seven and the Museum of Time, *she'd abruptly felt the impulse to move into another room; she wanted to get away from the sunlight glaring through the thin drapes covering the sliding glass doors of her study at the back of the house. On her way out of the room she picked up a loose-leaf notebook that contained, she thought, her entries in her daily journal. In the living room, Jane discovered that instead she'd chosen her notebook on "Heroics." It holds many of the notes on the heroic self, and heroic impulses, that she'd discussed in chapters 25–27 of* Psychic Politics, *which had been published in 1976. It also contains a number of ideas on heroics that she'd written after finishing that work. "When I looked at those notes I knew all of a sudden that I was to do that book —* Heroics *— that I was to keep on looking for the heroic self I'd written about in* Politics,*" she told me as we ate lunch. "Now's the time for it."*

(Yet she's not really sure why she gave herself the message to begin Heroics *at this time. We speculated that her creative self, knowing the completion of* Seven *is in sight, wanted her to have another project underway. She trusts her insight, though, and has already written a few pages for the new book. The irony of the situation is that she's been doing very well on* Seven; *just yesterday she'd remarked that she intended to begin typing finished copy for the chapters she's completed so far. But now she'd laid* Seven *aside — for who knows how long?*

(Jane isn't sure of the title, Heroics, *yet, or how she'll put the book together. "It'll have a lot of poetry, though, stuff I've been saving for years. My God, the whole morning changed when I got that idea. Everything looks charged, or new or something. . . ."*

(As for myself, since I mailed the corrected galley proofs for Emir *back to Delacorte Press five-and-a-half weeks ago [on April 9], I've been keeping up with the new sessions for* Mass Events, *as well as those on other general subjects and for ourselves. I've also been painting several hours a day, recording dreams, writing extensive notes on a variety of subjects, filing reference material I'd let pile up, and, lately, working in the yard of our hill house each day.)*

Good evening.

("Good evening, Seth.")

Dictation. Basically *(pause)*, a fanatic believes that he is powerless.

He does not trust his own self-structure, or his ability to act effectively. Joint action seems the only course, but a joint action in which each individual must actually be forced to act, driven by frenzy, or fear or hatred, incensed and provoked, for otherwise the fanatic fears that no action at all will be taken toward "the ideal."

Through such methods, and through such group hysteria, the responsibility for separate acts is divorced from the individual, and rests instead upon the group, where it becomes generalized and dispersed. The cause, whatever it is, can then cover any number of crimes, and no particular individual need bear the blame alone. Fanatics have tunnel vision, so that any beliefs not fitting their purposes are ignored. Those that challenge their own purposes, however, become instant targets of scorn and attack. *(Pause.)* Generally speaking in your society, power is considered a male attribute. Cult leaders are more often male than female, and females are more often than not followers, because they have been taught that it is wrong for them to use power, and right for them to follow the powerful.

I said *(in Session 846)* that you have religious and scientific cults, and the male-oriented scientific community uses its power in the same way that the male Jehovah used his power in a different arena, to protect his friends and destroy his enemies. I spoke rather thoroughly in my last book *(The Nature of the Psyche)* about the sexuality of your species, but here I want to mention how some of those sexual beliefs affect your behavior.

(With amusement:) The male scientist considers the rocket his private symbol of sexual power. *(Pause.)* He feels he has the prerogative to use power in any way he chooses. Now many scientists are

"idealists." *(Pause.)* They believe that their search for answers, however, justifies almost any means, or sacrifices, not only on their parts but on the parts of others. They become fanatics when they ignore the rights of others, and when they defile life in a misguided attempt to understand it *(see Session 850, with Note 3)*.

Women make a grave error when they try to prove their "equality" with men by showing that they can enter the armed forces, or go into combat as well as any man *(with more amusement)*. War always makes you less as a species than you could be. Women have shown uncommon good sense in not going to war, and uncommon bad sense by sending their sons and lovers to war. Again: To kill for the sake of peace only makes you better killers, and nothing will change that. In any war, both sides are fanatical to the extent that they are involved. I am quite aware that often war seems to be your only practical course, because of the set of beliefs that are, relatively speaking, worldwide. Until you change those beliefs, war will seem to have some practical value — a value which is highly deceptive, and quite false.

Fanatics always use ringing rhetoric, and speak in the highest terms of truth, good and evil, and particularly of retribution. To some extent capital punishment is the act of a fanatical society: The taking of the murderer's life does not bring back the victim's, and it does not prevent other men from [committing] such crimes. I am aware that the death penalty often seems to be a practical solution — and indeed many murderers want to die, and are caught because of their need for punishment. Many, now — and I am speaking generally — are in the position they are because they so thoroughly believe what all of you believe to a large extent: that you are flawed creatures, spawned by a meaningless universe, or made by a vengeful God and damaged by original sin.

Criminals act out those beliefs to perfection. Their "tendencies" are those that each of you fears you possess. Science and religion each tell you that left alone you will spontaneously be primitive creatures, filled with uncontrolled lust and avarice. Both Freud and Jehovah gave you that message. Poor Darwin tried to make sense of it all, but failed miserably.

Fanatics cannot stand tolerance. They expect obedience. A democratic society offers the greatest challenges and possibilities of achievement for the individual and the species, for it allows for the free intercourse of ideas. It demands much more of its people, however, for in a large manner each must pick and choose from amid a variety of life-styles and beliefs his and her own platform for daily life and action.

(10:08.) There are periods in which it certainly seems to some that all standards vanish, and so they yearn for old authorities. And there are always fanatics there to stand for ultimate truth, and to lift from the individual the challenge and "burden" of personal achievement and responsibility. Individuals can — they can — survive without organizations. Organizations cannot survive without individuals, and the most effective organizations are assemblies of individuals who assert their own private power in a group, and do not seek to hide within it *(all very emphatically)*.

Organized action is an excellent method of exerting influence, but only when each member is self-activating; only when he or she extends individuality through group action, and does not mindlessly seek to follow the dictates of others.

(Pause.) Fanatics exist because of the great gap between an idealized good and an exaggerated version of its opposite. The idealized good is projected into the future, while its exaggerated opposite is seen to pervade the present. The individual is seen as powerless to work alone toward that ideal with any sureness of success. Because of his belief in his powerlessness [the fanatic] feels that any means to an end is justified. Behind all this is the belief that spontaneously the ideal will never be achieved, and that, indeed, on his own man is getting worse and worse in every aspect: How can flawed selves ever hope to spontaneously achieve any good?

Let us see. Period. End of chapter. End of dictation.

(Then louder:) Yes, Ruburt has started up again. He is on the right track. He has his [new book] project, and you are doing well, and I bid you both a fond good evening.

("Good night, Seth."

(10:20. "I feel real good, and Seth did well finishing that material," Jane said. "I feel good about Heroics, *too. Before the session I was worried about what good stuff we might get, and whether we could put it in this book or if it would just lay there for years. But something you said helped —"*

("That I don't worry about things like that anymore," I repeated. "I discovered I don't want to spend the time being concerned, so I've changed my beliefs. I can't do that any longer." Whereupon Jane loudly and humorously returned as Seth, leaning forward for emphasis, her eyes wide and dark:)

You never should have [worried], and neither should he *(Jane)*. The book sessions will cover everything that needs to be covered.

("I know it," I said as Seth stared at me. Then he was gone.

(10:23 P.M. But, I told Jane with some humor of my own, I also knew that that knowledge wouldn't stop me from occasionally inserting what I think is a particularly good and appropriate nonbook session into whatever project Seth may have going at the time. She laughed.)

SESSION 855, MAY 21, 1979
9:15 P.M. MONDAY

(Last Thursday, Jane and I received from Prentice-Hall our first copies of the German translation of Seth Speaks. *Prentice-Hall authorized this venture by a foreign publisher well over a year ago, but we didn't know just when we'd see books within the two-year limit set for publication. This occasion signals the first appearance of the Seth material in another language, and we're happy to note that the translator, with whom Jane exchanged just a couple of letters, did an excellent, painstaking job. The publisher, Ariston Verlag, is actually located in Geneva, Switzerland; German is one of the four national languages of that country.*

(In addition, we expect that later this year the Dutch translation of Seth Speaks *will be published — but again, we don't know just when this will happen. We hope these two editions will lead to the publication of Seth's material in other languages.*

(In closing out the last session, Seth told us that he'd "cover everything that needs to be covered" in his books, and I wrote that sometimes I'd still choose to insert other particularly apropos material of his into whatever book he might be producing at the time. My chance to show how independent I am about doing just that arose much sooner than I'd expected it to — in tonight's session, in fact. So inserting this material puts off by one — at least — Seth's first session for Chapter 8 of Mass Events.

(At the end of the 852nd session I mentioned a letter Jane had received last month from a professor of physics, and that in a recent nonbook session

Seth had come through with a partial answer to some of the professor's questions. This afternoon Jane reread the letter, and wondered if Seth might give more material in reply; as she worked on Heroics *she did get a line or two from Seth, commenting on that possibility. My main reason for presenting the excerpts that follow is the same as it's been on other occasions: Seth's material fits into* Mass Events *very well. Nor do I want to wait an indefinite time before he may incorporate similar information in a book — even this one. Neither does Jane. In general, then, tonight Seth discusses questions many correspondents have asked; but specifically, his material is a continuation of an answer to some of the professor's questions. I know that eventually I'll mail to that gentleman whatever insights Seth gives us.*

(*Whispering:*) Dictation on Wednesday.

Now: Earlier today, Ruburt wondered if I might dictate more in reply to your scientist's letter. As he wondered, I very briefly responded to the effect that since we come from such different perspectives, it is actually quite difficult to give your scientist what I would consider a full response. I could dictate a reply that would satisfy him well enough, but it would (*pause*) perhaps be the more distorted the more it was geared for his understanding.

It is no coincidence that Ruburt does not possess a scientific vocabulary, though he does possess a scientific as well as intuitive mind. The very attempt to describe reality in scientific terms, as they are currently understood, pays, my dear friend, undue tribute to a vocabulary that automatically scales down greater concepts to fit its rigors. In other words, such attempts further compound the problem of considering a seemingly objective universe, and describing it in an objective fashion.

The universe is — and you can pick your terms — a spiritual or mental or psychological manifestation, and not, in your usual vocabulary, an objective manifestation.

There is presently no science, religion, or psychology that comes close to even approaching a conceptual framework that could explain, or even indirectly describe, the dimensions of that kind of universe. (*Pause.*) Its properties are psychological, following the logic of the psyche, and all of the physical properties that you understand are reflections of those deeper issues. Again, each atom and molecule — and any particle that you can imagine — possesses, and would possess, a consciousness. Unless you accept that statement at least as a theory upon which to build, then much of my material would appear meaningless.

That statement, therefore, must be the basis for any new scientific theories that hope to accomplish any performances at all leading to an acquisition of knowledge.

(9:30.) Since I must use [an] objective vocabulary I am always seeking for analogies. By objective I refer to the use of language, the English language, that automatically sets up its own screens of perception — as of course any language must do to some extent.

The universe expands, as I have said before, as an idea expands; and as sentences are built upon words, in your terms, and paragraphs upon sentences, and as each retains its own logic and continuity and evidence within that framework, so do all the portions of the universe appear to you also with the same cohesiveness (dash) — meaning continuity and order. Any sentence is meaningful. It seems to fall in order by itself as you say it. Its order is obvious. That one sentence is (underlined) meaningful because of its organization of letters, or if it is spoken, its organization of vowels and syllables. It makes sense, however, not only because of the letters or vowels or syllables that are used within it, but because of all of the letters or vowels or syllables that it excludes.

The same applies to your universe. It has meaning, coherence and order not only because of those realities that are obvious to you, and that appear, but also because of those inner realities that are "unspoken," or hidden. I am not speaking merely of hidden variables, in scientific terms, nor am I saying that the universe is an illusion, but a psychological reality in which "objectivity" is the result of psychological creativity.

(Pause.) It is not just that your view of reality is relative to your position within the universe, but that the universe itself is different according to your position within it, and that spiritual or psychological rules apply. The universe deals with different kinds of order, perceptions, and organizations, each dependent upon the others, yet each separate in its own domain.

(Pause.) In your realm of reality, there is no real freedom but the freedom of ideas, and there is no real bondage except for the

bondage of ideas *(intently)*, for your ideas form your private and mass reality. You want to examine the universe from the outside, to examine your societies from the outside. You still think that the interior world is somehow symbolic and the exterior world is <u>real</u> — that wars, for example, are fought by themselves or with bombs. All of the time, the psychological reality is the primary one, that forms all of your events.

It is not to say that you cannot understand the nature of the universe to some extent, but the answers lie in the natures of your own minds, in the processes of individual creativity, in studies that ask questions like: "Where did this thought come from? Where does it go? What effect does it have upon myself or others? How do I know how to dream, when I have never been taught to do so? How do I speak without understanding the mechanisms? Why do I feel that I have an eternal reality, when it is obvious that I was physically born and will physically die?"

Unscientific questions? I tell you that these are the most scientific of all. To some extent the attempt on the part of science to consider such material may possibly bring about those qualities of true scientific intuition that will help science bridge the gap between such divergent views as its own and ours.

(Pause at 9:53. This was the end of the regular session material for the evening. Seth came through with a good amount of information for Jane and me, however, then said good night at 10:15 P.M.)

CHAPTER 8

MEN, MOLECULES, POWER, AND FREE WILL

SESSION 856, MAY 24, 1979
8:23 P.M. THURSDAY

(O*nce again, see Note 1 on Three Mile Island.*
(The regularly scheduled book session for last night was not held. We sat for it as usual, but became involved watching the last episode of a television mini-series about events growing out of the Watergate break-in.[2] While we followed the drama, Jane reported to me a steady flow of comments about it from Seth. More often than not he was quite amused as he gave them to her. She also picked up from him the heading of Chapter 8 for Mass Events: *"Men, Molecules, Power, and Free Will." We decided to reschedule the session for this evening.*

(After supper tonight, however, Jane chose not to have the session because she felt so free and relaxed. Then a bit later she spontaneously announced she'd hold it after all — early, even. "I don't know how long I can hold out, though," she said. "I'm getting great bursts of stuff from Seth about all kinds of things. . . ." She described some of them to me, but I didn't have time to write them down and couldn't retain them. She laughed. She was very relaxed. Yet she launched into the session as easily as ever; I had to write fast to keep up with her delivery.)

Dictation: Next chapter *(8)*. Ruburt received it correctly the other *(last)* evening: "Men, Molecules, Power, and Free Will."

Before we end this particular section of the book, dealing with frightened people, idealism, and interpretations of good and evil, there is another instance that I would like to mention. It is the Watergate affair. Last evening, Ruburt and Joseph watched a *(television)* movie — a fictional dramatization of the Watergate events. Ordinarily a session would have been held, but Ruburt was interested in the movie, and I was interested in Ruburt's and Joseph's reactions to it.

To some extent or another, I watched the program with our friends. Actually, I allowed myself to become aware mainly of Ruburt's perceptions as he viewed the motion picture. By one of those curious coincidences that are not coincidences at all, another dramatic rendition of that same Watergate saga was simultaneously showing on another channel — this one depicting the second spiritual birth of one of the President's finest cohorts.

Let us look briefly at that entire affair, remembering some of our earlier questions: When does an idealist turn into a fanatic, and how? And how can the desire to do good bring about catastrophic results?

The President at the time, and through all of his life before *(pause)*, was at heart a stern, repressed idealist of a rather conventionally religious kind. He believed in an idealized good, while believing most firmly and simultaneously that man was fatally flawed *(loudly)*, filled with evil, more naturally given to bad rather than good intent. He believed in the absolute necessity of power, while convinced at the same time that he did not possess it; and further, he believed that in the most basic terms the individual was powerless to alter the devastating march of evil and corruption that he saw within the country, and in all the other countries of the world. No matter how much power he achieved, it seemed to him that others had more — other people, other groups, other countries — but their power he saw as evil. For while he believed in the existence of an idealized good, he felt that the wicked were powerful and the good were weak and without vigor.

(8:38.) He concentrated upon the vast gulf that seemed to separate the idealized good and the practical, ever-pervading corruption that in his eyes grew by leaps and bounds. He saw himself as just. Those who did not agree with him, he saw as moral enemies. Eventually it seemed to him that he was surrounded by the corrupt, and that any means at his disposal was justified to bring down those who would threaten the presidency or the state.

He was as paranoid as any poor deluded man or woman is who feels, without evidence, that he or she is being pursued by creatures from space, earthly or terrestrial enemies, or evil psychic powers. Those poor people will build up for themselves a logical sequence of events, in which the most innocent encounter is turned into a frightening threat. They will project that fear outward until they seem to meet it in each person they encounter.

It is obvious to most others that such paranoid views are not based on mass fact. *(Pause.)* Your President at that time, however, had at his command vast information, so that he was aware of many groups and organizations that did not agree with his policies. He used those as in other circumstances a paranoid might use the sight of a police car to convince himself that he was being pursued by the police, or the FBI or whatever. The President felt threatened — and not only personally threatened, for he felt that the good for which he stood in his own mind was in peril *(intently)*. And again, since the idealized good seemed too remote and difficult to achieve, any means was justified. Those who followed him, in the Cabinet and so forth, possessed the same kinds of characteristics to some degree or another.

(Pause.) No one is as fanatical, and no one can be more cruel, than the self-righteous. It is very easy for such persons "to become [religiously] converted" after such episodes *(as Watergate)*, lining themselves up once more on the side of good, searching for "the power of fellowship," turning to church rather than government, hearing in one way or another the voice of God.

So how can the well-meaning idealist know whether or not his good intent will lead to some actualization? How can he know, or how can she know, whether or not this good intent might in fact lead to disastrous conditions? When does the idealist turn into a fanatic?

Look at it this way: If someone tells you that pleasure is wrong and tolerance is weakness, and that you must follow this or that dogma blindly in obedience, and if you are told this is the only right road toward the idealized good, then most likely you are dealing with a fanatic. If you are told to kill for the sake of peace, you are dealing with someone who does not understand peace or justice. If you are told to give up your free will, you are dealing with a fanatic.

Both men and molecules dwell in a field of probabilities, and their paths are not determined. The vast reality of probabilities makes the existence of free will possible. If probabilities did not exist, and if you were not to some degree aware of probable actions and events, not only could you not choose between them, but you would not of course have any feelings of choice *(intently)*. You would be unaware of the entire issue.

(9:03.) Through your mundane conscious choices, you affect all of the events of your world, so that the mass world is the result of multitudinous individual choices. You could not make choices at all if you did not feel impulses to do this or that, so that choices usually involve you in making decisions between various impulses. Impulses are urges toward action. Some are conscious and some are not. Each cell of your body feels (underlined) the impulse toward action, response, and communication. You have been taught not to trust your impulses. Now impulses, however, help you to develop events of natural power. Impulses in children teach them to develop their muscles and minds [each] in their own unique manner. And as you will see, those impulses of a private nature are nevertheless also based upon the greater situation of the species and the planet, so that "ideally" the fulfillment of the individual would automatically lead to the better good of the species.

(9:10. Now Seth began some material on other matters, then ended the session at 9:19 P.M.

(I sat working on my notes for the beginning of the session while Jane left the room. When she returned, she said she had things to tell me. "I think it started with Seth, but then I went into another altered state of my own, like the time I got that dream material at the kitchen table — when was that, last March?" [See the 844th session for April 1.]

(Jane began to dictate what she'd just received. This certainly wasn't Seth coming through. Her voice was rather conversational, yet at the same time it was deliberate in a way quite different from her usual manner of speaking. I began to write at 9:47:

("As you learn to trust your natural impulses, they introduce you to your individual sense of power, so that you realize that your own actions do have meaning, that you do affect events, and that you can see some definite signs that you are achieving good ends. The idealized goal isn't as remote,

then, because it is being expressed. Even if that expression is by means of steps, you can point toward it as an accomplishment. Previously we distrusted our own impulses to such an extent that they often appeared in very distorted form."

(Jane said: "That's it as far as I got it. But the idea that each person tries to actualize the idealized good as much as they can through their daily lives — their work, social structures, and so forth — and in the meantime use certain criteria that will help them judge for themselves whether or not their actions are really in line with their ideals. The criteria are actually the ones given in the chapter. That's all. A whole lot of it was coming to me. I don't even know if it's right.

("Oh, that reminds me," she added. "Remember that letter we got today from a reader, about pollution? I picked up something about that, too: The real question, for example, isn't one of planetary pollution, or nuclear wastes, but the beliefs that make such questions even arise, and the attitudes that see an idealized good worth such risks. That is, people aren't polluting the world out of greed alone, but for the economic good of all. It's just that the means they often choose aren't justified by those ends. . . .")

NOTES: SESSION 856

1. Almost two full months have passed since Unit No. 2, one the two reactors at Pennsylvania's Three Mile Island nuclear power generating plant, overheated and came close to a catastrophic meltdown of its uranium fuel. The situation at TMI is as enigmatic as ever, with the damaged reactor's massive containment building sealed and holding within it large amounts of highly radioactive gasses, solids, and water. The contaminated water, some 600,000 gallons of it, floods the building's basement in a pool at least six feet deep.

There's plenty of action outside the Three Mile Island, however, with all of the investigations into the accident underway or planned. Scary stories abound about our nuclear dilemmas, ranging from tales of poorly designed plants, control rooms, and instruments, to the failure to promptly report potentially serious accidents, to the fact that in 1978 every one of the country's more than 70 nuclear power plants had at least one unexpected shutdown because of procedural errors, mechanical failures, or both. The increasing dependence of the United States upon nuclear power is being deeply questioned, even though that energy is supposed to help alleviate our growing reliance upon foreign oil. There's worry about the plants emitting constant radiation, and about their vulnerability to damage by sabotage, earthquakes, and — more likely — fires. There's debate about who's to pay for expensive nuclear accidents. Suits and countersuits are inevitable, processes that can continue for years. There will be fines and many tighter industry rules and regulations. And in all of this concern for safety there's much irony: for Three Mile Island, and the people of eastern Pennsylvania, were saved not by the plant's emergency cooling systems, but by nonsafety-related equipment that plant operators finally used to improvise cooling of the reactor's overheated core.

Beneath all of the frustrations and upsets we may feel at their surface manifestations, Jane and I are caught up in the deeper meanings of events like those at Jonestown and TMI, for they represent great challenges that our species has set for itself, through this century and beyond. Science and religion must ultimately be reconciled if we are to progress. These challenges aren't just national, of course, but worldwide: The scientific rationale embodied in TMI runs headlong into the western world's reliance upon energy supplies — mainly oil — from nations that are largely religiously oriented, and that profess all kinds of antipathy for social orders other than their own. In our lifetimes Jane and I look forward to our species at least making a start at grappling with such large areas of its own activity as science and religion. We must come to terms with those challenges we've created — and are creating.

2. Early on the morning of June 17, 1972, five men were arrested inside the headquarters of the Democratic National Committee, located in the Washington, D.C., apartment-hotel-office complex known as the Watergate. The men were employed by the "plumbers," a secret group working for the Republican President Richard Nixon's Committee to Re-Elect the President, and their tasks were to photograph records and to check upon listening devices — "bugs" — that had been planted in the offices during a first illegal entry in May. The detection of the break-in at Watergate both uncovered and perpetuated a labyrinthian series of events that culminated in the resignation of President Nixon on August 9, 1974.

SESSION 857, MAY 30, 1979
9:28 P.M. WEDNESDAY

(Monday night's session is a private one.

(In the opening notes for Session 852 I wrote that starting with the 846th session for April 4, "Seth has been dictating material for Mass Events *on Wednesday evenings only." Eight weeks later he's still following that arrangement, that "unspoken agreement" among the three of us. Even last Thursday night's session was displaced from the evening before. I took it upon myself to present material from two Monday night sessions — 853 and 855.*

(Earlier tonight Jane had picked up from Seth some of his material for the session, should she decide to hold it.)

Good evening.

("Good evening, Seth.")

Dictation: Impulses, therefore, provide impetus toward motion, coaxing the physical body and the mental person toward utilization of physical and mental power.

(Pause.) They help the individual impress the world — that is, to act upon it and within it effectively. Impulses also open up choices that may not have been consciously available before. I have often said that the c-e-l-l-s (*spelled*) precognate, and that at that level the body is aware of vast information, information not consciously known or apprehended. The universe and everything within it is composed of "information," but this information is aware-ized containing — I am sorry: information concerning the entire universe is always latent within each and any part of it.

The motive power of the universe and of each particle or wave or person within it is the magnificent thrust toward creative probabilities, and the tension that exists, the exuberant tension, that exists "between" probable choices and probable events. This applies to men and molecules, and to all of those hypothetically theorized smaller divisions with which scientists like to amaze themselves. Divisions or units.

In more mundane terms, impulses often come from unconscious knowledge, then. This knowledge is spontaneously and automatically received by the energy that composes your body, and then it is processed so that pertinent information applying to you can be taken advantage of. Ideally (underlined), your impulses are always in response to your own best interests — and, again, to the best interests of your world as well. Obviously there is a deep damaging distrust of impulses in the contemporary world, as in your terms there has been throughout the history that you follow. *(Pause.)* Impulses are spontaneous, and you have been taught not to trust the spontaneous portions of your being, but to rely upon your reason and your intellect — which *(amused)* both operate, incidentally, quite spontaneously, by the way.

When you let yourselves alone, you are spontaneously reasonable, but because of your beliefs it seems that reason and spontaneity make poor bedfellows.

Psychologically, your impulses are as vital to your being as your physical organs are. They are as altruistic, or unselfish, as your physical organs are *(intently),* and I would like that sentence read several times. And yet each impulse is suited and tailored directly to the individual who feels it. Ideally (underlined), by following your impulses you would feel the shape, the impulsive shape (as Ruburt says) of your life. You would not spend time wondering what your purpose was, for it would make itself known to you, as you perceived the direction in which your natural impulses led, and felt yourself exert power in the world through such actions. Again, impulses are doorways to action, satisfaction, the exertion of natural mental and physical power, the avenue for your private expression — the avenue where your private expression intersects the physical world and impresses it.

(9:49.) Many cults of one kind or another, and many fanatics, seek to divide you from your natural impulses, to impede their expression. They seek to sabotage your belief in your spontaneous being, so that the great power of impulses becomes damned up. Avenues of probabilities are closed bit by bit until you do indeed live — if you follow such precepts — in a closed mental environment, in which it seems you are powerless. It seems you cannot impress the world as you wish, that your ideals must always be stillborn.

Some of this has been discussed earlier in this book. In the case of the Jonestown tragedy, for example, all doors toward probable effective action seemed closed. Followers had been taught to act against their natural impulses with members of their families. They had been taught not to trust the outside world, and little by little the gap between misguided idealism and an exaggerated version of the world's evil blocked all doors through which power could be exerted — all doors save one. The desire for suicide is often the last recourse left to frightened people whose natural impulses toward action have been damned up — intensified on the one hand, and yet denied any practical expression.

There is a natural impulse to die on the part of men and animals, but in such circumstances [as we are discussing here] that desire becomes the only impulse that the individual feels able to express, for it seems that all other avenues of expression have become closed. There is much misunderstanding concerning the nature of impulses, so we will discuss them rather thoroughly. I always want to emphasize the importance of individual action, for only the individual can help form organizations that become physical vehicles *(intently)* for the effective expression of ideals. Only people who trust their spontaneous beings and the altruistic nature of their impulses can be consciously wise enough to choose from a myriad of probable futures the most promising events — for again, impulses take not only [people's] best interest into consideration, but those of all other species.

(Pause at 10:04.) I am using the term "impulses" for the understanding of the general public, and in those terms molecules and protons have impulses. No consciousness simply reacts to stimuli, but has its own impulse toward growth and value fulfillment. It seems to many of you that impulses are unpredictable, contradictory, without reason, the result of erratic mixtures of body chemicals, and that they must be squashed with as much deadly intent as some of you might when you spray a mosquito with insecticide.

Often the insecticide kills more than the mosquito, and its effects can be far-reaching, and possibly have disastrous consequences. However, to consider impulses as chaotic, meaningless — or worse, detrimental to an ordered life — represents a very dangerous attitude indeed; an attempt that causes many of your other problems, an attempt that does often distort the nature of impulses. Each person is fired by the desire to act, and to act beneficially, altruistically *(intently)*, to practically put his stamp, or her stamp, upon the world. When such natural impulses toward action are constantly denied over a period of time, when they are distrusted, when an individual feels in battle with his or her own impulses and shuts down the doors toward probable actions, then that intensity can explode into whatever avenue of escape is still left open.

I am not speaking of anything *(pause)* like "repression," as it is used by psychologists, but a far deeper issue: one in which the very self is so distrusted that natural impulses of any kind become suspect. You try to inoculate yourselves against yourselves — a nearly impossible situation, of course. You expect your motives to be selfish because you have been told that they are, and so when you catch yourselves with unkind motives you are almost comforted, because you think that at least you are behaving normally.

When you find yourself with good motives, you distrust them. "Surely," you think, "beneath this seeming altruism, there must indeed be some nefarious, or at best selfish, motives that escape me." As a people you are always examining your impulses, and yet you rarely examine the fruits of your intellects.

It may seem that (underlined) impulsive actions run rampant in society, in cultish behavior, for example, or in the behavior of criminals, or on the part of youth, but such activities show instead the power of impulses denied their natural expression, intensified and focused on the one hand into highly ritualized patterns of behavior, and in other areas denied expression.

(Pause.) A particular idealist believes that the world is headed for disaster, and [that] he is powerless to prevent it. Having denied his impulses, believing them wrong, and having impeded his expression of his own power to affect others, he might, for example, "hear the voice of God." That voice might tell him to commit any of a number of nefarious actions — to assassinate the enemies that stand in the way of his great ideal — and it might seem to him and to others that he has a natural impulse to kill, and indeed an inner decree from God to do so.

According to conditions, such a person could be a member of a small cult or the head of a nation, a criminal or a national hero, who claims to act with the authority of God. Again, the desire and motivation to act is so strong within each person that it will not be denied, and when it is denied then it can be expressed in a perverted form. Man must not only act, but he must act constructively, and he must feel that he acts for good ends.

Only when the natural impulse (*to act constructively*) is denied consistently does the idealist turn into a fanatic. Each person in his or her own way is an idealist.

(Pause at 10:28.) Power is natural. It is the force, the power of the muscle to move, or the eye to see, of the mind to think, the power of the emotions — these represent true power, and no accumulation of wealth or acclaim can substitute for that natural sense of power if it is lacking. Power always rests with the individual, and from the individual all political power must flow.

(Long pause.) A democracy is a highly interesting form of government, highly significant because it demands so much of individual

consciousness, and because it must rest primarily upon a belief in the powers of the individual. It is a tribute to that belief that it has lingered in your country, and operated with such vitality in the face of quite opposing beliefs officially held by both science and religion.

The idea [of democracy] expresses the existence of a high idealism — one that demands political and social organizations that are effective to some degree in providing some practical expression of those ideals *(emphatically)*. When those organizations fail and a gulf between idealism and actualized good becomes too great, then such conditions help turn some idealists into fanatics. *(Long pause.)* Those who follow with great strictness the dictates of either science or religion can switch sides in a moment. The scientist begins tipping tables or whatever, and suddenly disgusted by the limits of scientific knowledge, he turns all of his dedication to what he thinks of as its opposite, or pure intuitive knowledge. Thus, he blocks his reason as fanatically as earlier he blocked his intuitions. The businessman who believed in Darwinian principles and the fight for survival, who justified injustice and perhaps thievery to his ideal of surviving in a competitive world — he suddenly turns into a fundamentalist in religious terms, trying to gain his sense of power now, perhaps, by giving away the wealth he has amassed, all in a tangled attempt to express a natural idealism in a practical world.

How can you trust your impulses when you read, for example, that a man commits a murder because he has a strong impulse to do so, or because the voice of God commanded it? If some of you followed your impulses right now, for example — your first natural ones — it might seem they would be cruel or destructive.

How do your impulses affect your future experience, and help form the practical world of mass reality?

(Loudly, abruptly:) End of dictation.

(10:42.) Now Seth went into an analysis of a very vivid dream Jane had recently had, involving her deceased mother. He ended the session at 10:56 P.M.

(When I told her she'd delivered an excellent, often impassioned session, Jane said she'd written half a page this morning that sounded a lot like Seth's material. "Maybe he's going to do my own book," she said, referring to Heroics, *"but that's okay. I don't care which one of us does it. . . . ")*

SESSION 859, JUNE 6, 1979
9:14 P.M. WEDNESDAY

(Jane has really made an effort to recognize, study, and follow her impulses since Seth began emphasizing them two sessions ago in Mass Events. *She's become especially conscious of impulses while working on her new book,* Heroics, *for, strangely, she's found herself confronting a series of seemingly contradictory impulses to do other things, such as paint, or reread her old poetry.*

(For example, she spent Monday and Tuesday reading poetry she'd written before the sessions began [in 1963], wondering why she didn't have the impulse to work on Heroics *instead. Finally, last night she made her intuitive connection: She* had *been working on the book the entire time.* Heroics *isn't to be on how to reach some unattainable superself, but on the barriers that stand in the way of practical self-realization. That old poetry dealt with such impediments. "You can't find your heroic self unless you trust the self you have," she told me. "Seth's been telling us to be alert for negative Freudian and Darwinian beliefs — and suddenly I'm surrounded by my own. And all of those beliefs stand in the way of trusting my impulses. I finally see where the book is headed. I'm going to work out those beliefs for myself and for our readers.")*

Dictation.

Again, you have been taught to believe that impulses are wrong, generally speaking, or at best that they represent messages from a nefarious subconscious, giving voice to dark moods and desires.

For example: Many of you believe in the basis of Freudian psychology — that the son naturally wants to displace the father in his mother's attentions, and that beneath the son's love for his father, there rages the murderous intent to kill. Ridiculous idiocy!

Ruburt has been reading old poetry of his own, and he was appalled to find such beliefs in rather brutal, concentrated form. Until our sessions began, he followed the official line of consciousness, and though he railed against those precepts he could find no other solution. The self, so spectacularly alive, seemed equipped with reason to understand the great import of its own certain extinction. Such a tragedy to project upon the living personality.

You cannot begin to have a true psychology, again, unless you see the living self in a greater context, with greater motives, purposes and meanings than you now assign to it, or for that matter than you assign to nature and its creatures. You have denied many impulses, or programmed others so that they are allowed expression in only certain forms of action. If any of you do (underlined) still believe in the Freudian or Darwinian selves, then you will be leery about impulses to examine your own consciousness, afraid of what murderous debris might be uncovered. I am not speaking merely in hypothetical terms. For example, a well-intentioned woman was here recently. She worried about her overweight condition, and [was] depressed at what she thought of as her lack of discipline in following diets. In her dismay, she visited a psychologist, who told her that her marriage might somehow be part of the problem. The woman said she never went back. She was afraid that she might discover within herself the buried impulse to kill her husband, or to break up the marriage, but she was sure that her overweight condition hid some unfortunate impulse.

(Pause.) Actually the woman's condition hid her primary impulse: to communicate better with her husband, to ask him for definite expressions of love. Why did he not love her as much as she loved him? She could say it was because she was overweight, after all, for he was always remarking adversely about her fleshy opulence — though he did not use such a sympathetic phrase.

He could not express his love for her in the terms she wished for he believed that women would, if allowed to, destroy the man's freedom, and he interpreted the natural need for love as an unfortunate emotional demand. Both of them believed that women were inferior, and quite unknowingly they followed a Freudian dogma.

(9:35.) The ideas we have been speaking of, then, are intimately connected with your lives. The man just mentioned denies his personal impulses often. Sometimes he is not even aware of them as far as they involve the expression of affection or love to his wife.

In those areas where you cut down on your impulses, upon their very recognition, you close down probabilities, and prevent new beneficial acts that of themselves would lead you out of your difficulty. You prevent change. But many people fear that any change is detrimental, since they have been taught, after all, that left alone their bodies or their minds or their relationships are bound to deteriorate. Often, therefore, people react to events as if they themselves possessed no impetus to alter them. They live their lives as if they are indeed limited in experience not only to a brief lifetime, but a lifetime in which they are the victims of their chemistry — accidental members of a blighted species that is murderous to its very core.

Another woman [friend] found a small sore spot on her breast. Remembering well the barrage of negative suggestions that passes for preventative medicine — the public service announcements about cancer — she was filled with foreboding. She went to the doctor, who told her he did not believe there was anything wrong. He suggested X-rays, however, "just to be on the safe side," and so her body was treated to a basically unnecessary dose of radiation in the name of preventative medicine.

(Our friend did not have cancer. See Note 2 for Session 805.)

I am not suggesting that you do not visit doctors under such situations, because the weight of your negative beliefs about your bodies usually makes it too difficult for you to bear such uncertainties alone. Nevertheless, such actions speak only too loudly of your mass beliefs involving the vulnerability of the self and its flesh.

(Pause.) To me, it is almost inconceivable that, from your position, any of you seriously consider that the existence of your exquisite consciousness can possibly be the result of a conglomeration of chemicals and elements thrown together by a universe accidentally formed, and soon to vanish. So much more evidence is available to you: the order of nature; the creative drama of your dreams, that project your consciousness into other times and places; the very precision with which you spontaneously grow, without knowing how, from a fetus into an adult; the existence of heroic themes and quests and ideals that pervade the life of even the worst scoundrel — these all give evidence of the greater context in which you have your being.

(Pause at 9:51. Then loudly:) If the universe existed as you have been told it does, then I would not be writing this book.

There would be no psychological avenues to connect my world and yours. There would be no extensions of the self that would allow you to travel such a psychological distance to those thresholds of reality that form my mental environment. If the universe were structured as you have been told, the probability of my existence would be zero as far as you are concerned. There would have been no unofficial roads for Ruburt to follow, to lead him from the official beliefs of his time. He would never have acknowledged the original impulse to speak for me, and my voice would have been unheard in your world.

(Pause.) The probability that this book would ever exist, itself, would have remained unactualized. None of you would be reading it. The mass world is formed as the result of individual impulses. They meet and merge, and form platforms for action.

End of dictation.

(9:57. Now at my request Seth gave over a few paragraphs to what I think is a very perceptive interpretation of a dream I had had last night. I'd told Jane this morning that I knew the dream was quite significant in connection with the work we're doing with the Seth material, but that I was unable to adequately decipher it. End at 10:05 P.M.)

SESSION 860, JUNE 13, 1979
9:19 P.M. WEDNESDAY

(A private session was held on Monday evening.

(Four weeks ago, I wrote in the opening notes for the 854th session that Jane wasn't sure of Heroics *as the title for her new book. She's been using it ever since, though — until late last night, that is, when she finally agreed that she did have the definitive and very original title that she'd been searching for all along:* The God of Jane: A Psychic Manifesto. *"Is that too daring, too far out?" she asked me. No, I told her, I thought it was an excellent title, and that it said exactly what she wanted the reader to know.[1]*

(Once again now, Jane was quite relaxed. She had been most of the day, and by supper time she'd even thought of skipping the session. The situation wasn't without its humorous aspects, however, for Seth himself seemed eager to go: As we sat for the session Jane said she was getting material from him on several topics. "Over there — to my left — he's talking about the limitations of our kind of personality. That is, why would we say we're limited if we didn't feel there was more to being than we usually think there is?" It was another of those ideas that are quite obvious, once mentioned. Jane was also picking up on Seth's dictation for tonight. "But I don't care what he talks about," she said, "as long as he starts out with something and keeps me going."

(Whispering:) Good evening.

("Good evening, Seth.")

Dictation: Now let us return again to our discussion of impulses, in connection with probable actions.

(Pause.) You live surrounded by impulses. You must make innumerable decisions in your lives — must choose careers, mates, cities of residence. Experience can help you make decisions, but you <u>make</u> decisions long before you have years of experience behind you.

Overall, whether or not you are conscious of it — for some of you are, and some of you are not — your lives do have a certain psychological shape. That shape is formed by your decisions. You make decisions as the result of feeling impulses to do this or that, to perform in one manner or another, in response to both private considerations and in regard to demands seemingly placed upon you by others. In the vast arena of those numberless probabilities open to you, you do of course have some guidelines. Otherwise you would always be in a state of indecision. Your personal impulses provide those guidelines by showing you how best to use probabilities so that you fulfill your own potential to greatest advantage — and [in] so doing, provide constructive help to the society at large.

When you are taught not to trust your impulses you begin to lose your powers of decision, and to whatever extent involved in the circumstances, you begin to lose your sense of power because you are afraid to act.

Many people in a quandary of indecision write to Ruburt. Such a correspondent might lament, for example: "I do not know what to do, or what direction to follow. I think that I could make music my career. I am musically gifted. On the other hand *(pause)*, I feel a leaning toward psychology. I have not attended to my music lately, since I am so confused. Sometimes I think I could be a teacher. In the meantime, I am meditating and hoping that the answer will come." *(Pause.)* Such a person is afraid to trust any one impulse enough to act upon it. All remain equally probable activities. Meditation must be followed by action — and true meditation <u>is action</u> (underlined). Such people are afraid of making decisions, because they are afraid of their own impulses — and some of them <u>can</u> use meditation to dull their impulses, and actually prevent constructive action.

(9:35.) Impulses arise in a natural, spontaneous, constructive response to the abilities, potentials, and needs of the personality. They

are meant as directing forces. Luckily, the child usually walks before it is old enough to be taught that impulses are wrong, and luckily the child's natural impulses toward exploration, growth, fulfillment, action and power are strong enough to give it the necessary spring-board before your belief systems begin to erode its confidence. You have physical adult bodies. The pattern for each adult body existed in the fetus — which again, "luckily," impulsively, followed its own direction.

(With gentle irony:) No one told it that it was impossible to grow from a tiny cell — change that to a tiny <u>organism</u> instead of a cell — to a complicated adult structure. What tiny, spindly, threadlike, weak legs you all once had in your mother's wombs! Those legs now climb mountains, stride gigantic boulevards, because they followed their own impulsive shapes. Even the atoms and molecules within them sought out their own most favorable probabilities. And in terms that you do not understand, even those atoms and molecules made their own decisions as the result of recognizing and following those impul-sive sparks toward <u>action</u> that are inherent in all consciousness, what-ever their statuses in your terms *(all with intensity and feeling)*.

Consciousness attempts to grow toward its own ideal develop-ment, which also promotes the ideal development of all organiza-tions in which it takes part.

We are back, then, to the matter of the ideal and its actualization. When and how do your impulses affect the world? Again, what is the ideal, the good impulse, and why does it seem that your experience is so far from that ideal that it appears to be evil?

End of chapter, and give us a moment.

CHAPTER 9

The Ideal, the Individual, Religion, Science, and the Law

(**P**_ause at 9:45._) "The Ideal, the Individual, Religion, Science, and the Law" _(all with some humor and emphasis)._ That is the heading for our next chapter _(9)._

What is the law? Why do you have law?

("Law, or laws?")

Why do you have laws? You may follow it with that. Are laws made to protect life, to protect property, to establish order, to punish transgressors? Are laws made to protect man from his own cunning and chicanery? In short, are laws made to protect man from his own "basically criminal nature"?

Are laws made to protect man from the self as it is generally outlined by Freud and Darwin? Man had laws, however, far earlier. Are laws made then to protect man from his "sinful nature"? _(Pause.)_ If you were all "perfect beings," would you need laws at all? Do laws define what is unacceptable, or do they hint of some perhaps undifferentiated, barely sensed, more positive issues? Are laws an attempt to limit impulses? Do they represent society's mass definitions of what behavior is acceptable and what is not?

What is the difference between a crime and a sin, as most of you think of those terms? Can the state punish you for a sin? It certainly

can punish you for a crime. Is the law a reflection of something else —
a reflection of man's inherent search toward the ideal, and its actualization? When does the law act as a practical idealist? Why do you
sneer so when politicians show their feet of clay?

(Pause.) How does this concern you as an individual? We will start
with the individual.

(Pause at 9:59. Then whispering:) Each individual is innately
driven by a good intent, however distorted that intent may become,
or however twisted the means that may be taken to achieve it.

As the body wants to grow from childhood on, so all of the personality's abilities want to grow and develop. Each person has his [or
her] own ideals, and impulses direct those ideals naturally into their
own specific avenues of development — avenues meant to fulfill
both the individual and his society. Impulses provide specifications,
methods, meanings, definitions. They point toward definite avenues
of expression, avenues that will provide the individual with a sense of
actualization, natural power, and that will automatically provide
feedback, so that the person knows he is impressing his environment
for the better.

(Long pause.) Those natural impulses, followed, will automatically
lead to political and social organizations that become both tools for
individual development and implements for the fulfillment of the
society. Impulses then would follow easily, in a smooth motion, from
private action to social import. When you are taught to block your
impulses, and to distrust them, then your organizations become
clogged. You are left with vague idealized feelings of wanting to
change the world for the better, for example — but you are denied
the personal power of your own impulses that would otherwise help
direct that idealism by developing your personal abilities. You are left
with an undefined, persisting, even tormenting desire to do good, to
change events, but without having any means at your disposal to do
so. This leads to lingering frustration, and if your ideals are strong
the situation can cause you to feel quite desperate.

(Pause in a forceful delivery.) You may begin to exaggerate the gulf
between this generalized ideal and the specific evidences of man's
"greed and corruption" that you see so obviously about you. You may
begin to concentrate upon your own lacks, and in your growing sense

of dissatisfaction it may seem to you that most men are driven by a complete lack of good intent.

You may become outraged, scandalized — or worse, filled with self-righteousness, so that you begin to attack all those with whom you do not agree, because you do not know how else to respond to your own ideals, or to your own good intent *(with much emphasis).*

(10:15.) The job of trying to make the world better seems impossible, for it appears that you have no power, and any small private beneficial actions that you can (underlined) take seem so puny in contrast to this generalized ideal that you dismiss them sardonically, and so you do not try to use your power constructively. You do not begin with your own life, with your own job, or with your own associates. *(Louder:)* What difference can it make to the world if you are a better salesperson, or plumber, or office worker, or car salesman, for Christ's sake? What can one person do?

Yet that is precisely where first of all you must begin to exert yourselves. There, on your jobs and in your associations, are the places where you intersect with the world. Your impulses directly affect the world in those relationships *(intently).*

(Pause.) Many of you are convinced that you are not important — and while [each of] you feels that way it will seem that your actions have no effect upon the world. You will purposefully keep your ideals generalized, thus saving yourself from the necessity of acting upon them in the one way open to you: by trusting yourself and your impulses, and impressing those that you meet in daily life with the full validity that is your own.

Most criminals act out of a sense of despair. Many have high ideals, but ideals that have never been trusted or acted upon. They feel powerless, so that many strike out in self-righteous anger or vengeance against a world that they see as cynical, greedy, perverted. They have concentrated upon the great gaps that seem to exist between their ideals of what man should be, and their ideas of what man is.

On the one hand, they believe that the self is evil, and on the other they are convinced that the self should not be so. They react extravagantly. They often see society as the "enemy" of good. Many — not all, now — criminals possess the same characteristics you ascribe to heroes, except that the heroes have a means toward the expression of idealism, and specific avenues for that expression. And many criminals find such avenues cut off completely.

I do not want to romanticize criminals, or justify their actions. I do want to point out that few crimes are committed for "evil's sake," but in a distorted response to the failure of the actualization of a sensed ideal.

So we return to what is the nature of the ideal and the good. Who defines what is right and wrong, legal and illegal?

End of session, and a fond good evening *(louder).*

("Thank you very much."

(10:32 P.M. Jane's delivery had often been fast and impassioned, even with the indicated pauses. She's begun to slow up toward session's end, though. "There's more there, but I got so I couldn't get it," she said, referring to her very relaxed state, which she still enjoyed. "But I feel this generalized material, then Seth zeros in on it specifically. I think that the session tonight was one of those concentrated ones, where you get a lot in a short time. . . ." I told her she'd done well.)

NOTES: SESSION 860

1. Jane originated the key portion of the new title early last Sunday morning, when she got up at 4 A.M. to have breakfast and make some notes for her book. Through the open patio door she listened to the first bird calls, summoning her outside to watch the foggy dawn unfold. She was entranced. "No one else was watching what I watched from my personal viewpoint that morning," she wrote an hour later. "I felt as if I were being privileged to view a beginning of the world . . . or of my edge of it.

"Or, I thought suddenly, it was like seeing a new corner of your own psyche, transformed into trees, grass, flowers, sky and fog . . . I felt as if I were viewing that part of myself that I'm always pursuing, the part that is as clear-eyed as a child, fleet, at one with its own knowing. That part of us exists apart from our concerns about careers or business, money, fame, the opinion of family, friends, or the world. It's our direct connection with the universe . . . from which we emerge in each moment of our lives.

"So, in that moment, I named that part of me the God of Jane, and that designation makes sense to me, at least. In those terms, we each have our personal 'God,' and I *am* convinced that the universe knows us no matter who or where — or what — we are. I think there is a God of Mitzi, and a God of Billy, for each of our cats, and that each consciousness, regardless of its status, possesses this intimate connection with the universe. . . ."

SESSION 862, JUNE 25, 1979
8:37 P.M. MONDAY

(Jane and I have had two most pleasant surprises since Seth gave the 860th session on June 13. We'd expected both events, but not so soon. On the 14th we received from Prentice-Hall our complimentary copies, just off the press, of Seth's Psyche; *then on the 18th we received Volume 2 of* "Unknown" Reality.

(Volume 2 will be marketed a few weeks in advance of Psyche, *of course, as it should be, even though because of press scheduling the much shorter* Psyche *was printed first. Jane and I admired the books, looking so complete yet spontaneous in their shiny dust jackets. Volume 2 is a massive book, yet I still couldn't believe all the time — almost exactly five years — that had passed since Jane, Seth, and I began work on it. When one added the largely overlapping time spent on Volume 1, our temporal investment approached five-and-a-half years. Naturally we'd been involved in a number of other projects at the same time, as I've indicated in my notes for* Mass Events, *yet for me especially the publication of the two volumes of* "Unknown" Reality *meant that we had arrived at a certain point in the development and presentation of the Seth material: In those books, through correlating them in a modest way with our previous works, I'd attempted to show the reader just what the three of us had managed to achieve before Seth led us into* Psyche — *and, as it developed,* Mass Events.

(Last Wednesday night's regularly scheduled book session wasn't held because we had unexpected visitors after supper. They left late enough so that Jane decided to skip the session, even though earlier in the day she'd written notes on material that Seth had mentally informed her he'd cover.

(Tonight, Jane repeated an idea she'd started talking about before holding the 861st nonbook session just a week ago: She thinks Seth is in the process of finishing Mass Events. *"Not in the next couple of sessions, but he's heading that way. He's given all he can — or wants to — on the negative beliefs we hold as individuals and societies; he wants to start his* next book *[my emphasis] on how to positively work our way out of our challenges*

*and create a much better world . . . You know — that material I've been
telling you about, on therapy and value fulfillment. I was even messing
around with book titles today, though I know I shouldn't do that. "*[1]

*(Jane felt like beginning the session earlier than usual. A good portion
of it is deleted, however, since Seth discussed other subjects before coming
through with material for* Mass Events *at 9:09.)*

Briefly: Dictation.

The law in your country says that you are innocent until proven
guilty. In the eyes of that law, then, you are each innocent until a
crime is proven against you. There usually must also be witnesses.
There are other considerations. Often a spouse cannot testify against
the other. Opportunity and motive must also be established.

In the world of religion, however, you are already tainted by
original sin: "The mark of Cain" is symbolically upon your foreheads.
You come from a species that sinned against God. Automatically
condemned, you must do good works, or be baptized, or believe in
Christ, or perform other acts in order to be saved or redeemed.

According to other religions, you may be "earthbound" by the
"gross desires" of your nature, "bound to the wheel of life," condemned to endless reincarnations until you are "purified." As I have
said before, according to psychology and science, you are a living
conglomeration of elements and chemicals, spawned by a universe
without purpose, itself accidentally formed, and you are given a life
in which all the "primitive and animalistic" drives of your evolutionary past ever lurk within you, awaiting expression and undermining
your control.

So, dear reader, look at the law as it stands in this country with
somewhat more kindly eyes than you have before — for it at least
legally establishes a belief in your innocence, and for all of its failings, it protects you from the far more fanatical aspects, say, of any
religion's laws.

Religious laws deal with sin, whether or not a crime is committed
(pause), and religious concepts usually take it for granted that the
individual is guilty until proven innocent. And if you have not committed a crime in fact, then you have at least sinned in your heart —
for which, of course, you must be punished. A sin can be anything
from playing cards to having a sexual fantasy. You are sinful creatures.
How many of you believe that?

(Deliberately:) You were born with an in-built recognition of your own goodness. You were born with an inner recognition of your rightness in the universe. You were born with a desire to fulfill your abilities, to move and act in the world. Those assumptions are the basis of what I will call natural law.

You are born loving. You are born compassionate. You are born curious about yourself and your world. Those attributes also belong to natural law. You are born knowing that you possess a unique, intimate sense of being that is itself, and that seeks its own fulfillment, and the fulfillment of others. You are born seeking the actualization of the ideal. You are born seeking to add value to the quality of life, to add characteristics, energies, abilities to life that only you can individually contribute to the world, and to attain a state of being that is uniquely yours, while adding to the value fulfillment of the world.

(9:29.) All of these qualities and attributes are given you by natural law. You are a cooperative species, and you are a loving one. Your misunderstandings, your crimes, and your atrocities, real as they are, are seldom committed out of any intent to be evil, but because of severe misinterpretations about the nature of good, and the means that can be taken toward its actualization. Most individual people know that in some inner portion of themselves. Your societies, governments, educational systems, are all built around a firm belief in the unreliability of human nature. "You cannot change human nature." Such a statement takes it for granted that man's nature is to be greedy, a predator, a murderer at heart. You act in accordance with your own beliefs. You become the selves that you think you are. Your individual beliefs become the beliefs of your society, but that is always a give-and-take.

Shortly we will begin to discuss the formation of a better kind of mass reality — a reality that can happen as more and more individuals begin to come in contact with the true nature of the self. Then we will have less frightened people, and fewer fanatics, and each person involved can to some extent begin to see the "ideal" come into practical actualization. The means never justify the ends.

End of session. A fond good evening — and my hurrahs to Ruburt *(Jane).*

("He's doing very well.")

That is what I meant.

("All right. Thank you."

(9:40 P.M. Jane said that in his dictation this evening, Seth covered some of the information she'd picked up from him nonverbally, then written about prior to the session that wasn't held last Wednesday night. "But there's also more there he didn't get into yet.")

NOTES: SESSION 862

1. Just before giving the 861st session last week, Jane received from Seth some intriguing material on the idea that in psychological therapy, the good intents and impulses beneath the client's emotional and physical hassles should be searched out by the analyst. She made some notes about the information. It was very promising material, she told me, and could help change conventional ideas of therapy. A book could actually be involved — Seth's next — on "the therapy of value fulfillment." She was quite excited by the new ideas she'd presented herself with.

Then in the 861st session itself — which was not for *Mass Events*, as stated — Seth briefly mentioned the material on ideals and impulses he's been giving in recent book sessions. This in turn led him to comment on the notes Jane had just written. He certainly sounded as though he'd decided upon his next book:

"The therapy of value fulfillment will attempt to put individuals in touch with their basic instincts, to allow them to sense the impulsive shapes of their lives, to define their own versions of the ideal through the recognition of it as it exists in their own impulses and feelings and abilities, and to help them find acceptable and practical methods of exerting their natural power in the practical actualization of those ideals."

SESSION 863, JUNE 27, 1979
9:10 P.M. WEDNESDAY

(In my Introductory Notes for Volume 1 of "Unknown" Reality, I explained how Jane acknowledges the mail we get from our readers by sending them copies of letters from Seth and herself; to the latter she adds a few personal lines for each correspondent. She also encloses a list of her books, which many readers ask for. Seth dictated his letter in April 1975, just after finishing his part of the work for Volume 2 of "Unknown," and I presented it while introducing Volume 1. Jane still handles most of the mail herself, and she continues to send people Seth's letter because we still think he presented excellent ideas in it.

(In those notes I also referred to an earlier letter that Seth had dictated for readers in January 1973, and it can be found in Chapter 8 of Personal Reality. *Jane and I suggested then, as we do now, that when possible the two Seth letters be read together, since they compliment each other so well.*

(Jane receives 35 to 50 letters a week. The flow of mail to our hill house is surprisingly steady throughout the year, as we've often noticed: We never take in 100 letters one week, for instance, and none the next, or 70 one week and 15 the next. In some remarkable fashion, our correspondents space out their communications so that we get them on a steady basis. We have time to read each one. Each Saturday and Sunday Jane catches up with her replies for the week, brief as they often are, so that on Monday morning, when I put out that bundle of letters for the mailman, we're ready for the next week's accumulation. All of the mail doesn't need answering, of course, but the other day we estimated that with very little help from me Jane now replies to around 2,000 letters a year. That total is slowly increasing as her work becomes better known.

(In Note 2 for Session 801, I commented on the sociological implications represented by her correspondence.

(Whispering once again to start:) Good evening.

("Good evening, Seth.")

Dictation: When I speak of natural law, I am not referring to the scientists' laws of nature, such as the law of gravity, for example — which is not a law at all, but a manifestation appearing from the viewpoint of a certain level of consciousness as a result of perceptive apparatus. Your "prejudiced perception" is also built into your instruments in that regard.

(Pause.) I am speaking of the inner laws of nature, that pervade existence. What you call nature refers of course to your particular experience with reality, but quite different kinds of manifestations are also "natural" outside of that context. The laws of nature that I am in the process of explaining underlie all realities, then, and form a firm basis for multitudinous kinds of "natures." I will put these in your terms of reference, however.

(Long pause.) Each being experiences life as if it were at life's center. This applies to a spider in a closet as well as to any man or woman. This principle applies to each atom as well. Each manifestation of consciousness comes into being feeling secure at life's center — experiencing life through itself,[1] aware of life through its own

nature. It comes into being with an inner impetus toward value fulfillment. It is equipped with a feeling of safety, of security within its own environment with which it is fit to deal. It is given the impetus toward growth and action, and filled with the desire to impress its world.

(9:21.) The term "value fulfillment" is very difficult to explain, but it is very important. Obviously it deals with the development of values — not moral values, however, but values for which you really have no adequate words. Quite simply, these values have to do with increasing the quality of whatever life the being feels at its center. The quality of that life is not simply to be handed down or experienced, for example, but is to be creatively added to, multiplied, in a way that has nothing to do with quantity.

In those terms, animals have values, and if the quality of their lives disintegrates beyond a certain point, the species dwindles. We are not speaking of survival of the fittest, but the survival of life with meaning *(intently)*. Life is meaning for animals. The two are indistinguishable.

(Pause.) You say little, for example, if you note that spiders make webs instinctively because spiders must eat insects, and that the best web-maker will be the fittest kind of spider to survive. *(Long pause, then with humor:)* It is very difficult for me to escape the sticky web of your beliefs. The web, however, in its way represents an actualized ideal on the spider's part — and if you will forgive the term, an artistic one as well. *(Louder:)* It amazes the spiders that flies so kindly fall into those webs. You might say that the spider wonders that art can be so practical.

(Pause at 9:30.) What about the poor unsuspecting fly? Is it then so enamored of the spider's web that it loses all sense of caution? *(Whispering, and dryly:)* For surely flies are the victims of such nefarious webby splendors. We are into sticky stuff indeed.

(Still in trance, Jane paused to pour herself a little wine.)

For one thing, you are dealing with different kinds of consciousness than your own. They are focused consciousnesses, surely, each one feeling itself at life's center. While this is the case, however, these other forms of consciousness also identify then with the source of nature from which they emerge. In a way impossible to explain, the fly and the spider are connected, and <u>aware</u> of the connection. Not as hunter and prey, but as individual participants in deeper processes. Together they work toward a joint kind of value fulfillment, in which both are fulfilled.

(Pause.) There are communions of consciousness of which you are unaware. While you believe in theories like the survival of the fittest, however, and the grand fantasies of evolution, then you put together your perceptions of the world so that they seem to bear out those theories. You will see no value in the life of a mouse sacrificed in the laboratory, for example, and you will project claw-and-fang battles in nature, completely missing the great cooperative venture that <u>is</u> (underlined) involved.

(Pause.) Men can become deranged if they believe life has no meaning. Religion has made gross errors. At least it held out an afterlife, a hope of salvation, and preserved — sometimes despite itself — the tradition of the heroic soul. Science, including psychology, by what it has said, and by what it has neglected to say, has come close to a declaration that life itself is meaningless. This is a direct contradiction of deep biological knowledge, to say nothing of spiritual truth. It denies the meaning of biological integrity. It denies man the practical use of those very elements that he needs as a biological creature: the feeling that he is at life's center, that he can act safely in his environment, that he can trust himself, and that his being and his actions have meaning.

(9:44.) Impulses provide life's guide to action. If you are taught that you cannot trust your impulses, then you are set against your very physical integrity. If you believe that <u>your life</u> has no meaning, then you will do anything to provide meaning, all the while acting like a mouse in one of science's mazes — for your prime directive, so to speak, has been tampered with.

(Pause, then forcefully:) I am trying to temper my statements here, but your psychology of the past 50 years has helped <u>create</u> insanities by trying to reduce the great individual thrust of life that lies within each person, to a generalized mass of chaotic impulses and chemicals — a mixture, again, of Freudian and Darwinian thought, misapplied.

The most private agonies of the soul were assigned a more or less common source in man's primitive "unconscious" drives. The private

unquelled thrusts toward creativity were seen as the unbalanced conglomeration of chemicals within a person's most private being — a
twist of perversity. Genius was seen as a mistake of chromosomes, or
the fortunate result of a man's hatred for his father. The meaning of
life was reduced to the accidental nature of genes. Science thought
in terms of averages and statistics, and each person was supposed to
fit within those realms.

To some extent, this also applies to religion in the same time
period. Churches wanted sinners galore, but shied away from saints,
or any extravagant behavior that did not speak of man's duplicity.
Suddenly people with paranoidal characteristics, as well as schizo-
phrenics,[2] emerged from the wallpaper of this slickly styled civilization. The characteristics of each were duly noted. A person who feels
that life has no meaning, and that his or her life in particular has no
meaning, would rather be pursued than ignored. Even the weight of
guilt is better than no feeling at all. If the paranoid might feel that
he [or she] is pursued, by the government or "ungodly powers," then
at least he feels that his life must be important: otherwise, why would
others seek to destroy it? If voices tell him he is to be destroyed, then
these at least are comforting voices, for they convince him that his life
must have value.

At the same time, the paranoid person can use his creative abilities in fantasies that seemingly boggle the minds of the sane — and
those creative abilities have a meaning, for the fantasies, again, serve
to reassure the paranoid of his worth. If in your terms he were sane,
he could not use his creative abilities, for they are always connected
with life's meaning; and sane, the paranoid is convinced that life is
meaningless. It did little good in the past for Freudian psychologists
to listen to a person's associations (pause) while maintaining an
objective air, or pretending that values did not exist. Often the
person labeled schizophrenic is so frightened of his or her own
energy, impulses, and feelings that these are fragmented, objectified, and seen to come from outside rather than from within.

Ideas of good and evil are exaggerated, cut off from each other.
Yet here again the creative abilities are allowed some expression.
The person does not feel able to express them otherwise. Such
people are afraid of the brunt of their own personalities. They have

been taught that energy is wrong, that power is disastrous, and that the impulses of the self are to be feared.

What protection, then, but to effectively project these outside of the self — impulses of good as well as evil — and hence effectively block organized action?

(Pause at 10:07.) The term schizophrenia, with the authority of psychology, becomes a mass coverall in which the integrity of personal meaning is given a mass, generalized explanation. Those who are paranoid are, unfortunately, those who most firmly believe the worst idiocies of science and religion. The paranoid and the schizophrenic are trying to find meaning in a world they have been taught is meaningless, and their tendencies appear in lesser form throughout society.

Creativity is an in-built impetus in man, far more important than, say, what science calls the satisfaction of basic needs. In those terms, creativity is the most basic need of all. I am not speaking here of any obsessive need to find order — in which case, for example, a person might narrow his or her mental and physical environment — but of a powerful drive within the species for creativity, and for the fulfillment of values that are emotional and spiritual. And if man does not find these *(louder),* then the so-called basic drives toward food or shelter will not sustain him.

I am not simply saying that man does not live for bread alone. I am saying that if man does not find meaning in life he will not live, bread or no. He will not have the energy to seek bread, nor trust his impulse to do so.

There are natural laws, then, that guide all kinds of life, and all realities — laws of love and cooperation — and those are the basic needs of which I am speaking.

(Whispering:) End of session.

("Okay. Good night."

(10:17 P.M. "Now that's weird," Jane said as soon as Seth withdrew, "It's only a quarter after ten, but I feel that what we got is way beyond in proportion to the time involved. Before the session I knew he was going into schizophrenia and so forth, but he went past those inklings. . . ." Indeed, her delivery had often been intense, and quite demanding as far as my writing speed went.)

NOTES: SESSION 863

1. In recent weeks Jane herself has been quite intrigued by the idea of "personal centering," as she put it in her notes for *God of Jane.* She also wants to study the subject for her book in connection with reincarnation, the origins of our species — and even of our world. She's already written several poems about her own view of reality. The one that follows charmed me as soon as she produced it last May 31. It'll probably end up in *God of Jane,* but I'd like to present it here, too:

No Matter Where I Look

No matter where I look, I seem to be
at the center of a world that forms
perfectly around me.
No lopsided vision ever shows
the world spread only to my left,
with my image on the last right edge,
nor has the world
ever appeared just ahead,
while nothingness began
just behind my back.

I sit in a swivel chair
with smooth ball bearings.
Without warning, I turn myself
around in a complete circle,
but nothing disturbs
my world vision,
and objects appear on all sides
with sweet precision,
as if a projector in my head
sends out invisible rays that turn
into images, so I
always seem inside
dimensions of depth
and weight.

2. Seth discussed paranoia in the 812th session; see the beginning of Chapter 6.

These brief definitions are very general: A paranoid is afflicted with systematic, logically-reasoned delusions of grandeur or persecution; the personality can be relatively stable otherwise. A schizophrenic suffers from a division between thought processes and emotions. The cause of schizophrenia is unknown, and the victim usually ends up hospitalized because of the severity of symptoms, which can include motor malfunctions, perceptual distortions involving hallucinations and delusions, strange behavior, and a withdrawal from reality. Yet the schizophrenic can also keep the use of his or her primary intellectual capacities.

SESSION 866, JULY 18, 1979
9:04 P.M. WEDNESDAY

(Since the 863rd session was held three weeks ago, Seth has given us but two regular sessions — both on subjects other than those for Mass Events — *and two private sessions.*

(According to him, tonight's session after 9:52 isn't book material either, but Jane and I are presenting it here because in it Seth returns to questions I'd asked earlier in Mass Events: *What about the roles played in human affairs by viruses like smallpox? As I quoted myself in the opening notes for the 840th session: "What is the* real *relationship between the host organism and disease?" See Session 840 itself, and certain parts of Session 841.*

(My questions had been rearoused because of an article I'd read a few days ago in a scientific journal; in their piece the authors explained that a certain significant percentage of women can develop cervical cancer from contact with a virus carried by the sperm of males who haven't had vasectomies — or who haven't been sterilized, in other words. I found the whole premise or situation strange indeed, I told Jane — that the male of our species actually has the potential to pass on cancer to the female. We've heard of the theory before, by the way — but transmitting cancer in such a fashion seems to be one of the most deadly results that can follow from the union of a man and a woman. We became intensely curious as to how Seth would explain the whole matter, and he gave us excellent information on it. The chances for ironies abound in our belief systems, I said to Jane. What if researchers next find out that in some as-yet-unsuspected manner, the female can in turn pass on a cancer-causing virus to her mate?

(The evening was a bit cooler than evenings have been lately. Jane was rather quiet as we waited for Seth to come through. "All those questions," she said when I asked her about her silence. "All those things I'm supposed to answer . . . I guess I've been brooding because I fell into that trap Seth talks about — of thinking that I've got to save the world. . . . "

(Then we both laughed. There isn't any saving of the world necessary, we agreed. The world doesn't need to be saved. It's perfectly capable of surviving even while it's home to a species as obstreperous as man. After all, I said, man is but one species who creates his perception of the living earth in concert with nearly innumerable other species — and each other species does the same thing from its viewpoint. Even with his seemingly destructive ways, man can injure that joint reality only to a minor extent, regardless of such potential fiascos as that posed by Three Mile Island, or even nuclear war. In particular, I reminded Jane of a paragraph of material Seth gave in the 865th nonbook session, which she held a week ago from last Monday evening:

("Fortunately, the power of constructive action and thought is indeed paramount in nature and in your world. Otherwise, you would simply not exist. The cooperative ventures that crisscross this community of Elmira, in biological, social, spiritual, economic, political and artistic ways are staggering. That cooperation goes unnoticed, largely, yet it rests firmly upon the stability that is characteristic within all life. Period. ")

Dictation.

(Pause.) Each species is endowed with emotional feelings, immersed in an interior system of value fulfillment. Each species, again, then, is not only concerned with physical survival and the multiplication of its members, but [with] an intensification and fulfillment of those particular qualities that are characteristic of it.

As far as this discussion is concerned, there are biological ideals, imprinted within the chromosomes, but there are also in-built ideals much more difficult to define, that exist as, say, mental blueprints for the development of other kinds of abilities. I use the word mental, meaning that all species possess their own kinds of interior mental life, as opposed to the physical characteristics of plants or animals with which you are familiar. Your official views effectively close you off from the true evidence you might perceive of the cooperation that exists among the species, for example. Nor am I speaking of an enforced cooperation — the result of "instinct" that somehow arranges the social habits of the animals; for their habits are indeed social and cooperative.

Ruburt was recently scandalized upon reading that orthodox science still does not grant man with volition. According to its tenets, any such feeling of conscious choice is instead the reflection of the brain's attitude at any given time. Yet I am saying that man has free will within the framework of his existence, and that all other species do also within the frameworks of their existences (underlined).

The chicken cannot read a book. It cannot choose to read. The plant cannot choose to walk down the street. The chicken and the plant can choose to live or die, however — rather important issues in the existence of any entity. They can choose to like or dislike their environment, and to change it according to their individual circumstances. It is fashionable to say that some scientific laws can be proven at microscopic levels, where, for example, small particles can be accelerated far beyond [their usual states]. But you quite studiously ignore that feeling exists on microscopic levels, that there can be psychological particles, much less come to the conclusion that all particles are psychological particles, with their own impetuses for development and value fulfillment. That is why atoms join together to form matter. They seek the fulfillment of themselves through form. They cooperatively choose the forms that they take.

(9:23.) If the simplest particle is so endowed with impetus, with hidden ideals that seek fulfillment, then what about the human being? You have the propensity to search for meaning, for love, for cooperative ventures. You have the propensity to form dazzling mental and psychological creations, such as your arts and sciences and religions and civilizations. Whatever errors that you have made, or gross distortions, even those exist because of your need to find meaning [in] your private existence and [in] life itself.

Any scientist who believes that life has no meaning has simply provided himself with what he thinks of as an unfailing support against life's vicissitudes. If he says: "Life has no meaning," he cannot be disappointed if such is the case, for he is ensconced in a self-created cocoon that has meaning (underlined), because it provides a cushion against his deepest fears *(all very intently).*

When a civilization does not support creativity it begins to falter. When it distrusts its gifted people, rather than encouraging them, a nation is at least in trouble. Your psychologies, stressing "the norm," made people frightened of their individual characteristics and abilities, because psychology's norm did not fit the contours of any one human being. It did not touch the heights or the depths of human experience. People became afraid of their own individuality.

Ruburt today read an article about gifted children — their background and development. Gifted children do not fit psychology's picture. Gifted children do not fit the portrait of children that is sold to parents. The fact is that for many reasons gifted children merely show the latent quickness, mental agility, and curiosity and learning capacity, that is inherent in the species. They are not eccentric versions of humanity at all, but instead provide a hint of mankind's true capacities.

(Pause.) Your brains are not empty, but well-oiled machines ready to whirl into activity at your births. They are provided with a propensity to learn — and the rudiments of knowledge as you understand it exits within the brain *(intently)*. In those terms, now, the brain thinks before birth. It does not simply react. Each individual has its own unique abilities. Some that involve relationships with others, you do not even have words for. Parents, however, often half-disapprove of their children if they show unusual gifts. They are afraid their children will not get along with others. They are upset because the children do not fit the norm — but no child ever fits "the norm."

Many adults, sensing their own abilities in one field or another, deliberately play down those abilities because they are afraid of standing out from "the masses" — or they are afraid they will be attacked by their peers. They have been taught by religion and science alike that any kind of greatness is suspect. Yet each person alive contains an element of greatness; and more, a desire to fulfill those inner abilities.

I am not speaking of greatness in terms of fame, or in terms of usually understood artistic or intellectual abilities alone, but also of people whose lives have the capacity for great emotional content. I am speaking also of other natural abilities — that of dream communication, the conscious utilization of dreams and creativity in daily life. There are dimensions of human sentiment and psychological experience, that remain latent simply because you focus your attention so closely within the idea of "the norm." Any unofficial experience must then remain bizarre, eccentric, outside of your main concerns, and ignored by your sciences *(quietly)*.

Many children, for that matter, who are regarded as retarded by their teachers, are instead highly gifted. The same also applies to disruptive children, who are overactive and put on drugs. Their rebellion is quite natural. Autistic children, in many cases, now, are those who have picked up the idea that the world is so unsafe that it is better not to communicate with it at all, as long as their demands or needs are being met. When the child is fed and clothed and cared for, then it continues its behavior, and the behavior itself does (underlined) serve its needs.

(Pause at 9:46.) The child feels that it is not safe to interact with the world, however. No one is going to deprive a child of food, and yet food can be used in such cases, in terms perhaps of treats, if the child must ask for them, or in some way indicate a choice. Autistic children are afraid of making choices. Some of this is often picked up from parents, so that the child expresses their own unacknowledged fears. The autistic child [can be] highly intelligent, however.

To some extent, such a child symbolizes what happens when an individual believes that he or she is unworthy, that he or she cannot trust impulses, that choices present more problems than advantages. That it is safer to hide abilities than it is to use them. Life is expression.

End of dictation.

(9:52.) I will give the beginning of an answer *(to my question about the relationship between the host organism and disease).* You make your own reality. That should be your complete answer *(with humor),* but obviously it is not.

First of all, if (underlined) a sperm carrying cancer entered a woman's uterus, and if she had no intentions of getting the disease, her body's own system would make the cancer completely ineffective. In the second place, however, referring to the article, that is not what happens to begin with — and I am somewhat at a loss to explain, simply because of certain invisible assumptions that it seems to me you must necessarily make.

(Pause.) I will explain as best I can, though some of what I say will certainly seem contradictory to scientific knowledge.

Though scientists might find "cancer cells," and though it might seem that cancer is caused by a virus, cancer instead involves a relationship, say, between what you might think of as a host and parasite, in those terms — and to some extent the same applies to any disease, including smallpox, though the diseases themselves may appear to have different causes completely. A host cell, say, is not simply attacked. It invites attack, though I am not pleased at all with

the connotations of the word "attack." I am trying to use words familiar to you to start.

It is not simply that a cell suddenly "relaxes its defenses" against
disease. As easily as I can, I will try to explain. A cell mirrors a psychological state. A cell exists by itself, as its own entity, but also in
context with all of the other cells in the body. There are literally
uncountable psychological states mixing and interchanging constantly, with the overall psychological stance being one of biological
integrity (colon): The organism holds together, maintains its functions, and so forth.

Your body is the physical mirror of your psychological state *(quietly intent)*. It is <u>powered</u> by the energy of the universe. It actually
springs into being in each moment. Your mind and your body come
from the same source, from universal energy. You are powered with
vitality. You must seek meaning in your lives. When you lose the
sense of life's meaning, for whatever reason, this is reflected in your
body. *(Pause.)* It is very difficult to separate all of this from the many
connotations placed about disease, and I do not want the material to
be misread *(still intently)*. Cancer, for example, has become the
symbol for the body's vulnerability, in current years — the proof of
man's susceptibility to the body. It is a disease that people have when
they want to die — when they are ashamed to admit that they want
to die, because death seems to fly against sane behavior. If the
species struggles to survive, then how can individuals want to die?

I have mentioned before that many people have had cancer and
recovered without knowing it. In your belief system, however, it is
almost imperative to see a doctor in such circumstances *(as Jane wrote
in Note 2 for Session 805)*, for many fears are unsubstantiated, and the
fear alone, found groundless, gives the person new life symbolically
and physically.

In the case of your article, a woman's cells would already have
had to prepare themselves for the guest — granted that guest was
cancerous, and was a sperm. There is not an attack. There is an
<u>acceptance</u>, and a preparation for certain changes.

(Pause at 10:13.) A life crisis is formed. The "parasite," or virus,
plays its part in setting up such a psychologically-desired position. It
is an emotionally-charged position, an imminent crisis. I am aware of
the tormenting questions involved in such issues, and also of the gap

between my explanations and the daily experiences of many people. The fact is that when death comes it is wanted; it has been chosen.

The fact is that death in its way is the culmination of life, leading toward a new birth and new experience. The cells know this. So does the heart. People cannot admit that they want to die at certain times. If they could accept the fact of their own wishes, some could even change their minds. Many do: The psychological condition changes for the better, and the body cells are no longer amiable to the cancerous condition.

Women whose husbands have had vasectomies have themselves often resolved sexual problems that have bothered them. Fear is reduced in that area. *(Long pause.)* Cervical cancer can involve — can involve — distortions of the growth process itself, because of the complicated distortions of belief on the woman's part. In a way the very pain of cancer — of some cancers — often acts through its intensity as a reflection of the person's belief that life is painful, tormenting. At the same time, the pain is a reminder of feeling and sensation.

(Pause.) That is all for this evening. A fond good evening to you both.

("Thank you very much. Good night.")

(End at 10:23 P.M.)

SESSION 867, JULY 23, 1979
9:28 P.M. MONDAY

(The evening was very humid but cool after a late-afternoon thunderstorm. Jane felt the humidity as we sat for the session at 9:15. She had no questions for Seth, but expected him to continue his material of last Wednesday night, when he'd started an answer to my question about the relationship between the host organism and disease. This idea had come to her "pretty strongly" after supper: "It won't be dictation. I think there's a whole lot there — but you know, it's not quite here yet," she said.

(Neighbors stopped in at 8:45, however, and Jane explained afterward that because of the visit, brief as it was, the material had "retreated away" from her internal perception somewhat. "So I'm just waiting for it to come forward again," she said. When it did, Seth followed the nonbook portion of the last session so well that we want to include it in Mass Events. Finally:)

Now: Good evening.

("Good evening, Seth.")

I can be perplexed *(wryly)*, and it was my perplexity that Ruburt felt, for there is indeed much information that I want to give you along certain lines. And yet I must contend with modes of thought that are habitual to you, and those modes make it difficult for you to combine various elements of speculation.

As always, I will do the best that I can *(smiling)*, using concepts with which you are familiar, at least to begin. I realize that current experience may perhaps seem contradictory to some of these ideas, so bear with me. I will, therefore, combine the idea of a disease with the idea of creativity, for the two are intimately connected.

(Pause.) Briefly, remember analogies I have made in the past, comparing the landscape of physical experience to the painter's landscape — which may be dark, gloomy, filled with portents of disaster, and yet still be a work of art. In that regard, every person paints his or her own portrait in living color — a portrait that does not simply sit in a tranquil pose at a table, but one that has the full capacity for action. Those of you now living, say, are in the same life class. You look about to see how your contemporaries are getting along with their portraits, and you find multitudinous varieties: tragic self-portraits, heroic self-portraits, comic self-portraits. And all of these portraits are alive and interacting, and as they interact they form the planetary, mass social and political events of your world.

These portraits obviously have a biological reality. In a manner of speaking, now, each person dips into the same supplies of paint, and so forth — which are the elements out of which your likenesses emerge. There must be great creative leeway allowed for such portraits. Each one interacting with each other one helps form the psychological and physical reality of the species, so you are somehow involved in the formation of a multitudinous number of portraits. I simply want you to keep that analogy in the background.

(Pause.) These portraits, however, are the result of creativity so inborn and miraculous that they are created automatically — an automatic art. At certain levels the species is always creatively embarked upon alternate versions of itself. The overall patterns will remain. Biological integrity is [everywhere] sustained. What you think of as diseases, however, are quite creative elements working at different levels, and at many levels at once.

(9:46.) Many viruses are vital to physical existence, and in your terms there are gradations of activity, so that only under certain conditions do viruses turn into, say, what you think of as deadly ones. The healthiest body contains within it many so-called deadly viruses in <u>what you may call</u> (underlined) an inactive form — inactive from your viewpoint, in that they are not causing disease. They <u>are</u>, however, helping to maintain the body's overall balance. <u>In a way</u> (underlined) in each body, the species settles upon a known status quo, and yet experiments creatively at many levels with cellular alterations, chromosomal variations, so that of course each body is unique. There are kinds of gradations, say, in the lines and kinds of disease. Certain diseases can actually strengthen the body from a prior weaker state, by calling upon the body's full defenses. Under certain conditions, some so-called disease states could insure the species' survival.

(Long pause, one of many.) Give us a moment . . . *(Long pause.)* It is very difficult to explain. *(Pause.)* In a way, some disease states help to insure the survival of the species — not by weeding out the sickly but by introducing into large numbers of individuals the conditions needed to stabilize other strains within the species that need to be checked, or to "naturally inoculate" the species against a sensed greater danger.

At the minute levels — microscopic levels — there are always some biological experiments being carried out, in a creative effort to give the species as much leeway as possible for effective action. Your body is changed biologically by your thoughts.

(Long pause at 10:01.) Your culture has its biological effect upon the species. I am not speaking of obvious connections in a derogatory manner, such as pollution and so forth. If you were thinking in old terms of evolution, then I would be saying that your cultures and civilizations actually alter the chromosomal messages. Your thoughts affect your cells, again, and they can change what are thought of as hereditary factors. Give us a moment . . . Your imaginations are intimately connected with your diseases, just as your imaginations are so important in all other areas of your lives. You form your being by imaginatively considering such-and-such a possibility, and your thoughts affect your body in that regard. In a way, illness is a tool used on behalf of life, for people have given it social, economic,

psychological, and religious connotations. It becomes another area of activity and of expression.

I have told you that at microscopic levels there is no rigid (under-lined) self-structure like your own. There is identity. A cell does not fear its own death. Its identity has traveled back and forth from phys-ical to nonphysical reality too often as a matter of course.

It "sings" with the quality of its own life. It cooperates with other cells. It affiliates itself with the body of which it is part, but in a way it lends itself to that formation. *(Pause.)* The dreams of the species are highly important to its survival — not just because dreaming is a bio-logical necessity, but because in dreams the species is immersed in deeper levels of creativity, so that those actions, inventions, ideas that will be needed in the future will appear in their proper times and places. In the old terms of evolution, I am saying that man's evolu-tionary progress was also dependent upon his dreams.

(10:20.) Give us a moment . . . Now many of the characteristics you consider human — in fact, most of them — appear to one extent or another in all other species. It was the nature of man's dreams, however, that was largely responsible for what you like to think of as the evolution of your species. *(Intently:)* You learned to dream differ-ently than other creatures. I thought you would like that quotation.

("It's very good.")

You dreamed you spoke languages before their physical inven-tion, of course. It was the nature of your dreams, and your dreams' creativity, that made you what you are, for otherwise you would have developed a mechanical-like language — had you developed one at all — that named designations, locations, and dealt with the most simple, objective reality: "I walked there. He walks there. The sun is hot." You would not have had that kind of bare statement of physical fact. You would not have had *(pause)* any way *(pause)* of conceiving of objects that did not already exist. You would not have had any way of imagining yourselves in novel situations. You would not have had any overall picture of the seasons, for dreaming educated the memory and lengthened man's attention span. It reinforced the lessons of daily life, and was highly important in man's progress.

Using the intellect alone, man did not simply learn through daily experience over the generations, say, that one season followed the other. He lived too much in the moment for that. In one season he dreamed of the others, however, and in dreams he saw himself spreading the seeds of fruits as he had seen the wind do in daily life.

His dreams reminded him that a cold season had come, and would come again. Most of your inventions came in dreams, and, again, it is the nature of your dreams that makes you so different from other species.

(10:35.) Give us a moment . . . The creativity of the species is also the result of your particular kind of dream specialization. It amounts to — amounts to — a unique state of existence by itself, in which you combine the elements of physical and nonphysical reality. It is almost a threshold between the two realities, and you learned to hold your physical intent long enough at that threshold so that you have a kind of brief attention span there, and use it to draw from nonphysical reality precisely those creative elements that you need. Period.

Animals, as a rule (underlined) are less physically-oriented in their dreaming states. They do dream of physical reality, but much more briefly than you. Otherwise, they immerse themselves in dreams in different kinds of dreaming consciousness that I hope to explain at a later date *(louder)*.

(Pause.) End of session — but I will continue with the material. I bid you a fond good evening, and we have opened up a fine kettle of metaphysical fish.

(Very good. Good night, Seth, and thank you.")

(10:42 P.M. I've indicated but a few of the many long pauses Jane took while speaking for Seth; in fact, the session had been her slowest one in many months. "Now I see why I felt so puzzled before the session," she said, "even with the company. I just had to sit there and wait for things to be put together in a new way. It was really funny."

(She paused. Then: "I seem to get things that are different toward the ends of books, like where one is leading into the next one. Take the idea of the book Seth mentioned on therapy and value fulfillment, and so forth, and what you said today about body consciousness. Everything's related."

(See the brief references to the therapy of value fulfillment in the opening notes for Session 862, with its Note 1. Today I'd mentioned to Jane how I remembered Seth's saying — perhaps a couple of years ago — that still

untouched in his material is the whole question of the body consciousness, and its role in health and many other fields. Seth had indicated that he had available a vast amount of material on the body consciousness, and that he could give it to us at any time. I've been curious about the subject ever since.

(Now, however, when I remarked that I like tonight's material on dreaming and language, Jane replied: "I wish you hadn't said that. As soon as you did, I felt a circle of information open up — a lot of it — about when ancient man had a series of mass dreams in which he learned how to speak. The dreams were like glossolalia — you know, speaking in unintelligible speech sounds — yet they made sense, and man began to speak. . . ."

(Then a minute later: "Another thing I just got was that when man was with other men in the physical world, he could point to stuff to share descriptions with others, but that he learned to really speak when he tried to describe dreams. It was the only way — speech — by which he could share data that couldn't be seen. He could point to a tree and grunt, but there wasn't anything in a dream he could point to. He had to have a method of expression to describe invisible things. Inventions could have come about when he tried to tell others what he saw in his dreams, too.")

PART FOUR

THE
PRACTICING
IDEALIST

CHAPTER 10

THE GOOD, THE BETTER, AND THE BEST.
VALUE FULFILLMENT VERSUS COMPETITION

SESSION 868, JULY 25, 1979
9:15 P.M. WEDNESDAY

(O*nce again, Jane was uncomfortable because of the very humid evening.)*

(As we prepared for the session I mentioned that I wouldn't mind if Seth commented on a particularly vivid dream I'd had last night. I'd written a detailed account of it upon arising, as I do with all dreams I recall, and Jane had read it as we ate breakfast. I wasn't sure that she heard me now, though. "I think Seth's going to add a Part 4 to this book," she said, "and he's going to call it 'The Practicing Idealist.' And I want to keep changing it to 'Practicing Idealism,' because his heading sounds too much like it's already been used. Wasn't that a book? I think it might have been written by a political figure, though I'm not sure. . . ."

(I could only reply that I didn't know of a book called The Practicing Idealist. *Then:)*

Good evening.

(Good evening, Seth.")

Dictation. *(With humor:)* Part 4: "The Practicing Idealist."

(Pause.) New chapter *(10):* "The Good, the Better, and the Best. Value Fulfillment Versus Competition."

Give us a moment . . . Most readers of this book can be considered idealists in one way or another by themselves or others. Yet certainly in these pages we have presented several pictures of social and political realities that are far from ideal. We have tried to outline for you many beliefs that undermine your private integrity as individuals, and contribute to the very definite troubles current in the mass world.

(*Pause.*) Very few people really act, again, from an evil intent. Any unfortunate situations in the fields of medicine, science, or religion result not from any determined effort to sabotage the "idea," but instead happen because men often believe that any means is justified in the pursuit of the ideal.

When science seems to betray you, in your society, it does so because its methods are unworthy of its intent — so unworthy and so out of line with science's prime purpose that the methods themselves almost amount to an insidious antiscientific attitude that goes all unrecognized. The same applies to medicine, of course, when in its worthy purpose to save life, its methods often lead to quite unworthy experimentation (*see Note 3 for Session 850*), so that life is destroyed for the sake of saving, say, a greater number of lives. (*Pause.*) On the surface level, such methods appear sometimes regrettable but necessary, but the deeper implications far outdo any temporary benefits, for through such methods men lose sight of life's sacredness, and begin to treat it contemptuously.

You will often condone quite reprehensible acts if you think they were committed for the sake of a greater good. You have a tendency to look for outright evil, to think in terms of "the powers of good and evil," and I am quite sure that many of my readers are convinced of evil's force. Evil does not exist in those terms, and that is why so many seemingly idealistic people can be partners in quite reprehensible actions, while telling themselves that such acts are justified, since they are methods toward a good end.

(*Long pause at 9:32.*) That is why fanatics feel justified in their (underlined) actions. When you indulge in such black-and-white thinking, you treat your ideals shabbily. Each act that is not in keeping with that ideal begins to unravel the ideal at its very core. As I have stated [several times], if you feel unworthy, or powerless to act, and if you are idealistic, you may begin to feel that the ideal exists so far in the future that it is necessary to take steps you might not otherwise take to achieve it. And when this happens, the ideal is always eroded. If you want to be a true practicing idealist, then each step that you take along the way must be worthy of your goal.

In your country, the free enterprise system originated — change the word to "immersed" — is immersed in strange origins. It is based upon the democratic belief in each individual's right to pursue a worthy and equitable life. But that also [became] bound up with Darwinian ideas of the survival of the fittest, and with the belief, then, that each individual must seek his or her own good at the expense of others, and by the quite erroneous conception that all of the members of a given species are in competition with each other, and that each species is in further competition with each other species.

The "laws" of supply and demand are misconceptions based upon a quite uncomplimentary belief in man's basic greedy nature. In the past you treated the land in your country as if your species, being the "fittest," had the right to survive at the expense of all other species, and at the expense of the land itself. The ideal of the country was and is an excellent one: the right of each individual to pursue an equitable, worthy existence, with dignity. The means, however, have helped erode that ideal, and the public interpretation of Darwin's principles was, quite unfortunately, transferred to the economic area, and to the image of man as a political animal.

(Pause, then all intently:) Religion and science alike denied other species any real consciousness. When man spoke of the sacredness of life — in his more expansive moods — he referred to human life alone. You are not in competition with other species, nor are you in any natural competition with yourselves. Nor is the natural world in any way the result of competitiveness among species. If that were the case you would have no world at all.

Individually, you exist physically because of the unsurpassed cooperation that exists just biologically between your species and all others, and on deeper levels because of the cellular affiliations that exist among the cells of all species. Value fulfillment is a psychological and physical propensity that exists in each unit of consciousness, propelling it toward its own greatest fulfillment in such a way that its individual fulfillment also adds to the best possible development on the part of each other such unit of consciousness. (Also see Session 863 *at 9:21.)* This propensity operates below and within the framework of matter. It operates above as well, but I am here concerned with the cooperative nature with which value fulfillment endows all units of consciousness within your physical world.

(9:54.) While you believed in competition, then competition became not only a reality but an ideal. Children are taught to compete against each other. The child <u>naturally</u> "competes" against herself or himself *(amused)* in an urge to outdo old performance with new. Competition, however, has been promoted as the ideal at all levels of activity. It is as if you must look at others to see how you are doing — and when you are taught not to trust your own abilities, then of course you need the opinions of others overmuch. I am not speaking of any playful competition, obviously, but of a determined, rigorous, desperate, sometimes almost deadly competition, in which a person's value is determined according to the number of individuals he or she has shunted aside.

(Pause.) This is carried through in economics, politics, medicine, the sciences, and even the religions. So I would like to reinforce the fact that life is indeed a cooperative venture, and that all the steps taken toward the ideal must of themselves be life-promoting.

End of dictation.

(10:01. Seth did discuss my dream of last night, explaining in some detail how I'd busily constructed a second dream self so that I could carry on a dialogue expressing creative impatience with myself: I was eager to embark upon new ventures in painting and writing, even while I was recording Mass Events *for Jane and Seth, and preparing for publication.)*

End of session, and a fond good evening.

(But I didn't want Seth to go yet. "Can I ask you another question?")
You may.

("Why is Jane so sensitive to the summer weather?")
As I have said before, Ruburt considers summer a time of vacations and beautiful distractions. He does not work well with it. He is afraid that it can lead to laxness. He yearns toward the cool hours, which then become significant.

People often respond to the seasons in individualistic fashion, of course, using certain elements to spur them on or hold them back, using the sessions as sounding boards. No season is itself only. It exists in relationship to all the people within its boundaries, and Ruburt enjoys summer thoroughly, the cooler hours being used as a contrast.

End of session.

("Okay. Thank you.")

Again, a fond good evening.

("The same to you. Good night."

(End at 10:14 P.M.)

SESSION 869, JULY 30, 1979
9:05 P.M. MONDAY

(Just two months ago, I mentioned in the 857th session that Seth was continuing to dictate material for Mass Events *on Wednesday evenings only. With one exception [involving a portion of Session 862], he's kept to that policy, setting aside Monday nights for other regular or private information.*

(Even though Seth didn't call last Monday's 867th session book dictation, then, Jane and I presented it because his material on viruses, disease, health, and biological experimentation obviously complemented his themes for Mass Events. *The excerpts from tonight's session continue that presentation.*

(First, though, let me explain an odd development. In the opening notes for Session 855, which was held on May 21, I wrote that a few days earlier we'd received our complimentary copies of the German translation of Seth Speaks. *I added that we expected the Dutch translation of the same book to be published later this year, but that we didn't know just when this would happen — so Jane and I were understandably surprised last Thursday to receive a letter from a reader in Holland, informing us that he'd just purchased a copy of the Dutch edition of* Seth Speaks! *Usually we're notified well in advance of a book's publication, but not this time — if the event has actually taken place. Could our correspondent have meant the German edition instead? No doubt a confusion of communications has come about. We've had no correspondence with the Dutch publisher, Ankh-Hermes, about a publication date. Jane called her editor at Prentice-Hall, Tam Mossman, who had no knowledge of the Dutch* Seth Speaks *being marketed either; he's to check with Ankh-Hermes and let us know. Jane and I are pleased, though, since if Seth isn't available yet in two foreign languages, he soon will be.*

(On the same day we received the letter from Holland, Jane also heard from Eleanor Friede, her editor at Delacorte Press: Eleanor sent the first color

proof of the jacket design for Emir. *Jane really likes it, since it conveys very well the feeling of her little story "for readers of all ages."*

(Here are the excerpts from tonight's nonbook session.

(9:28.) A small note — for this will be a brief session — to add to your material on disease: All biological organisms know that physical life depends upon a constant transformation of consciousness and form. In your terms I am saying, of course, that physically death gives life. This biological knowledge is intimately acknowledged at microscopic levels. Even your c-e-l-l-s (*spelled*) know that their deaths are necessary for the continuation of your physical form.

The entire orientation is strange or alien only to your conscious belief systems. In one way or another, most people are aware of a desire for death before they die — a desire they usually do not consciously acknowledge. To a large measure, the sensations of pain are also the results of your beliefs, so that even diseases that are indeed accompanied, now, by great pain, need not be. Obviously, I am saying that "deadly" viruses do not "think of themselves" as killers, any more than a cat does when it devours a mouse. The mouse may die, and a cell might die as a result of the virus, but the connotations applied to such events are also the results of beliefs. In the greater sphere of spiritual and biological activity, the viruses are protecting life at their level, and in the capacity given them.

In one way or another, they are always <u>invited</u> (underlined) — again, <u>always invited</u> — in response to that greater rhythm of existence in which physical life is dependent upon constant transformation of consciousness and form. Some early chapters in our latest book (*Mass Events*)[1] throw light on reasons other than biological ones, for such circumstances.

(9:40.) Give us a moment . . . The phase of death is, then, a part of life's cycle. I mentioned evolutionary experiments,[2] as you think of evolution. There is a disease you read about recently, where the skin turns leathery after intense itching — a fascinating development in which the human body tries to form a leathery-like skin that would, if the experiment continued, be flexible enough for, say, sweat pores and normal locomotion, yet tough enough to protect itself in jungle environments from the bites of many "still more dangerous" insects and snakes.[3] Many such experiments appear in certain stages as diseases, since the conditions are obviously not normal physical ones.

To some extent (underlined twice), cancer also represents a kind of evolutionary experiment. But all such instances escape you because you think of so-called evolution as finished.

(*Pause.*) Some (underlined) varieties of your own species were considered by the animals as diseased animal species, so I want to broaden your concepts there. In the entire natural scheme, and at all levels — even social or economic ones — disease always has its own creative basis. Abnormalities of any kind in birth always represent probable versions of the species itself — and they are kept in the gene pool to provide a never-ending bank of alternates.

(*Pause.*) There are all kinds of interrelationships. So-called Mongoloid children, for example, are reminders of man's purely emotional heritage, as separate from his intellectual achievements. They often appear more numerously in industrialized civilizations for that reason . . .

(*Pause, then with amusement:*) In our next book, we will try to acquaint people with the picture of their true nature as a species, as they exist independently of their belief systems. We will hope to show man's origin as existing in an inner environment, and emphasize the importance of dreams in "evolutionary advancement," and as the main origin of man's most creative achievements.

End of session, and a fond good evening.

(*"Okay, Seth. Good night."*

(*9:56 P.M. "Boy, how he got all that out of me, I don't know," Jane laughed, for she had been very relaxed before the session. Her delivery had moved right along. I've deleted a few portions of the session that don't apply to disease and evolutionary experimentation. Jane reported that when Seth gave the material on onchocerciasis she "really felt that the people's skins were trying to turn into some sort of leathery protection. I don't know whether I got those sensations from Seth, picked them up on my own, or just created them myself to go along with the material." She hadn't been aware of any feelings involving her own skin.*

(*For the last five weeks Jane has been intrigued by ideas about Seth's next book, which, she said, would concern "the therapy of value fulfillment." Seth has also used the phrase in connection with a next work.[4] Now it appears that he's settled upon a formal title for his book — one that Jane has received from him several times lately:* Dreams, "Evolution," and Value Fulfillment.*)

NOTES: SESSION 869

1. See the first three sessions, 801–3, in Chapter 1 of *Mass Events*.

2. See Session 867 after 9:46.

3. The disease Seth referred to is onchocerciasis, which is caused by a filarial parasite spread by the bite of the blackfly. In his passing reference to it, Seth didn't mention that besides producing the gruesome leathery skin, onchocerciasis can cause blindness — hence its common name, river blindness. This most serious affliction appears to be centered in West Africa, and infects many millions of people there. Four centuries ago, it was carried to the Western Hemisphere by slaves, and is now found in certain areas of Mexico, south to Brazil.

Onchocerciasis doesn't kill, and the percentage of victims who lose their sight varies according to location. We'd like to get more data from Seth on the experimental evolutionary aspects of the blindness, however, since we don't understand how such a debilitating state could really lead to something better. (Perhaps in this particular biological experiment, the blindness represents an evolutionary dead end, in those terms.) We may ask Seth to elaborate before he finishes *Mass Events*.

Indeed, it seems that he probably has available enough information on the evolutionary aspects of disease to fill a book. To use his own word, it would be "fascinating," should the three of us ever find the time to get to it. The whole idea of such biological experimentation makes us wonder just how, and to what extent, those impetuses may be involved with any of the "ordinary" diseases we're so used to thinking of as just that — diseases.

4. See Note 1 for Session 862, and the closing notes for Session 867.

SESSION 870, AUGUST 1, 1979
9:21 P.M. WEDNESDAY

(I'm just waiting," Jane said at 9:19, after we'd been sitting for the session for perhaps fifteen minutes. "Come on, Seth, for Christ's sake," she said, with unintentional humor. "It really bothers me when I don't start a session within a reasonable time: I wonder what kind of a block is there, you know . . ." Then: "I think that right now there's some material I sense, but it hasn't fallen into the right slot yet. I just want dictation . . . Well, I guess I'm ready. . . ." She was in trance before she laid her glasses on the coffee table between us. Her eyes were very dark now when she stared at me as Seth.)

Now: Dictation.

The blueprints for "ideal" developments exist within the pool of genetic knowledge, providing the species with multitudinous avenues for fulfillment. Those blueprints exist mentally as ideals. They express themselves through the impulses and creativity of the species' individual members.

Your natural athletes, for example, show through their physical expertise certain ideal body conditions. They may personify great agility or strength or power: individual attributes, physical ideals *(pause)* which are held up to others for their appreciation, and which signify, to whatever extent, abilities inherent in the species itself.

(Louder, when I asked Seth to repeat a phrase:) I believe that man runs the mile much quicker now *(by about 12 seconds)* than he did, say, thirty years ago. Has the body's effective speed suddenly quickened? Hardly. Instead, mental beliefs about the body's performance have changed, and increased physical speed resulted. The body can indeed run faster than the current record *(of 3:49)*. I merely want to show the effect of beliefs upon physical performance. All people do not want to be expert runners, however. Their creativity and their ideals may lie in quite different fields of endeavor, but individual performance always adds to the knowledge of the species. Good, better, best. Is it bad to be a poor runner? Of course not, unless running is your own particular avocation. And if it is, you improve with practice.

Now your ideals, whatever they may be, initially emerge from your inner experience, and this applies to the species as a whole. Your ideas of society and cooperation arise from both a biological and spiritual knowledge given you at birth. Man recognized the importance of groups after observing the animals' cooperation. Your civilizations are your splendid, creative, exterior renditions of the inner social groupings of the cells of the body, and the cooperative processes of nature that give you physical life. This does not mean that the intellect is any less, but that it uses its abilities to help you form physical civilizations that are the reflections of mental, spiritual, and biological inner civilizations. You learn from nature always, and you are a part of it always.

Your searches toward understanding excellent performance in any area — your idealisms — are all spiritually and biologically ingrained. If many of the conditions we have mentioned in this book are less than ideal in your society, then you can as an individual begin to change those situations. You do this by accepting the rightness of your own personhood. You do this by discarding ideas of unworthiness and powerlessness, no matter what their sources. You do this by beginning to observe your own impulses, by trusting your own direction. You start wherever you are, today. Period.

(9:42.) You do not dwell upon the unfortunate conditions in your environment, but you do take steps in your own life to express your ideals in whatever way is given. Those ways are multitudinous.

Generally speaking, for example, if you are seriously worried about a physical condition, go to a doctor, because your own beliefs may overfrighten you otherwise. Begin with innocuous but annoying physical conditions, however, and try to work those out for yourself. Try to discover why you are bothered. When you have a headache or a simple stomach upset, or if you have a chronic, annoying but not serious condition, such as trouble with your sinuses, or if you have hay fever — in those situations, remind yourself that your body does indeed have the capacity to heal itself.

Do the exercises in my book, *The Nature of Personal Reality,* to discover what conditions of a mental nature, or of psychological origin, are causing you distress. Instead of taking an aspirin for a headache, sit down, breathe quietly, and remind yourself that you are an integral part of the universe. Allow yourself to feel a sense of belonging with nature. Such an exercise can often relieve a headache in no time. But each such experience will allow you to build up a sense of trust in your own body's processes.

Examine the literature that you read, the television programs that you watch, and tell yourself to ignore those indications given of the body's weaknesses. Tell yourself to ignore literature or programs that speak authoritatively about the species' "killer instincts." Make an effort to free your intellect of such hampering beliefs. Take a chance on your own abilities. If you learn to trust your basic integrity as a person, then you will be able to assess your abilities clearly, neither exaggerating them or underassessing them.

(Pause.) You will not feel the need, say, to "justify your existence" by exaggerating a particular gift, setting up the performance of one particular feat or art as a rigid ideal, when in fact you may be pleasantly gifted but not greatly enough endowed with a certain ability to give you the outstanding praise you think you might deserve.

On the other hand, there are many highly gifted people who continually put down their abilities, and are afraid to take one small step toward their expression. If you accept the rightness of your life in the universe, then your ideals will be those in keeping with your nature. They will be fairly easily given expression, so that they add to your own fulfillment and to the development of the society as well.

(Pause.) Your impulses are your closest communication with your inner self, because in the waking state they are the spontaneous urgings toward action, rising from that deep inner knowledge of yourself that you have in dreams. *(Intently:)* You were born because you had the impulse to be. The universe exists because it had the impulse to be. There was no exterior cosmic Pied Piper, singing magical notes or playing a magical tune, urging the universe into being. The urge to be came from within, and that urge is repeated to some extent in each impulse, each urge toward action on the part of man or molecule. If you do not trust the nature of your impulses, then you do not trust the nature of your life, the nature of the universe, or the nature of your own being.

(10:01.) Any animal knows better than to distrust the nature of its own life, and so does any infant. Nature exists by virtue of faith. The squirrels gather nuts in the faith that they will have provisions, in the faith that the next season will come, and that spring will follow winter. Your impulses are immersed in the quality called faith, for they urge you into action in the faith [that] the moment for action exists. Your beliefs must interact with your impulses, however, and often they can erode that great natural beneficial spontaneity that impulses can provide.

(Pause.) When I speak of impulses, many of you will automatically think of impulses that appear contradictory or dangerous or "evil" — and that is because you are so convinced of the basic unworthiness of your being. You have every right to question your impulses, to choose among them, to assess them, but you must be aware of them, acknowledge their existence, for they will lead you to your own true nature. This may involve a lengthy journey for some of you, with your belief systems, for many of your impulses

now are the result of the pressure caused by perfectly normal unacknowledged ones in the past. But your impulses reflect the basic
impulse of your life. Even if they appear contradictory at any given
time, overall they will be seen to form constructive patterns toward
action that point more clearly towards your own clear path for fulfillment and development.

(Long pause at 10:10.) Natural attributes show themselves quite
clearly in early childhood, for example, when you are allowed greater
freedom to do what you want to do. As children, some people love to
work with words, some with images, some with objects. Some show
great ability in dealing with their contemporaries, while others naturally lean toward solitude and private meditations. Look back toward
the impulsive behavior of your childhood, toward those activities that
mostly pleased you.

If you painted pictures, this does not mean that you necessarily
should be an artist. Only you know the strength of those impulses —
but if they are intense and consistent, then pursue them. If you end
up simply painting as a hobby, that will still enrich your life and
understanding. If your impulses lead you toward relationships with
others, then do not let fears of unworthiness stand in your way. It is
very important that you express your idealism actively, to whatever
extent you can, for this increases your sense of worth and power.

Such action serves as a safeguard so that you do not overempha-
size the gaps that may exist in yourself or in society, between the reality and the ideal condition. Many people want to change the world
for the better, but that ideal seems so awe-inspiring that they think
they can make no headway unless they perform some great acts of
daring or heroism, or envision themselves in some political or religious place of power, or promote an uprising or rebellion. The ideal
seems so remote and unreachable that, again, sometimes any means,
however reprehensible, eventually can seem justified *(see Session 850,
for example)*. To change the world for the better, you must begin by
changing your own life. There is no other way.

You begin by accepting your own worth as a part of the universe,
and by granting every other being that same recognition. You begin
by honoring life in all of its forms. You begin by changing your
thoughts toward your contemporaries, your country, your family,
your working companions. If the ideal of loving your neighbor like

yourself seems remote, you will at least absolutely refrain from killing your neighbor — and your neighbor is any other person on the face of the planet *(louder)*.

You cannot love your neighbor, in fact, until you love yourself, and if you believe that it is wrong to love yourself, then you are indeed unable to love anyone else.

For a start you will acknowledge your existence in the framework of nature, and to do that you must recognize the vast cooperative processes that connect each species with each other one. If you truly use your prerogatives as an individual in your country, then you can exert far more power in normal daily living than you do now. Every time you affirm the rightness of your own existence, you help others. Your mental states are part of the planet's psychic atmosphere.

End of dictation.

(10:27. Now Seth came through with a couple of paragraphs of material for Jane, here deleted. Then at 10:31:)

A note: Your exterior civilizations do indeed mirror and reflect the great cellular civilizations, so that you try to exteriorize that kind of order and creativity.

Many of your technological advances — all of them, for that matter — are rather interpretations of the inner mechanisms of nature: sonar, radar, and so forth, as you attempt to physically or objectively reproduce the inner realities of nature. I have mentioned civilizations often before. But it is sometimes almost impossible to verbally describe civilizations of scent, civilizations built upon temperature variations, alphabets of color, pressure gradations — all of these highly intimate and organized, but quite outside of verbal representation. You would have to have additional material, nonverbal, to approach an understanding of such matters.

In your lives, anything you want is possible within the contours of your natures, if only you understand that this is so.

Do you have any questions?

("No." Actually, I did — a lot of them — particularly concerning certain themes I've been writing about lately, but I was tiring so I let the questions go. After a few comments about Jane's and my belief systems, Seth said good night at 10:40 P.M.

("You did well tonight," I told Jane. Her delivery had often been fast and, obviously, deeply felt. More than once I've seen her produce excellent

material like she had tonight even though, before a session, she'd announce a reservation about holding it for one reason or another.

("Yes. Tonight I just did it to do it," Jane said. "I have sessions now at times when I wouldn't have bothered to in the past. I was getting stuff from Seth before the session, but I haven't the slightest idea of what he said in the session itself — I don't remember anything. But it was good, huh?")

SESSION 872, AUGUST 8, 1979
9:15 P.M. WEDNESDAY

(Monday evening's 871st session was not for Mass Events.

(As we waited for tonight's session to begin I read to Jane a letter I've just written to a prominent biologist. I'm asking his help in obtaining source material for the visual "evidence" for evolution — showing the forms involved, say, as little by little the descendants of the reptile changed into the bird. By evidence in this case I mean drawings, *based upon the best scientific assumptions as to what all of those intermediate creatures must have looked like. I also wanted estimates as to how they survived for so many millennia while the changes took place. As far as I've been able to learn, no such transitional fossils have been found, like the discrete forms of reptiles and birds that* have *been discovered, so I decided to search out the next best thing: the visual representations as to what they must have looked like. But what good were the developing stages of a wing, I wondered, and how many uncounted generations of reptiles-turning-into-birds had to carry those appendages, before a fully-formed bird was finally hatched that could* fly? *Would nature do things that way?*

("I'm a professional artist," I wrote to the scientist, "and at times have been puzzled enough by questions about evolution to consider making my own series of drawings that would show the transformation from reptile to bird, for instance, just to see if I could do it convincingly . . . But each time I start visualizing the results, I end up with two notions: First, that as I work with those intermediate forms I'll become involved with myth and fantasy, rather than 'fact.' Just how did *reptiles change into birds? What kind of intermediate forms were there? Second, the idea of my drawings makes me think that others must have done it already, not once but many times. So what I really want to ask you for are references to later textbooks, that are more clear and precise than those I have on the origin of major new species. I'm especially interested in visual data. . . . "*

(I wrote about evolution in Appendix 12 for Volume 2 of "Unknown" Reality. Following all the studying I had to do in order to produce that piece, I've become very cautious in considering the theory — after all, even the dictionaries still refer to it as the theory [my emphasis] of evolution! "It seems to me," I said to Jane, "that if science wants to be believed, it should offer some data that are at least reasonably convincing. If science wants to talk about the tree of life, of reptiles turning into birds, then we've certainly got the right to see all — or at least most — of the leaves on the tree, not just those at the tips of the branches." Meaning, of course, that many of those invisible leaves would represent the missing, physical, intermediate forms demanded by evolutionary theory.

(The scientist in question may never answer my letter, but it's already had one unexpected beneficial effect: Tonight, after he finished book dictation, Seth gave an excellent summation of his own version of what our species like to call evolution. I intend to copy it for use whenever the need arises, as well as to simply remind myself periodically of its contents.

(Whispering:) Good evening.

("Good evening, Seth.")

Dictation: It may seem to some readers that the subject matter of this book *(pause)* is far divorced from any discussion of the specific development of psychic abilities.

Many people write requesting that I outline the proper methods for achieving astral projection, for example, or psychic advancement, or spiritual understanding. In its fashion, however, this book is geared to bring about the development of such abilities, for it is not a lack of methods that inhibits such activities. Instead, "psychic progress" is hampered by those very negative beliefs that we have tried to bring to your attention.

Many of you keep searching for some seemingly remote spiritual inner self that you can trust and look to for help and support, but all the while you distrust the familiar self with which you have such intimate contact. You set up divisions between portions of the self that are unnecessary.

Some correspondents write: "I realize that I am too egotistical." There are many schools for spiritual advancement that teach you to "get rid of the clutter of your impulses and desires," to shove aside the self that you are in search of a greater idealized version. First of all, the self that you are is ever-changing and never static. There is an inner self in the terms of those definitions, but that inner self, which is the source of your present being, speaks through your impulses. They provide in-built spiritual and biological impetuses toward <u>your most ideal development</u> (underlined). You must trust the self that you <u>are</u>, now.

If you would know yourself in deepest terms, you must start with your own feelings, emotions, desires, intents and impulses. Spiritual knowledge and psychic wisdom are the natural result of a sense of self-unity.

Again, impulses are inherently good, both spiritually and biologically. They emerge from Framework 2, from the inner self, and they are based on the great inner webwork of communication that exists among all species on your planet. *(Pause.)* Impulses also provide the natural impetus toward those patterns of behavior that serve you best, so that while certain impulses may bunch up toward physical activity, say, others, seemingly contradictory, will lead toward quiet contemplation, so that overall certain balances are maintained.

Some people are only aware of — or largely aware of — impulses toward anger, because they have inhibited those natural impulses toward love that would otherwise temper what seemed to be aggressive desires. When you begin trusting yourselves, you start by taking it for granted that to some extent at least you have not trusted yourself or your impulses in the past: You have thought that impulses were dangerous, disruptive, or even evil. So as you begin to learn self-trust, you acknowledge your impulses. You try them on for size. You see where they lead you by allowing them some freedom. You do not follow urges through that would hurt others physically, or that seem in direct contradiction to your present beliefs — but you <u>do</u> acknowledge them. You <u>do</u> try to discover their source. Behind them you will almost always find an inhibited impulse — or many of them — that motivated you to move in some ideal direction, to seek a love or understanding so idealized in your mind that it seemed impossible to achieve. You are left with the impulse to strike out.

If you examine such troublesome stimuli, you will always find that they originally rose after a long process, a process in which you were afraid to take small positive steps toward some ideal. Your own impulses naturally lead you to seek creative fulfillment, the expansion of your consciousness, psychic excursions, and the conscious knowledge and manipulation of your dreams.

(All intently at 9:40:) No methods will work if you are afraid of your own impulses, or of the nature of your own being. Most of you understand that All That Is is within you, that God is within creation, within physical matter, and that "He" does not simply operate as some cosmic director on the outside of reality. You must understand that the spiritual self also exists within the physical self in the same fashion. The inner self is not remote, either — not divorced from your most intimate desires and affairs, but instead communicates through your own smallest gesture, through your smallest ideal.

This sense of division within the self forces you to think that there is a remote, spiritual, wise, intuitive inner self, and a bewildered, put-upon, spiritually ignorant, inferior physical self, which happens to be the one you identify with. Many of you believe, moreover, that the physical self's very nature is evil, that its impulses, left alone, will run in direct opposition to the good of the physical world and society, and fly in the face of the deeper spiritual truths of inner reality. The inner self then becomes so idealized and so remote that by contrast the physical self seems only the more ignorant and flawed. In the face of such beliefs the ideal of psychic development, or astral travel, or spiritual knowledge, or even of sane living, seems so remote as to be impossible. You must, therefore, begin to celebrate your own beings, to look to your own impulses as being the natural connectors between the physical and the nonphysical self. Children trusting their impulses learn to walk, and trusting your impulses, you can find yourselves again.

(Pause.) End of dictation.

(9:49.) Give us a moment . . .

Consciousness predates physical forms. Consciousness predates the physical universe. *(Long pause.)* Consciousness predates all of its manifestations.

The impulse to be, in any terms that you can understand, is without beginning or end. What you have in your physical species are the manifestations of inner species of being, or creative groupings originated by consciousness as material patterns into which consciousness then flows. In those terms, the world came into being and the species appeared in a completely different framework of activity than is imagined, and one that cannot be scientifically established — particularly within those boundaries with which science has protected itself.

The patterns for the earth and for its creatures were as real before their physical appearances, and far more real than, say, the plan for a painting that you might have in your mind. The universe always was innately (underlined) objective in your terms, with its planets and creatures. The patterns for all of the species always existed without any before or after arrangement.

(Pause.) I am not pleased with those analogies, but sometimes they are all I can use to express issues so outside of normal channels of knowledge. It is as if, then, the earth, with all of its species, existed in complete form as a fully dimensioned cosmic underpainting, which gradually came alive all at once. Birds did not come from reptiles. They were always birds. They expressed a certain kind of consciousness that sought a certain kind of form (all intently). Physically the species appeared — all species appeared — in the same way that you might imagine all of the elements of a highly complicated dream suddenly coming alive with physical properties. Mental images — in those terms, now — existed that "in a flash of cosmic inspiration" were suddenly endowed with full physical manifestation.

To that extent, the Bible's interpretation is correct. Life was given, was free to develop according to its characteristic conditions. The planet was prepared, and endowed with life. Consciousness built the forms, so life existed within consciousness for all eternity. There was no point in which chemicals or atoms suddenly acquired life, for they always possessed consciousness, which is life's requirement.

In the terms that you can understand (underlined), all species that you are aware of (underlined) appeared more or less at once, because the mental patterns had peaked (gesturing). Their vitality was strong enough to form differentiation and cooperation within the framework of matter.

(Pause at 10:07.) I understand that it appears that species have vanished, but again you must remember probabilities, and that those species simply "developed" along the patterns of probable earths. You are not just dealing with a one-line development of matter, but of an unimaginable creativity, in which all versions of your physical world exist, each one quite convinced of its physical nature. There are ramifications quite unspeakable, although in certain states of trance, or with the aid of educated dreaming, you might be able to glimpse the inner complications, the webworks of communications that connect your official earth with other probable ones. You choose your time and focus in physical reality again and again, and the mind holds an inner comprehension of many seemingly mysterious developments involving the species.

Even the c-e-l-l-s *(spelled)* are free enough of time and space to hold an intimate framework of being within the present, while being surrounded by this greater knowledge of what you think of as the earth's past. In greater terms, the earth and all of its species are created in each moment. You wonder what gave life to the first egg or seed, or whatever, and think that an answer to that question would answer most others; for life, you say, was simply passed on from that point.

But what gives life to the egg or the seed now, keeps it going, provides that energy? Imagining some great big-bang theory *(to explain the creation of the universe)* gives you an immense explosion of energy, that somehow turns into life but must wear out somewhere along the line — and if that were the case, life would be getting weaker all the time, but it is not. The child is as new and fresh today as a child was 5,000 years ago, and each spring is as new.

What gives life to chemicals now? That is the more proper question. All energy is (underlined) not only aware-ized but the source of all organizations of consciousness, and all physical forms. These represent frameworks of consciousness. *(Long pause.)* There was a day when the dreaming world, in your terms, suddenly awakened to full reality as far as physical materialization is concerned. The planet was visited by desire. There were ghost excursions there — mental buildings, dream civilizations which then became actualized.

End of session. There is much left unsaid.

("Yes. ")

My fondest regards to each of you — and tell Ruburt to remember the power of thought.

("Okay. Good night."

(10:23 P.M. "I don't know where the hell I was tonight," Jane said. "I might as well have been without a body, I was so far out. The only thing

I could feel was that he was trying to find analogies to make clear that sec-
tion about evolution. Actually, what I got was — my feeling is — that we
don't have the concepts yet for something that seems so alien to our ordinary
reality. No matter how hard we try, even you and me. But I don't mean that
personally or anything.

("I guess the feeling I was getting was that some part of consciousness
dreamed of the earth, and visited it all the time; and then some part woke
up in it and became it for a while, with whatever it needed already
there. . . ."

("Do you realize the transformations in belief that would have to take
place before this material was even considered by the elite — let alone
accepted?" I asked. "It would destroy the world of a scientist who believed in
evolution. That is, if he would pay any attention to it to begin with."

(My remark reminded Jane that this afternoon she'd found herself
thinking that science should at least consider any *information, no matter*
where it came from. Then from Seth she'd picked up that she was wrong —
that her kind of information would be considered "noninformation," and
so would be ignored.

(But no matter, for it certainly seemed that with his material on evolution
this evening Seth was preparing for his next book: Dreams, "Evolution,"
and Value Fulfillment. *See the closing notes for Session 869.)*

SESSION 873, AUGUST 15, 1979
9:31 P.M. WEDNESDAY

(Since holding last Wednesday's 872nd book session, Jane has given
two more sessions. Both of them are private, however, and came through on
Sunday and Monday evenings.

("I'll tell you one thing," she said as we sat for tonight's session, "I
don't have an idea in my head . . . I'm just waiting. Come on, Seth. . . ."
Nevertheless, we knew that Seth would soon finish Mass Events; *he's been*
very neatly summing it up in recent sessions.

(Yesterday, with two good friends helping us move all of the furniture,
Jane switched rooms. That is, the living room in the hill house is now her
writing room, and her one-time writing room at the back, north side of the
house has become the living room — or call it the den-and-television room.
The new arrangement seems to be a very comfortable one. Jane has been

restless lately, and looking for a change. Our friends very accurately picked
up on her need, likening the room changes to a mini-vacation for her.

(Over two years ago, in Note 2 for Session 801, and in the opening
notes for Session 805, I described our decision to add the writing room to the
house. All four of us involved in the moving were quite amused, then — for
the friends who helped Jane and me carry the furniture yesterday are the
father-and-son contracting team that built the room in the first place.

(Whispering:) Good evening.

Dictation, in your cozy new den.

In a manner of speaking, you must be a practicing (underlined)
idealist if you are to remain a true idealist for long. You must take
small practical steps, often when you would prefer to take giant ones
— but you must move (underlined) in the direction of your ideals
through action. Otherwise you will feel disillusioned, or powerless,
or sure, again, that only drastic, highly unideal methods will ever
bring about the achievement of a given ideal state or situation.

(Pause.) Life at all levels of activity is propelled to seek ideals,
whether of a biological or mental nature. That pursuit automatically
gives life its zest and natural sense of excitement and drama. Developing your own abilities, whatever they may be, exploring and ex-
panding your experience of selfhood, gives life a sense of purpose,
meaning, and creative excitement — and also adds to the understanding and development of the society and the species.

It is not enough to meditate, or to imagine in your mind some
desired goal being accomplished, if you are afraid to act upon the
very impulses to which your meditations and imaginings give rise.
When you do not take any steps toward an ideal position, then your
life does lack excitement. You become depressed. You might become
an idealist in reverse, so that you find a certain excitement in contemplating the occurrence of natural disasters, such as earthquakes.
(Pause.) You may begin to concentrate your attention on such activities. You may contemplate the end of the world instead, but in either
case you are propelled by a sense of personal frustration, and perhaps
by some degree of vengeance, seeing in your mind the destruction of
a world that fell so far beneath your idealized expectations.

None of the unfortunate situations discussed in this book have
any power over you, however, if you understand that events do not

exist by themselves. All events and situations exist first within the mind. At the deepest levels of communication no news is secret, whether or not you receive it by way of your technological gadgets.

Your thoughts and beliefs and desires form the events that you view on television. If you want to change your world, you must first change your thoughts, expectations, and beliefs. If every reader of this book changed his or her attitudes, even though not one law was rewritten, tomorrow the world would have changed for the better. The new laws would follow.

(Long pause at 9:48.) Any new law always follows the change in belief. It is not the other way around.

Give us a moment . . . There is no civilization, no system of science, art, or philosophy, that did not originate in the mind. When you give lip service to ideas with which you do not agree, you are betraying your own ideals, harming yourself to some extent, and society as well, insofar as you are denying yourself and society the benefit of your own understanding. Each person is an idealist. I simply want to help you practice your idealism in the acts of your daily life.

Each person alive helps paint the living picture of civilization as it exists at any given time, in your terms. Be your own best artist. Your thoughts, feelings and expectations are like the living brush strokes with which you paint your corner of life's landscape. If you do your best in your own life, then you are indeed helping to improve the quality of all life. Your thoughts are as real as snowflakes or raindrops or clouds. They mix and merge with the thoughts of others, to form man's livingscape, providing the vast mental elements from which physical events will be formed.

As you learn to allow your impulses some freedom, you will discover their connection with your own idealized version of what life should be. You will begin to discover that [those spontaneous urges] are as basically good and life-giving as the physical elements of the earth, that provide the impetus for all biological life.

Beyond that, however, those impulses, again, connect you with the original impulse from which all life emerges.

(9:59.) Give us a moment . . . You will discover the natural, cooperative nature of your impulses, and you will no longer believe that they exist as contradictory or disruptive influences. Your impulses are part of the great multi-action of being. *(Pause.)* At deeper levels, the

impulsive portion of the personality is aware of all actions upon the earth's surface. You are involved in a cooperative venture, in which your slightest impulse has a greater meaning, and is intimately connected with all other actions. You have the power to change your life and the world for the better, but in doing so you must, again, reevaluate what your ideals are, and the methods that are worthy of them. Science and religion have each contributed much to man's development. They must also reevaluate their ideals and methods, however.

(Pause.) In larger terms, there are really only scientific and religious men and women, however, and fields of science and religion would be meaningless without those individuals who believe in their positions. As those men and women enlarge their definitions of reality, the fields of science and religion must expand. You must be reckless in pursuit of the ideal — reckless enough to insist that each step you take along the way is worthy of that ideal.

You will understand, if you are a practicing idealist, that you cannot kill in the name of peace, for if you do so your methods will automatically undermine your ideal. The sacredness of life and spirit are one and the same. You cannot condemn the body without ultimately condemning the soul. You cannot condemn the soul without ultimately condemning the body.

I would like each of my readers to be a practicing idealist, and, if you are then you will automatically be tolerant of the beliefs of others. You will not be unkind in the pursuit of your own ideals. You will look upon the world with a sane compassion, with some humor, and you will look for man's basic good intent. You will find it. It has always been there. You will discover your own basic good intent, and see that it has always been behind all of your actions — even in those least fitted to the pursuit of your private ideals *(with gentle irony).*

The end does not justify the means. If you learn that lesson, then your good intent will allow you to act effectively and creatively in your private experience, and in your relationships with others. Your changed beliefs will affect the mental atmosphere of your nation and of the world.

(Long pause at 10:13.) Give us a moment . . . You must encounter the selves that you are now. Acknowledge your impulses. Explore their meanings. Rely upon yourselves. You will find far greater power, achievement, and virtue than you suppose.

End of session. End of chapter. Get our friend some cigarettes.

(After I'd done so at 10:16:) Rest your fingers.

(Pause at 10:17, eyes closed.) Conclusion: You are individuals, yet each of you forms a part of the world's reality. Consciously, you are usually aware only of your own thoughts, but those thoughts merge with the thoughts of all others in the world. You understand what television is. At other levels, however, you carry a picture of the world's news, [one] that is "picked up" by signals transmitted by the c-e-l-l-s *(spelled)* that compose all living matter. When you have an impulse to act, it is your own impulse, yet it is also a part of the world's action. In those terms, there are inner neurological-like systems that provide constant communication through all of the world's parts. If you accept the fact that man is basically a good creature, then you allow free, natural motions of your own psychic nature — and that nature springs from your impulses, and not in opposition to them.

There is no event upon the face of the earth in which each of you has not played some part, however minute, because of the nature of your thoughts, beliefs, and expectations.

There is no public act in which you are not in that same manner involved. You are intimately connected with all of the historic events of your time.

(Long pause.) To some extent you participated in putting a man on the moon, whether or not you had any connection at all with the physical occurrence itself. Your thoughts put a man on the moon as surely as any rocket did. You can become involved now in a new exploration, one in which man's civilizations and organizations change their course, reflecting his good intents and his ideals. You can do this by seeing to it that each step you personally take is "ideally suited" to the ends you hope to achieve. You will see to it that your methods are ideal.

If you do this, your life will automatically be provided with excitement, natural zest and creativity, and those characteristics will be reflected outward into the social, political, economic, and scientific worlds. This is a challenge more than worth the effort. It is a challenge that I hope each reader will accept. *(Pause.)* The practical idealist *(pause)* . . . Give us a moment . . . When all is said and done, there is no other kind.

I bid each of you success in that endeavor.

End of book. End of session *(louder).*

"*Thank you.*")

I put the concluding statements separate, since I thought they would be more effective that way. *(Humorously:)* And I bid both of you practicing idealists a fond good evening.

(10:36 P.M. And on that gentle note Seth brought Mass Events *to a close. To the end he stayed with his practice of giving book dictation on Wednesday evenings. Jane and I had expected him to finish his work soon, yet when the moment arrived we still felt a certain surprise, a certain nostalgic letdown: Something we'd counted upon as part of our weekly routine wouldn't be there any more.*

("I always feel funny when he ends a book," Jane couldn't help saying. "I can never believe it. At the same time I want to race through it and see how it all came out. . . ."

("Okay," I said, teasing her. "You'd better hurry up, though, 'cause he's already got his next one planned. On dreams, evolution, and value fulfillment — remember? But I should be careful," I added. "You and your boy might start in on it too soon, and then the joke would be on me." Somewhat ruefully, I considered all of the work I still had to do to prepare the manuscript of Mass Events *for publication.*

(Actually, both of us will continue to be as busy as ever. Jane plans to write an introduction for Mass Events *next month, as summer draws to a close. In the meantime she's occupied with her own latest book,* The God of Jane: A Psychic Manifesto, *which she started last May under the* Heroics *title [see the opening notes for the 854th session]. She's written the first drafts for many of the chapters of the book by now, and has planned most of the rest of them — although she may change any of her work at any time. Now she reminded me that "a lot of* God of Jane *is written as my own response to stuff Seth gives in* Mass Events." *Jane's editor, Tam Mossman, hasn't seen any of her new book yet, although he's well acquainted with it through a series of lengthy telephone exchanges. Jane thinks she may sign the contracts for it later this year — before Christmas, that is. And her third Seven novel,* Oversoul Seven and the Museum of Time, *waits for her to return to work on it.*

(While I'm doing my own work on Mass Events *we'll hold the sessions for Seth's* Dreams, "Evolution," *and* Value Fulfillment, *of course. My own long-range goal in working with the Seth books is one that I've found very difficult to achieve: I want to catch up on the backlog of work involved*

with the books so that I can devote most of my efforts to whatever the current Seth book is — *while Seth is still producing it.* This would certainly be a luxury for me; in my notes for Mass Events *I've shown how complicated affairs could get for Jane and me when I had to juggle several projects at once over long periods of time.*

(And these final notes: We still don't know whether the Dutch edition of Seth Speaks *has been published* — *but we do know that our good friend Sue Watkins is presently working on Chapter 15 of* Conversations With Seth, *the book she's writing about Jane's ESP classes. Sue has a few chapters to go, plus some appendix material, and Tam is due to receive her manuscript in January 1980. I also know that as I prepare these notes our 7-month-old kittens, Billy Two and Mitzi, are racing through the house.*

(Through all of our personal activities, Jane and I are intensely conscious of the cultural, scientific, artistic, and economic aspects of the world we've chosen to live and work in. Each other individual is just as focused in his or her own unique reality, also. Right now, we're very much aware of all of the good things the people of our world are providing for us and for millions of others, every minute of every day — yet a certain portion of our joint interest in that "outside" world is also directed toward the situation at Three Mile Island, the nuclear power generating plant located some 130 airline miles south of us. Four-and-a-half months ago, one of the two nuclear reactors at TMI malfunctioned and came close to a meltdown of its uranium fuel. The whole world was a spectator at the worst accident in the history of our country's nuclear power program.

(The latest, Jane and I gather from a variety of reports, is that Three Mile Island's damaged reactor, Unit No. 2, is still a sealed enigma, just as it was when I described it in Note 1 for Session 856. A great amount of radiation is trapped within the reactor's containment building, so "many months" still must pass before it can even be entered. And "several years" will pass before scientists and engineers pronounce the site finally and safely decontaminated, at who knows what enormous expense, for each step in that cleanup process will have to be scrupulously managed for maximum safety.

(I left my thoughts about Three Mile Island, and began to consider a closing statement about Seth finishing Mass Events *as summer passed its zenith and prepared to blend into fall. Then I had it. Of course: The change of seasons meant that while I would be doing my own work on the book, the geese would be flying south. Already I looked forward to their migration, that ancient movement I've become especially fond of since we moved into the hill house over four years ago. Through the geese I want to associate Jane's and my activities with nature rather than technology, for in nature I sense a great, sublime, ultimate peacefulness and creativity that far surpasses technology, can we but ever manage to approach an understanding of what nature really means for us physical creatures. To me, without getting into questions about the magnificent overall originality embodied in All That Is, nature is the basic physical environment which all "living" species jointly create and manipulate within. And my personal, symbolic way of trying to grasp a bit of nature's ultimate mystery lies in my admiration for the twice-yearly flights of the geese.*

(I can't think of a better way to bring Mass Events *to an end.)*

INDEX

on criminals, 222, 230, 255
on cults, 165, 168, 197, 204, 210, 211,
    220, 230, 243
on death, 9–10, 12–13, 14, 19, 20, 21,
    29–30, 31, 32, 138, 164, 177, 186, 187,
    188, 272, 285, 286
on disasters, 83, 84, 97, 98, 99, 211
on disease, 41, 48, 49, 53–55, 68–69,
    101, 274, 275, 285, 286
on dreams, 59, 75, 104, 109–110, 132,
    271, 276, 277
on ego, 104, 105, 106, 109, 110, 115,
    126
on evil, 259, 282
on fanaticism, 215, 217, 218, 220, 221,
    222, 229, 230, 237, 282
on fear, 40–41, 48, 100
on God, 67, 96, 97, 103, 143, 150, 157,
    158, 159, 226, 227, 230, 238, 245, 297
on idealism, 207, 211, 212, 215, 216,
    217, 236, 237, 245, 282, 290–292, 300,
    301, 303–305
on imagination, 39–40, 135, 137, 139,
    140, 141, 142, 144, 276
on impulses, xv, xvi, 241–246, 250, 251,
    252, 254, 290, 291, 296, 297, 303, 304
on life, 39, 41–42, 43, 44–46, 94,
    156–157, 206, 249, 261, 262, 264, 269,
    299, 303
on nature, 30, 32, 82, 97, 98, 113,
    136–138, 139, 258, 260, 261
on paranoia, 173–174, 175
on reality, 89, 102, 148–149, 150, 232,
    302, 303
on religion, 47, 48, 66–67, 84, 93, 96,
    97, 156, 157, 159, 205, 207, 225, 226,
    230, 258, 264, 283, 303
on science, 66, 84, 85, 97, 197–198, 205,
    206, 210, 230, 262, 282, 283, 303
on self, 166, 167, 168, 198, 290, 296, 297
on universe, 94, 113, 114, 120, 121, 205,
    233, 249, 298
Seth Material, The (Roberts), 52, 102
Seth Speaks: The Eternal Validity of the Soul
    (Roberts), 15, 52, 102, 145
    Dutch edition, 285
    German edition, 231
*Seven Two, see The Education of Oversoul
    Seven*
Sin, 258, 264
Smallpox, 182, 183
Society, 51
    beliefs of. 160–161
    importance of, 290

Soul, 159
Species, creation of, 298, 299
Speech, beginning of, 278
Spontaneity, 199, 242, 243
Stress, 49
Suggestion, power of, 176
Suicide, 13–14, 243
Supply and demand, laws of, 283
Survival of species, 44–45, 158
Suspicion, 48

Talent, 131
Technological advances, 150, 293
Television, 49, 73–74
Three Mile Island (nuclear plant), xvi,
    192, 193, 196–197, 201, 211, 218, 219,
    226, 239, 306
Therapy, psychological, 259
Time, 57, 77, 87
Tornadoes, 208, 211
Truth, search for, 205

Unconscious, 104, 109
Universe, 233, 242, 249, 250, 298
    creation of, 112–113, 114, 120, 122, 205
    expansion of, 94
    functioning of, 120, 121
    meaning of, 141
    "Unknown" Reality, The: A Seth Book
        (Roberts) 7, 15, 16, 17, 26, 55, 95, 108

Value fulfillment, 258, 259, 260, 261
Values, 6
Violence, justification for, 218
Viruses, 182, 183, 184, 185, 189, 190, 272,
    274, 286
    relationship to mental states, 20, 21
Voodooism, 190

Wallace, Alfred, 27
Wars, 176, 230
Watergate, 236, 237, 238
Watkins, Sue, 55–56, 60, 63, 72, 86, 95,
    153, 155, 159–160, 191, 195, 306
Weather, 98
Willy (cat), 183
Witch hunts, Salem, 222
Women, 225, 230
World
    changing, 293, 302, 303
    improving, 255
World Health Organization (WHO), 182
*World View of Paul Cézanne, The: A Psychic
    Interpretation* (Roberts), 16, 17

New Seth Books, Online Seth Courses
Seth Conferences & Workshops

"THE EARLY SESSIONS" – BY JANE ROBERTS

"The Early Sessions" are the first 510 sessions dictated by Seth during the first six years of his relationship with Jane Roberts and her husband, Robert F. Butts. Published in nine volumes, these new Seth books offer fresh insights from Seth on a vast array of topics.

"THE PERSONAL SESSIONS" – BY JANE ROBERTS

"The Personal Sessions," originally referred to as "the deleted sessions," are Seth-dictated sessions that Jane Roberts and Robert F. Butts considered to be of a highly personal nature, and therefore kept separate from the main body of the Seth material.

THE SETH AUDIO COLLECTION

These audios consist of rare recordings of Seth speaking through Jane Roberts during her classes in Elmira, New York in the 1970s, and recorded by her student, Rick Stack. This collection represents the best of Seth's comments gleaned from over 120 class sessions.

ONLINE SETH COURSES

This in-home learning experience offers an intensive immersion into some of the most important concepts presented in the Seth material. (Includes live online interactive webinars with instructor Rick Stack.)

SETH CONFERENCES & WORKSHOPS

These gatherings offer a unique opportunity to meet people of like mind, increase your understanding of both inner and outer reality, and enhance your ability to create your ideal life.

For further information, contact New Awareness Network, Inc.
(516) 869-9108 between 9:00 A.M. – 5:00 P.M. ET
email: sumari@sethcenter.com, or visit our websites:
www.sethcenter.com
www.sethlearningcenter.org

ALSO FROM AMBER-ALLEN PUBLISHING

Seth Speaks by Jane Roberts. In this essential guide to conscious living, Seth clearly and powerfully articulates the concept that we create our own reality according to our beliefs.

The Nature of Personal Reality by Jane Roberts. Seth explains how the conscious mind directs unconscious activity, and has at its command all the powers of the inner self.

The Nature of the Psyche by Jane Roberts. Seth reveals a startling new concept of self, answering questions about many aspects of the psyche, including love, dreams, sexuality, and death.

The Magical Approach by Jane Roberts. Seth discusses how we can live our lives spontaneously, creatively, and according to our own natural rhythms.

The "Unknown" Reality, Volumes One and Two by Jane Roberts. Exploring the interdependence of multiple selves, Seth explains how understanding unknown dimensions can change the world as we know it.

Dreams, "Evolution," and Value Fulfillment, Volumes One and Two by Jane Roberts. These books answer crucial questions about the entire significance of Seth's system of thought, as he takes us on an odyssey to identify the origins of our universe and our species.

The Oversoul Seven Trilogy by Jane Roberts. The adventures of Oversoul Seven are an intriguing fantasy, a mind-altering exploration of our being, and a vibrant celebration of life.

The Way Toward Health by Jane Roberts. In this final "Seth Book," Jane channels the teachings of Seth from her hospital bed as her husband shares the intimate story of her final days. Includes Seth speaking about self-healing and the mind's effect upon physical health.

The Seven Spiritual Laws of Success by Deepak Chopra. In this perennial bestseller, Chopra gathers his most powerful pearls of wisdom, and offers a life-altering perspective on the attainment of success.

ALSO FROM AMBER-ALLEN PUBLISHING

The Four Agreements by don Miguel Ruiz with Janet Mills. Based on ancient Toltec wisdom, The Four Agreements offer a powerful code of conduct that can rapidly transform our lives to a new experience of freedom, true happiness, and love.

The Four Agreements Companion Book by don Miguel Ruiz with Janet Mills. This companion book offers additional insights, practice ideas, questions and answers about applying The Four Agreements, and true stories from people who have already changed their lives.

The Mastery of Love by don Miguel Ruiz with Janet Mills. Using insightful stories to bring his message to life, don Miguel Ruiz shows us how to heal our emotional wounds, recover the freedom and joy that are our birthright, and restore the spirit of playfulness that is vital to loving relationships.

The Circle of Fire by don Miguel Ruiz with Janet Mills. This beautiful collection of prayers, guided meditations, and powerful prose, will inspire and transform your life.

The Voice of Knowledge by don Miguel Ruiz with Janet Mills. In this life-altering book, don Miguel Ruiz reminds us of a profound and simple truth: the only way to end our emotional suffering and restore our joy in living is to stop believing in lies — mainly about ourselves.

The Fifth Agreement by don Miguel Ruiz and don Jose Ruiz with Janet Mills. Ruiz joins his son to encourage us to see the truth, to recover our authenticity, and to change the message we deliver to ourselves and to everyone around us.

For information about other bestselling titles from
Amber-Allen Publishing, please visit us online.
www.amberallen.com